Hoccleve's Works.

Early English Text Society.

Extra Series, LXXII.

1897.

Hunc Librum scripsit Thomas Hoccleue (fol. 34) circiter annum domini 1400, eumque dedit et dicauit Henrico Monmouthiæ, realiæ principi. Erat hic Tho. Hoccleue familiaris—ut ipse hoc opere testatur— discipulus Galf. Chauceri et Joannis Gower, quorum ingenium et eloquentiam mirificè laudat, folio 36 & 38. Posuit etiam Iconem Galf. Chauceri in margine huius Libri folio 91, cum Laudibus eiusdem Chauceri, &c.

Fuit etiam Thomas Hoccleue, Clericus Sigilli priuati regii, vide fol 15ᵗᵒ, vbi videas quanta in officiariis mutatio, & de eorum tam annua pensione, quam tenuitate : vide fol 17. b. & 32 b., 33. a. & fol 79. b. &c.

[*This is written on the page opposite fol.* 1. *a, in a 17th-century hand.* *A later hand adds:* See another copy of this Book in this Library, marked 35. A. 17.]

Hoccleve's Works.

:——◆——

III. THE REGEMENT OF PRINCES

A.D. 1411—12,

FROM THE HARLEIAN MS. 4866,

AND

FOURTEEN OF HOCCLEVE'S MINOR POEMS

FROM THE EGERTON MS. 615.

EDITED BY

FREDERICK J. FURNIVALL,

FOUNDER AND DIRECTOR OF THE EARLY ENGLISH TEXT SOCIETY.

LONDON:

PUBLISHED FOR THE EARLY ENGLISH TEXT SOCIETY

By KEGAN PAUL, TRENCH, TRÜBNER & Co.,

PATERNOSTER HOUSE, CHARING-CROSS ROAD, W.C.

1897.

TO

Olive Butlin.

Extra Series, LXXII.

R. CLAY & SONS, LIMITED, LONDON & BUNGAY.

CONTENTS.

Hoccleve's Introduction to his Regement.

Contents.

Hocclebe's Regement of Princes.

FOREWORDS.

§ 1. The first new point about Hoccleve's work that has turnd up since my edition of his *Minor Poems* I was issued by the Society in 1892 is, that his first poem in that volume is part of the 1413[1] englishing of Jn. Gallopez's prose version of the second of De Guilleville's three Pilgrimages[2]—1. of Human Life, 2. of the Soul, 3. of Jesus Christ—in the Egerton MS. 615 in the British Museum.[3] This MS. was long ago copied for the Society by Mrs. Kellner, and the transcript has been since in her husband's hands for editing; but time has faild him, and money the Society, to print the text. The work is mainly in prose, with fourteen poems intersperst. I suppose that in or before 1413 Hoccleve englisht the *Compleynte* before the whole Soul-Pilgrimage was translated, and that he then lent his copy to the englisher of the treatise. The other thirteen poems or set of verses in 7-line stanzas in Egerton 615 did not at first strike me as Hoccleve's (nor did the prose), and I meant to leave Dr. Kellner to print them; but Mr. Gollancz urged that they ought to be printed at once, for comparison with Hoccleve's acknowledgd works. The result of this printing (in the Appendix, p. xxiii—lxii), and of afterworking at the Poems has been, that I accept them as genuine. So this is the second new point. Members can judge for themselves. The only bother is that this Appendix-printing renders needless the next two and a half pages (viii—x) which were set long before the Appendix; but as they were so set, they may as well stand. It is odd that Hoccleve did not use the other 13 poems again in one of his later begging volumes, as he did his *Cupid*, his Envoy to the *Regement*, &c. As to the prose english of Egerton 615, Dr. Kellner will give us his opinion on Hoccleve's authorship of it when he edits the MS.

[1] Here endith the dreem of the pilgrimage of the soule translated owt of frensche in to Englysche, the yeer of our lord m¹cccc xiiiᵐᵒ, lf. 106.—Ward, ii. 583.

[2] See Ward's Catalog of MS. Romances in the Brit. Mus. ii. 580-5.

[3] Years ago, Dr. Helwig of Vienna read for our Dictionary, Caxton's 'pylgremage of the sowle' 1483, generally attributed to Lydgate. One of his slips was the same as one of my Hoccleve extracts. Dr. Murray sent them to me ; and on looking up the Caxton *Pylgremage*, I found that its poem was Hoccleve's *Compleynte of the Virgin*.

A lamentacion' of the grene tree, complaynyng' of the losyng' of hire appille. Capit*ulum* xxj^{mum}.

(Egerton MS. 615, leaf 63.)

(1)

O fader god, how fers and how cruel,   1
   In whom the list' or wilt', canst' þou the make !
Whom wilt' thu spare, ne wot' I neuer' a deel,
   Sithe thu thi sone hast' to the deth be-take,
   That' the offended neuere, ne dide wrake,   5
   Or mystook' him to the, or disobeyde ;
Ne to non) other' dide he harme, or seide.   7

(2)

I had Ioye entier', & also gladnesse,   [leaf 63, back]   8
   Whan þou be-took' him me to clothe & wrappe
In ma*n*nes flesch : I wend in sothfastnesse
   have had for eu*er*e Ioye þe the lappe ;
   But' now hath sorwe caught' me with his trapp*e* ;   12
   Mi ioye hath made a p*er*mutacion)
With wepyng' & eek' lamentacion).   14

(3)

O Holy gost' þat' art' alle confortou*r*e   15
   Of' woful hertes that' woful be,
And art' hire verry helpe & coúnceylou*r*e,
   That' of' hey vertue shadowist' me,
   Whan þat' the clernesse of' thi diuinite   19
   So shynyng' in my fearful gost' alight',
Which that' me sore agasted & affright'.   21

(4)

Whi hast' thu me not' in thi remembraunce,   22
   Now, at this tyme, right' as thu had tho ?
Or whi is it' noght' to thin pleasaunce
   Now for to schadwe me as weel also,
   That', hid from me, myght be my sones woo,   26
   Wherof', if' þat' I may no counfort' haue,
From deth-is strok' there may no thing' me save.   28

(5)

O Gaubriel, whan þat' thu come a place,   29
   And madest' vnto me thi salewyng',
And seidist' thus, "heil, Mary, ful of' grace ! "
   Whi, ne had thu govë me warnyng'
   Of' þat' grace that' beyn is and faylyng',   33
   As thu now seest', & sey it weel beforne,
Sith my ioye is me rafte,[1] my grace is lorn*e*.   35

---

[1] ? MS. raste

(6)

O thu Elizabeth, my cosyn dere,   36
  The word þatͤ thu spakͤ in the mowntayne
Be ended al in a-nothere manere
  Than thu had wened : my blissyngͤ in-to peyne
Retorned is : ofͤ ioye am I bareyne :   40
  I songͤ to sone ; for I sangͤ be the morwe
And now at evene, I wepe and make sorwe.   [leaf 64]   42

(7)

[O woman þat amongͤ the poepil speke,
  How that the wombe blissed was þat bere, &c.]

The last 5 verses of the Complaint, after Hoccleve ends, *Minor Poems,*
I, p. 8, are

(36)   [Egerton MS. 615, leaf 67.]

My dere childe, my fruytͤ þatͤ on me growed,   246
  Mynῠ lusty appil, blisful, faire, and sweetͤ,
Now deth hath him be-clapped with his clowde,
  Thatͤ him [hath] persed to the hertë rote :
Go toſ thow man, þere thu myghtͤ haue thi bote ;   250
  Go suke the Iuce ; the is no thing so sweetͤ ;
  Go take thin partͤ ; I rede the notͤ for-gete.   252

(37)

Go nere, & see how þatͤ he is for-bete,   253
  And alle for-persed sore and pietously :
See how there rennë fyvë stremës grete,
  Thatͤ yelde[n] owtͤ the Iuce habundauntly :
Go sowke therofͤ, I say you faithfully :   257
  In good tyme was he bore, þatͤ hath þatͤ grace,
  In tho woundës to make his dwellyngͤ place.   259

(38)

O Aduersari ! [t]how cruel drye tree !   260
  To the speke I ; nowe hastͤ þou thi ententͤ :
My sweet[e] fruytͤ þou hastͤ be-reved me
  A-geynῠ my will, nothingͤ ofͤ myne assentͤ :
I se how al to-Raced and to-rentͤ   264
  On the he hongith : is this weel I-doo ?
  I bare him monethis nyne, but no-thingͤ so.   266

(39)

O cruel tree, sith thu hastͤ thi desire,   267
  Whi wiltͤ þou notͤ to my fruytͤ be fauorabille,
To saue itͤ hool ? butͤ feruentere than the fiere
  He findeth [it] ; & no thing agreable
Itͤ is to me, butͤ alle discounfortable,   271
  To se myne herte attacched the vponῠ ;
  For he & I, oure hertͤ is butͤ one.   273

(40)

Now w*ith* my fruytᵗ artᵗ þou here openly,   274
   Thatᵗ alle the world itᵗ may be-holde & see
Restored ; whicħ, I sey the sekerly,
   Is more ofᵗ vertue and ofᵗ dignyte
Than was the fruytᵗ þat spoyled was from the ;   278
   Thu hastᵗ thi wiħ ; thin hono*u*re schal suffice
To the ; yelde me my fruytᵗ in goodly wise   [leaf 67, back]

𝕿han answere𝖉 the 𝖉r𝖞e tree & sei𝖉 in this manere.
Cap*itulu*m xxij.   (&c. &c.)

As a sample of how close the englishing is to the French original, take
a dozen lines that I happened to copy into my *Minor Poems* when I was
looking at the De Guilleville MS :

French (Addit. 22,937).	*Hoccleve.*	
Et mes mamelles alletes,	Eek thee, to sowke, on my breestes yaf y,	
Souuent gisant entre mes bras	Thee norisshyngᵗ fair*e* & tendrely	77
(12)	(12)	
Et te depart de moi la mort	Now thee fro me, withdrawith bittir deeth	78
(28)	(28)	
Hee iehan, beau tresdouz amis	O Iohn, my deare frend ! . . .	190
(32)	(32)	
Non marie, mais marrie	Marie ? nay / but 'marred' I thee caħ	218
(35)	(35)	
Mere, ne veystes pieca	A modir þat so soone / hir cote taar	239
Qui si tost sa cotte fendist	Or rente / sy men neu*e*re noon or this,	
Pour enfant quelle nourrist,	For chyld / which þat shee of hir body baar,	
Et pour mamelle lui donner	To yeue her tete⦂ as my chyld, that heere is,	
Comme sest tost laissie forer,	His cote hath torn / for your gilt, nat for his,	243
Et son escorce hors percier,	And hath his blood despent in greet foysoun ;	
Pour vous faire son ius succier.	And al it was for your Redemcioun.	245
Venez, quar ma pomme foraige	¶ Cest tout	
Est mise a partuy saige &c. &c.		

Hoccleve's change in his last line is surely justifiable.

§ 2. On Hoccleve's writing his *Regement of Princes*, doubtless in
1412, to Henry, Prince of Wales, who became King Henry V on 21
March, 1413 ; on his clerkship in the Privy Council Office (l. 802) ; his
meaning to be a priest (l. 1147-8) ; his having but six marks or £4 a year
(l. 935, 974, 1217) ; on his living in Chester's Inn in the Strand (l. 5) ;
on his marriage (l. 1453) ; his prodigality in youth (l. 4355-4396) ; his
grievances over his writing or copying work (l. 988-1029), and his poverty
(l. 960-973), I have dwelt in my Forewords to his *Minor Poems*, p. ix-
xii, xiii-xviii, and on his love and praise of Chaucer in p. xxx-xxxiv, so
that on these points I need say no more here. But note may well be
made 1. of the hold that anxiety for his future had taken of Hoccleve at
44 or 45, when he ought to have been in full vigour ;—it had well nigh
fainted him to death, 1/14 ; he was destitute of joy and hope, 2/34 ; his

life was but a deadly gladness, 3/70; his great desire was to be alone, 4/86; he had often longd for death, 5/112; he took no heed of a man speaking to him, 5/124, and had to be shaken before he would attend and answer, 6/132; the topic occurs again and again;—2. of the orthodoxy[1] of Hoccleve's views of the Sacrament, 11/344-50, 15/379—385, and the duty of swallowing all the nonsense and pious frauds of Holy Church, because "oure goode faders olde" did so, 14/351-7; 3. of Hoccleve's fresh and gay small-pleated gown, like a lord's, 16/409-10, 17/435-7; 4. of his strong praise of John of Gaunt, young prince Henry's grandfather, p. 19-20, st. 74-5. Eight pages are then taken up by a discourse of the Beggar with whom Hoccleve is chatting; and then the poet on p. 28 begins to talk about his own troubles, and want of money, as notist above and in my Forewords to his *Minor Poems*. He goes on, with intervals of the Beggar's chat, to p. 73, where his Proem to his *Regement* begins. In the kind young prince is his one hope of redress, p. 67-9. More than a third of his poem—73 pages out of 197—does Hoccleve take up in preliminary talk about himself and with his Beggar; and near the end of his *Regement* he recurs to his prodigality in youth, his poverty, and his annuity in arrear, on pages 157-8, 172-3.

§ 3. Most of the political and social questions treated by Hoccleve in his *Regement* are sumd up by Thomas Wright in the passage reprinted in the note on p. xix of the *Minor Poems* I; but we may notice here our poet's allusion to the Deposition of Richard II in 1399, p. 2, l. 22-4; to the martyrdom of John Badby, an artificer (? tailor or blacksmith) of Evesham, Worcestershire,[2] burnt at Smithfield on March 1, 1410, p. 11—13; to the extravagant scarlet gowns then worn, 12 yards wide, with sleeves hanging on the ground (and sweeping the streets, p. 20, st. 77), and £20 (now over £250) worth of fur on them, p. 16, st. 61-2, which leave the owners penniless[3] when they've paid for em, 16/430; to lower-class men dressing like lords, p. 17, st. 64; to the "foul waste of cloth in a man's tippet," even a yard of broad cloth, p. 17, st. 65; to the impos-

---

[1] This was natural, as he was first meant for a priest, 53/1447-8.

[2] "In the middle of the next century, two of the most illustrious martyrs of Protestantism had been Bishops of Worcester,—Hugh Latimer and John Hooper."— *Daily News*, 16 March, 1897, p. 6, col. 2, reviewing the Rev. W. Urwick's *Nonconformity in Worcester*, 1897. This book assumes, without authority, that John Badby was of the family of Robert Badby, who held the honourable office of Escheator for the county of Worcester in 13 Ric. II, 1389-90.—Nash's *Worcestershire*, Introduction, p. xiii. See also Badby's Life in *Dict. Nat. Biog.*

[3] Compare *Henry VIII*, I. i. 83-5,

O, many
Have broke their backs with laying manors on em
For this great journey.

sibility of long-sleevd retainers defending their lord when he's attackt in the street, p. 18, st. 67; to the houses of London skinners being too small, so that they have to go into the country to carry on their trade, p. 68, st. 69, and curse their debtors who don't pay, st. 70; to the often-repeated complaint of the decay of households and hospitality thro' extravagance in dress, p. 19, st. 71-2; to common folk copying the newest fashions among lords, p. 19, st. 73; to long sleeves (instead of brooms) sweeping the streets, p. 20, st. 77; to a flatterer or bawd in fine clothes being preferd to Truth and Purity, p. 21, st. 79.

Then the Beggar, who has been talking about these things to Hoccleve, sketches his own life, that of Hoccleve and other fast young men of the day. He went to the Tavern,—which carries the lantern before Unthrift, p. 23, st. 88,—paid it his tithes, st. 89, playd at dice all night there and swore, st. 90, and spent 100 marks a year at this, say £700 now (st. 93), but kept clear of fighting, p. 24, st. 92; had women of all kinds, wives, maids, and nuns, st. 93-4; and altho' he had a good post, he spent all he got, whether rightly or wrongly, p. 25, st. 95, and at last lost everything but one old russet suit he stood in, p. 25, st. 95-7, and had but a needle and thread, and a leather thimble in his purse, st. 98. So his finery and his friends have all gone, p. 26, and he lives to repent and amend, p. 27. He recurs to his wealth in youth, and his poverty in age, on p. 48, st. 189, 190.

On pages 32, 33, Hoccleve appeals for help to the poor gentlemen who fought in France and were then left to starve,—reminding us of the state of some of our own Balaclava heroes. On pages 51-3 the evils of unjust Church-promotion and the holding of pluralities are dealt with; on pages 54-6 the bad treatment of the Privy-Seal Clerks; on p. 58—61 the ills arising from marriages for money, winding up with the declaration on p. 64, st. 252, that for Adultery 'wers peple is non undir the sonne' than Englishmen. So Robert of Brunne's comparison no longer held, that Frenchmen's sin was Lechery; Englishmen's, Envy (*Handlyng Synne* 131/4154-5). At the top of p. 60 is an interesting confirmation of the practice of Child-Marriages in England: see my volume in the E.E.T.S., Original Series, 1897.

In the *Regement* itself, Hoccleve gives the young Prince Henry advice on his conduct under the 15 heads notist in the Contents above, p. vi. The chief political and social allusions in the poem are, that if a poor man breaks his promise, he's sent to prison, while a lord isn't punisht, but only thought ill of, p. 87, st. 343-4; that knights are losing honour (p. 89, st. 351), and England righteousness, st. 352; that—in contrast to

Henry IV, no doubt—benign Edward III often went alone in simple array among his people to hear what they said of him,[1] p. 93, st. 366; that good Duke Henry, the first Duke of Lancaster (unlike Henry IV's nobles, implied), did justice, and had all that belongd to knighthood in his excellent manhood, p. 96, st. 379; that Law is nigh banisht out of England, armd folk assembling in nearly every shire, taking the law into their own hands, doing wrong, and harrying the poor, while the rich go free, p. 101-2; that the Chapters ought freely to elect their own bishops, p. 105-6; that flatterers are the curses of lords, p. 110—112; that pardons for murder are too lightly given, p. 115, st. 455; that the Prince should recollect how merciful and benign his grandfather John of Gaunt was, and his father Henry IV is, p. 121, st. 479-81; that though good wives are as hard to find as a wind blowing south and north at once, p. 135, l. 3756-9, yet Hoccleve can't sufficiently express the virtue of Women, p. 137, st. 542; that luxurious living and lechery rob us 'reasonable beasts of our reason, p. 138-40; that he, Hoccleve, is poor, and his annuity in arrear, p. 158; that too frequent money Aids to the King for war, &c., are a curse, p. 159-60; that hearts are now as hard as stones, p. 169, and that many lords don't care a blackberry for folks' misfortunes, p. 170, st. 674; that the Prince should never grant a pension, and then stop the payment of it, as in Hoccleve's case, p. 172-3; that the kiss of Judas is widely spread in England, but small love had (p. 183, l. 5081-2), as men speak honied words, but their acts are gall, st. 727; that internal wars in England have slain thousands, and wasted our wealth, p. 188-9; that worthy Oxford and Cambridge clerks get no promotion, the prebends being held by flatterers, p. 190, st. 754; that men who've shed their blood in war can get no favour unless they flatter, st. 755; that sharp war, and hard, is at the door, p. 191, l. 5288-9; that France is in an agony of distress, and Hoccleve, tho' its foe, pities it, p. 191; that France and England should be one at heart, p. 192, st. 761; that peace should be made at once between them, p. 194, st. 769, and this can be done by Prince Henry marrying Princess Katherine, st. 771 :—

> For love of him that died upon the tree,
> And of Mary, his blisful mother dear,
> Follow that way, & your strife lay on bier;
> Purchase ye peace by way of marriage,
> And ye therin shall find your advantage.

The above sketch of the *Regement's* contents shows how valuable the book is for the social life of the England of its time, and how right Mr.

---

[1] Has this got into any ballad like 'Edw. IV and the Tanner of Warkworth' in Percy? Edw. III and the Countess of Salisbury are in vol. iii of the Percy Folio as well as in the play of 'Edward III,' &c.

Wylie has been in using it and Hoccleve's *Minor Poems* for his ' History of England under Henry IV.' And surely the statesmanlike view that the poet takes in his last pages of the urgent need of union between England and France by peaceful means, the marriage of Henry and Katherine—ultimately brought about on 2 June, 1420, by long-fought wars—must be reckond to his credit. We may well believe too that Hoccleve's counsels to the young prince may have had some effect in turning him from his wild ways when he became King. For though Ewald and others have tried to show that Prince Henry was too busy in affairs of state to have time for larks,[1] yet here is an extract from a MS Chronicle of Henry V, written about twenty years after Hoccleve's *Regement*, by a contemporary of his, which shows that Shakspere was, as usual, about right in his judgment of Prince Hal, as well as all other folk :—

c. 1430, Cotton MS, Claudius A 8, leaf 11.

Of the lawde of Kyng Henry the fyfte . . . . .

Here is to be noted that this Kyng Henry the .v. was a noble prince after he was Kyng and crouned, how-be-it, be-fore in his youthe he had bene wylde, recheles, and spared nothyng of his lustes ne desires, but Accomplysshed theym after his lykyng . . but as sonne as he was crouned, enoynted & sacred, anone sodenly he was chaunged in-to a new man, and all his intente, to lyff vertuously in mayntenynge of holy church, destro-yng of heretikes, kepyng iustice, and defendyng of his Reame and subgettes.

Tho Mr. C. L. Kingsford quotes this passage in the *Dict. Nat. Biog.*, xxvi, 46/1, and admits ' some youthful follies' in the Prince, he yet says that Henry's " youth was spent in the battlefield and council chamber "

---

[1] Ewald, *Stories from the State Papers*, i. 42-3 :

1409, Nov. 18.   Grant to Henry, Prince of Wales of 500 marks yearly for the custody of Edmund, Earl of March, and his brother.

1410, March 18.   Grant to Henry, Prince of Wales, of the house called Coldherbergh (Coldharbour), in the City of London.

1410, March 18.   Henry, Prince of Wales, appointed Captain of Calais, vice John, Earl of Somerset, deceased.

1410, March 23.   The King's officers and subjects ordered to obey the Prince of Wales as Captain of Calais.

1411, June 10.   Appointment of the Captain of Calais as conservator of the truce between England and Burgundy for the security of the merchants of England and Flanders.

1412, May 1.   Mandate from the King to the Prince of Wales, Constable of Dover and Warden of the Cinque Ports, to summon the barons of the ports to provide the service of ships.

1412, March 11.   The King orders the Prince of Wales to publish the truce with Flanders.

1412, July 12.   Appointment of the Prince as one of the conservators of the truce with Flanders.

1413, March 20.   Henry becomes King, on the death of his father, Henry IV.

1422, Aug. 31, Henry V dies. (See other details in *Dict. Nat. Biog.*)

—a good deal of it certainly was—" and the popular tradition (immortalised by Shakespeare [that is, Shakspere]) of his riotous and dissolute conduct is not supported by any contemporary authority." Let the reader judge.

§ 4. As to the main sources of the Poem, Hoccleve states these himself, and quotes from them in his side-notes,—1. (p. 74, st. 292) the supposititious Aristotle's Epistles to Alexander, or *Secreta Secretorum*[1]; 2. (p. 75, st. 294) Gyles of Regyment of Princes, D. Aegidius Romanus, Ordinis Fratum Eremitarum S. Augustini, *De regimine Principum* lib. 3[2]; 3. (p. 77, st. 302) 'the Chesse moralised' of Iacob de Cessoles, his *Libellus de ludo scachorum*. But to these have to be added, as the Latin side-notes or the text show, Boethius (p. 3, 132), Marcialis Cocus (p. 4, st. 13), Valerius Maximus (p. 83, st. 329; p. 93, st. 368; p. 117, st. 465; p. 146, st. 579), St. Chrysostom's 12th Homily on Matthew (p. 85), the 22nd Canon (p. 85), Quintilian (p. 86), St. James (p. 87, 88), Proverbs[3] and Ecclesiasticus (p. 88, 104, 123, 129, 163, 168, 176, 178, 181, 187), St. Anselm (p. 89, 130), the Book of Wisdom (p. 93, st. 367), St. Gregory (p. 48, 125), the Life of John the Almoner (p. 103, st. 409), Seneca[4] and St. Jerome[5] (p. 111), Hugo de St. Victore (p. 112), St. Augustine,[6] St. Matthew, and St. Ambrose[7] (p. 120), the Sermon on the Mount (p. 121, st. 480), St. Bernard and Seneca (p. 122), the Book of Judges (p. 126), Saints Bernard, Basil, and Isidore[8] (p. 129), Caesarius (p. 130), the Epistles to the Ephesians and Hebrews (p. 132, st. 525), the books of Daniel, Judges, and Genesis[9] (p. 139), Isaiah and Jeremiah (p. 162, l. 4500; p. 164, st. 651), Sallust (p. 164, st. 653; p. 165, st. 655), the Books of Tobias (p. 178, st. 706), of Kings (p. 178, l. 4948), of Job (p. 182, st. 721), the Psalmist (p. 183, st. 725), the Revelations of St. Bridget (p. 194, st. 770), besides several quotations, " Scriptum est," &c., some of which, at least, are from the Vulgate, as on p. 183, ' Et factus est in pace locus ejus,' Psalm lxxv. 3.[10] On p. 178, 'Cum fatuis consilium non habes' is from Eccli. viii. 20. I cannot find any of the other ' Scriptum est's' in the Concordance to the Vulgate.

---

[1] See p. 88, st. 347; p. 99, st. 390 (this eye story is also in *Secreta Secretorum*, Pt. I, ch. 3, 'de Obseruacione legum').
[2] See p. 91, st. 358; p. 112, st. 444; p. 166, st. 659—665; p. 174, st. 692, 693.
[3] p. 9, st. 32 is from Proverbs xvii. 22, and st. 33 from Prov. xxv. 20.
[4] Also on p. 147, l. 4075.
[5] Also on p. 135, st. 534; p. 181, st. 718.
[6] Also on p. 130, st. 515; p. 160, st. 637; p. 161, st. 638; p. 186, st. 738.
[7] Also on p. 163, st. 649.   [8] Also on p. 130, st. 514.   [9] Also on p. 184, st. 731.
[10] The lower side-note there is from Psalm lxxii. 3, 'Quia zelavi super iniquos, pacem peccatorum videns.' And 'Qui loquuntur pacem cum proximo suo' is from Psalm xxvii. 3. 'Initium sapientiae, timor Domini,' p. 175, is from Psalm cx. 10.

Besides these, we have mentions or stories of Pompey (p. 117), Julius Cæsar (p. 117, 118, 127), Scipio Africanus (p. 127, 133, from *Secreta*, Pt. III. ch. 3), Marcus Marcellus (p. 134, st. 531), Plato and Demosthenes (p. 136, st. 538-9), Codrus (p. 142, st. 565), Marcus Curtius (p. 145, st. 577), Diogenes (p. 147, st. 583), Tully (183/583), Judas Iscariot and the traitor Ganelon (183/5084), &c.

Stanza 523, p. 132, on lechery being a hog's life, destruction of body, corruption of virtue, and a scandal to a man who'd take the ways that reasonless beasts hold, is, as Hoccleve hints, Ca. viii of the *Secreta:*

"De castitate & continentia regis.

"Clemens imperator, *noli inclinare* femora tua *ad coitum meretricum; quia coitus est porcorum quidam proprietas.* Quae gloria regni erit *si exerceat uicium irrationabilium bestiarum* & actus brutorum? Credes michi indubitanter, quia coitus est abbreuiatio uite, *destructio corporis, uirtutum corruptio,* legis transgressio, & postremo, mores femineos generat." —Louvain Ed. 1485?

Again, st. 444, p. 112, on a Prince restraining his anger, is, as the side-note shows, from the *Secreta*, Ca. vi :

"Decet etiam regem pium esse, & iras ciuium cohibere, ne improuisa commotione siue deliberacione progrediatur ad actum."

Stanza 445, p. 112, is from Ch. x of the *Secreta:*

"O Alexander, caue, quantum poteris, humanum sanguinem effundere. Noli etiam assumere diuinum officium . . . 'da michi uindictam, & ego retribuam.' . . .

The quotation from the *Secreta* in the Latin side-note to st. 590-4, p. 149—150, is from ch. i,[1] while that to st. 630, p. 159, is from chapter ii, somewhat alterd, according to the Louvain edition, 1485? :—

"O Alexander, firmiter dico tibi, quod quicunque rex facit superfluas expensas ultra quod regnum suum possit sustinere, talis rex proculdubio destruit et destruitur."

The first side-note and footnote on p. 160—which have little to do with the text—are from ch. ii of the *Secreta:*

"Hoc enim fuit causa subuersionis & destructio principum & regni Anglorum. Nonne quia superfluitas expensarum superabat redditus ciuitatum. Et sic, deficientibus redditibus & expensis, extenderunt rex & principes manus ad possessiones subditorum rapiendas. Subdifi uero, propter iniurias, clamauerunt ad deum excelsum & gloriosum, qui, mittens uentum calidum, afflixit illos tirannos uehementer, & insurrexit contra eos populus, & nomina eorum deleuit de terra."

---

[1] The last word should be 'hominum': the text continues, for the English lines following, "Debes igitur largiri bona tua iuxta posse tuum hominibus indigentibus atque dignis," and then continues nearly as the side-note to st. 591.

Mr. Steele states that Stanzas 700—703 are also from the *Secreta*, tho' I cannot find them in the Louvain edition of 1485 (?).

The story of John of Canace and his three daughters, or 'John de Ganazath' as Caxton calls him, is from 'the Chesse moralised,' Bk. III, ch. 8 of Caxton's 'Game and Playe of the Chesse,' 1474, p. 148—150, ed. Axon, 1883; and that of Marcus Regulus, p. 82-3, is also from the *Chess* and *Secreta*, ch. iv (from Augustine, *de Civitate Dei*, lib. i, ca. 16, and Cicero, *de Officiis*, lib. i and iii).

§ 5. I have printed the text from the Harleian MS. 4866, because it has the best portrait of Chaucer, and fewer superfluous final *es*, and some older readings, than Reg. 17 D vi, which Thomas Wright edited for the Roxburghe Club in 1860.

The absence of many final *es* may be due to a partly-Northern scribe, as *knawit* for *knoweth* (13/338), *mak* for *make* (11/294), *spak, cum*, &c. No doubt I ought to have put-in more of these final *es*, as in 'styng' infinitive, ryming with the participial nouns 'throwyng, lawhyng' in the oblique case[1]; but any one who likes can do this for himself. I'm on the side of those sensible scribes who didn't sound the *e* at the end of the line in their own reading—save in cases like 'tymë . . by me' 5/120-2, &c.—and therefore didn't write it. The Harleian man's dropping of the *e* where it was wanted metrically inside the line, and of syllables and words now and then, I cannot defend.

As to the older and better readings of H,—compare its cleft or 'chynnèd lippës drye' 15/405, with R's 'thynne'; its 'Nessheth your hertes' 195/5412, with R's 'softeth'; its prosperous or 'weleful and wys' 33/908, with R's 'wilfull' (which makes nonsense); its 'pref' (proof, trial, trouble) with R's 'myschief' weakly repeated from the line above, with which it rymes; its 'iettë forth' 16/428, with R's 'gode,' went; its 'outen his langage' 140/3889, with R's 'uttre'; its thirstest or 'thristist sore, a rychë man to be' with R's 'trustest sone'; its 'y hertë-depe gan wade' 5/118, with R's '(wo)fulle hert deepe'; its 'þis bare olde russet' 25/675, with R's 'þis oldë,'[2] &c. &c. Of course there are instances on the other side, as R's eyes or 'yen,' 38/1027, for H's 'than,' which is nonsense (the MS. *y* and þ are often so alike that scribes often took the one for the other). But on the whole, I prefer the Harleian to the Royal MS.; and that was already in type.

Of the wrong or thwarted stress which I notist in the *Minor Poems*, p. xli, take a few instances from this *Regement:*

---

[1] But see 'may spring . . is pesible suffryng' (*nom.*), 187/5194. See also 'al, fal, gal' for 'alle, falle, galle,' 195/5413-16, &c. &c.   [2] H lite, R right 75/2079.

He was in no þing ábassht, ne eschu, 11/290.
As he þat was to þé fende acceptáble, 12/319.
Of reson, or what he can ýmagine, 13/347.
Byleue, as fer as þat holý writ seiþ, 15/385.
A foul wast óf cloth, and an éxcessyf, 17/450.
He may not stand him in steed óf a man, 18/469.
The skynner vnto þé feeld moot also, 18/477.
To beddë, thán lakke óf array outrage, 19/499.
Syn sydë sleuës óf penýlees gromes, 20/535.
By þat sette I naght þé worth óf a flye, 23/613.
In tymë dare by redë óf nature, 23/625.
And encheson of my woful murnynge, 29/795.
To lakkë mercy, ánd ben vnpitous, 122/3371.

Of ë before a vowel (see *Minor Poems* I, p. xlii) cases occur, as

It is synnë outragïous and vyl 17/460,
And walke at largë out of þi prisoun 11/277.

The pronoun *herë*, her, as two syllables (*Minor Poems*, p. xli) occurs in 9/238, 'Or louest herë þat not loueþ þe,' &c. The noun *honour* is *honur* in 4/97, 21/549.

The double vowel for length (*Minor Poems*, p. xl, xli) is not a characteristic of Harleian 4866. Its scribe sometimes writes *v* for *w*; *vas, vel, velthy* for ' was, well, wealthy,' 215/2.

Words which I suppose new, are *unresty*, restless 5/116, *syncope* (v. t. cut down their wages) 170/4727, perhaps *thoghty*, anxious 4/80, *unsyte* (sb. not-seeing), 180/5002, *cercly*[1] (circular, curvd) 185/5127, *harrageous* (obstreperous), 187/5191, &c.

Of course the *Regement* isn't without some chaff on the Woman-question, and evidence that in Hoccleve's case the grey mare was the better horse. As he says, in pages 184-7, 'it's no wonder that women want to rule their husbands; they're choicer folk. Man was made only of slime; woman of a rib, a much finer thing. And as to suggesting that this crooked rib made woman's temper crooked, that's nonsense; all perfect things—the Heaven, Sun, Moon, the Heart, &c.—are round and crooked. Moreover, man was made out of Paradise, woman in it; and as Christ servd his mother for 30 years, so men ought to serve their wives. As to women being "contrarious" to their husbands, it's only when the husbands go wrong. And even if they do bully their husbands,

"Goode is, he suffre : therby pees may spring,
Housbondës pees is pesible suffryng." '

---

[1] Our Oxford Dict. has the word only as an adverb, from Huloet. 1552. Here is the adjective in 1412.

So Thomas Hoccleve grind and bore it; said 'anything for a quiet life':
see _Minor Poems,_ p. xxxviii.

§ 6. I am sorry that these Forewords are so slight and scrappy; but
they have been written at intervals, other work or laziness coming between
the bits, and putting the details of this text out of my head. Dictionary
work is always going on; and marking words and cutting slips out of
books and papers is so pleasant and easy, that it makes one neglect work
that needs effort. Then there was the starting of my Hammersmith
Girls' Sculling Club[1] in May 1896, for working-girls in shop sewing-
rooms, and their brothers and friends, with the after housing of them, and
the getting-up Sunday whole-day outings,[2] Socials, dances and classes.
Last August I took my bundle of Hoccleve papers down to the pleasant
farm in which we spent our holiday month, Axhill House, Ashill, 8½
miles south of Taunton. But, alas, I never untied the string. There
was the nice soft lawn to walk on barefooted, or lie on, all the morning;
beautiful lanes and cross-country paths to stroll over in the afternoon or
evening; songs and pieces to listen to at nightfall; crops and cattle to look
at and chat about; a grand view round three-fourths of the horizon to see
from our hill; visits to pay, churches to inspect, neighbours' stories to

---

[1] "Its object was to give healthful exercise and innocent enjoyment to hard-
working girls; and without question this object has been fully attained. . . .

"The boats have been out on afternoons with Home-Girls, on evenings with
Work-Girls, and with both on moonlit nights and whole and half-day trips as far as
the Tower Bridge down-river, and Kingston up. One big double-sculler was largely
used during the girls' holidays, being out every day and all day, full of members,
relations and friends; and it made some members declare that it had given them the
happiest holiday they'd ever had in their lives. . . .

"Difficulty was at first experienced in getting Meeting and Dressing rooms for
the members. It was met by the President (F. J. F.) taking the house on the River-
bank, 19 Lower Mall, where the Club has been since August 1st, 1896, and letting the
members use it free till they can pay rent and gas (£45 a year), which they hope soon
partly to do. The first-floor rooms were fitted with gas-fires, incandescent lights,
mirrors and pictures, and made as homelike as the donations and funds available
allowed. The President sent down one of his pianos; and many pleasant Teas,
Social Meetings, and Dances have been held. Friends at Petersham, Kingston, and
Hammersmith Terrace have also frequently entertained boats' crews. Lately, the
front ground-floor room of the Club has been fitted up for men Honorary Members.

"During the winter months, Dr. Batteson has kindly taken a Shakspere Class;
Miss Lillie Davis an Elocution Class; and Mr. Jessurun a Singing Class, each meet-
ing one evening a week for two hours. To these teachers the members are deeply
indebted.

"The Club has thus benefited the minds as well as the bodies of members. It
has enlarged their sympathies and their circle of friends; it has developed their
muscles and their pluck, has strengthened their feeling of comradeship, and has
given them a new and healthy interest in life."—_Extract from the First Report,_
May, 1897.

[2] I manage to get these weekly from May to October (less August) from Rich-
mond, and from Nov. to April from Hammersmith whenever there's a tide to suit.
When there isn't, I get the morning for a shorter scull.

hear ;—bother Hoccleve ! where could he come in, with the sunshine, flowers, apple-orchards and harvest about? But here, in his London— his, and yet how different from his,—the present scraps have been put together, mainly under the electric light in the British Museum. Let them serve till the old poet's next editor treats him thoroughly, as Prof. Schick treated Lydgate.

Brit. Mus., 9 Dec., 1897.

§ 7.   *The Englisht De Guilleville Poems.*

Are the 14 poems that follow in the Appendix[1] Hoccleve's? I think they are, as they show some of his characteristics, and I cannot distinguish between the style of the Virgin's *Lamentation* or *Complaynte*, No. 7, p. xxxvii—xlv, which we know is his, and that of the other 13 Poems.

In them we find 1. his two-syllable 'hirë' for *their* (tho' not *her* as in *Minor Poems*, p. xli) :—

Some of hem, but at hirë lyvës ende, xxix/30.
In heven is assigned hirë place, xxxiv/35.
Rewardyng hem with blisse for hirë mede, xxxvii/33.
Ne will cessyn of hirë felle corage, lviii/214.

2. His ë before a vowel and *h* (*Minor Poems*, p. xlii) :—

Sest thu noght Agë, with his whightë eres, xxv/66.
Shamë hath he, þat at the cheker pleith, xxvi/113.
And is to meward fallë[2] in trespace, xxvii/131.
The falsë feend so sorë hem asseyled, xxxiii/10.
ffor he & I, our hertë is but one, xlv/273.
me schapyng to appelë and accuse, li/6.
Schul failë here, liii/44.   he and allë his, lix/252.
That thu for me purveyë and purchase, liii/66.
He will hem castë in-to hellë dike, lvii/188.
But mercie, pite, goodnessë and grace, lviii/223.
My quarell now to helpë and excuse, lviii/236.
That is abowt to noyë and mysbede, lxii/346.

3. His spelling *honure* (tho' not his ryme : *Minor Poems*, p. xxxix),

---

[1] Mr. Henry Littlehales, our Editor of the *Primer* or *Lay Folks' Prayer-Book*, has kindly copied all but the first for me. This first, left out through a misunderstanding, I have transcribed, and printed last, to avoid shifting the 13 poems set before it. As Mr. L. copied the already printed 'Compleynte to the Virgin' among his lot, I let it stand.

[2] The right emendation may be 'fallen,' as in certain cases of the infinitive in the poems, now ending with ë.

among several of *honówre* (xxx/1, 8, 22, &c.) and *honóure* (noun xxxi/7):—

> For euere hónured be thi maieste, xxxii/14.   And, &c., xxxiv/7.
> honúred be thu, Ihesu souereyn̄, xxxiv/24. H. &c., saueour̄, xlviii/1.
> Honúred be the blissed Trinité, xlviii/28.
> The thriddë festë, with̄ his highe persone
> To hónure, turnyng watir into wyne, xlviii/16, 17.
> (*The noun*) All hónure, vertue, and alle myght̄ynesse, xxxiv/3.
> Who is honúrë, may no thing deface, xxxvi/5.
> Now be we glad, in hónure of this maide, xlvi/15.
> In hónure of this [highe] solemnite, xlviii/27.

4. His thwarted accent or stress (*Minor Poems*, p. xli):—

> And castith̄ him nought̄ ámendis to make, xxvii/132 (aménded, xxxv/26 ; ámendid, lxii/362).
> Whil þát we in purgátory haue be, xxxii/25 (púrgatory xxxv/27).
> But wonder schort, in régard of oure synne, xxxii/28.
> In a good áccorde with̄owt ony peyne, xxxv/46.
> And youre labourë nobly díspended, xxxv/23 ; lxii/361.
> Youre selffë myght̄ely haue défendid, xxxv/25.
> Be ended al in á-nothére manére, xxxviii/38.
> So sore as this martírdam smertith̄ me, xxxviii/55.
> it semith̄ þat thu makist départyng, xlii/174.
> Weel fele I thát deth̄ hís vengeábilt bowe, xlii/179.
> And ámendith̄ right be his ownë deth̄, xliv/237.
> To gret distresse & gret desólacioun, xlvi/36.
> A maidë first was déceyvëd be the, xlvi/37.
> This ffischeres alle be ávoyded of slowthe, li/15.
> If þat I shalt myne réwarde vnderfonge, lii/27.
> To éxcuse me have I none audience, lii/38.
> If I hire, in oný place myght a-spie, liii/56.
> I knowe nought̄, tó whom I shal mý selffe dresse, liv/86.
> To the, will I now áppelë beforne, liv/95 ; lvi/168.
> Was neuere yitte none, tó whom it was warned, liv/105.
> That to haue spokë of aduócacie, lvi/150.
> So be myne helpe to ávoide and represse, lvi/171.
> To prócede in his accïon̄ as nowthe, lviii/242.
> With̄ tho that so be déformed in kende, lix/273.
> The rélieff of youre excellent merites, lxii/351.

The reader must judge for himself of the worth of the evidence above. It satisfies me that these 13 Poems are Hoccleve's.

The scribe writes *ie* for *i* in 'piete' pity, and its compounds, in xxiv/53, xxxvi/4, xli/131, xliv/254, lvii/180, pietous lxi/325, lxii/348, and in pietaunce (pittance), lx/301, &c.; and the same *ie* for *e*, in 'modier,' xxxii/15, 18, 19, &c., xlvi/16, lvi/162, and in 'fadier,' xxxiii/2 ; while in xliii/221, 'fery' is for 'fiery.'   He has *ea* for *e* in 'veari,' very, xxiii/18, xxvi/98, xlvii/3, lvii/207 ; vearili, lvii/177 ; and *ei* for *ë* in lxi/315, 330. Shirley's participial *e* for *i* is seen in ' e-graunted,' 113/3124, and his *eo* for *e* in 'fleobotomy,' xxii/28.

Of new words, I note only ' this infame' (scamp, rascal) for Satan, lix/258. ' Stealthless,' 66/1809, is also new, I suppose.

9 April, 1898.

CORRECTIONS.

PAGE

14/378. *Put the comma after* ' vnto '

19/507. *Read* ' If lordes wolden [cessyn] in þis wyse '

111/3063. *For* ' ffye ' *read* ' fflye '

For Works I. *Minor Poems :* p. x, l. 17, *for* l. 1147, *read* l. 1447.

APPENDIX.

The XIII Poems in the englisht De Guilleville's 'Pilgrimage of the Soul.'

Egerton MS. 615, Brit. Mus.

(1) The epistle of grace sent to the seek man. littera. [leaf 17, back]

[26 stanzas of 7 lines each, *ababb, cc.*]

(1)

I, Gracë quen), and heuenly princesse,—   1   I, Grace,
  As depute[1] be the souereyn kyng eterne,
In erthe a-lowe to be the gyderesse   the Guide of Pilgrims,
  That[2] liste the redy wey[ë]s for to lerne,
  In pilgrymagë him selff to gouerne—   5
    Gretyng, with yerde & lore of disciplyne,   greet you as one of mine.
    To the that hast, and must be, one of myn).   7

(2)

It is me don) to knowe & vnderstonde,   8   You are now sick.
  þat, this dethës seruaunt, malady,
The hath arrest, and holdith now in hande,
  And the oppressith, nought knowyng the forwhi.
  I wil therfore, as for thi remedy,   12   I'll tell you the remedy.
    Ordeyne[n] in my best[ë] manere wise ;
    I rede þe that thi self þou wel aduyse.   14

(3)

I haue be with the whan thu knewe it nought,   15
  Enserchyng, lo, thi poin[t]is of conscïence,
Be wich I knewe the innermost of thought.
  Thu hauest, thi self, with veari neclegence,   By neglect and sloth
  And also for defawte of diligence,   19
    Noght take heed to thi gouernaunce,
    Thi selffë brought in anguysshe & greuaunce.   21   you've come to grief.

[1] ? MS. deprite.
[2] That = of him that. (Tags tᵗ rᵗ fᵗ &c. are not printed.)

(4)

You've livd in surfeit and lust.

[leaf 18]

Thu hast, with surfeet, leuyng sobirnesse,   22
   fful greuously encombred thi corage,
In lust dispending al thin besynesse,
   Syñ þat thu were a childe of tender age,

That the now doth ful gret disauauntage ;   26

You must be bled.

   Wherfore the nature of thi maladye
   Wil askë sothly a fleobotomye.   28

(5)

You're full of corrupt humour,

Also I see, þat ful art thu withinne   29
   of córrupte humour' al a-bowt[ë] spred,
That rennyth ay betwyn [þi] flesch and skynne,
   That causith þat thu kepist now thi bedde :

Than ydilnesse and slouthë hath this bred ;   33

and have not sweated out 1 tear.

   Thu hast nought swet owt of thin eye one tere ;
   Wich thing to the ful necessary were.   35

(6)

And if you don't sweat

For if thu myghtist, dayës two or thre,   36
   With mynde upon thi foulë wrechidnesse
haue suche a sweet, it wolde availë the ;
   ffor leue it weel,—I sey it the expresse—

but if thu do the rathere thi besynesse,   40

and mend, you'll die.

   with suche a swet thi self[ë] to amende,
   This malady wiłł of the make an ende.   42

(7)

Look what rottenness is in you.

Take heed[ë] nowe, and to thi self conuerte,   43
   And see what wrechidnesse is the withinne,
Or dethë take thi liffe out of thin herte ;
   To be my reed, anoñ þat thu be-gynne

To make the clenë of thi sory synne,   47

Wash it out with weeping.

   As ferrë [forth] as þou canst think or spye,
   And wasshe hem out with terës of thin eye.   49

(8)

Death won't hear

For if þat deth the sudeynly assaile,   50
   beleue it weel, he sparith no persone ;

any excuse.

With him to trete, it may no thing avayle ;
   On the hath he no piete, thow thu grone ;
   Complayntis sothly he rewardith none,   54

But buskiþ you vnto the pittës brynk :
On this, I rede, thu besely bethink.　　56

(9)

Take heed, and here, how þat to euery wiȝt　　57
　With-in[në]-forth he clepiþ preuely :
" Arayeth you, and be al redi diȝt,
　ffor I wil come—beleve it sikerly—
　Or ye be ware, parauenture sudeynly :　　61
　　And me by-for' ther may [no] praiere spede
　　Ne now ne wele : I sparë for [no] mede."　　63

Death has warnd you [leaf 18, back] to be ready, as he'll come suddenly.

(10)

" Beholde and see, how þat this messageres,　　64
　lo, in awaitë, [now] be leyd for the.
Sest thu noȝt Agë, with his whightë eres,
　hath had[1] himselff ful nye,—canst thu not see ?—
　And maladi[ë] hath arrest par-de.　　[1 ? hid]　　68
　　Herist thu nowt, how thei crie lowde alwey,
　　' what eiliþ vs, to tarye so al day ?'　　70

Death's messengers, Age and Sickness, lie in wait for you.

(11)

" How oftë haue I warned the be-for',　　71
　Som while apert, somtymë preuely,
That redy schuldist thu have be euermor' :
　Witnesse upon thi self, I say the, whi
　Thu miȝt the nouȝt excusë vtterly :　　75
　　Synderesis, she knowith euery deel ;
　　Sche wiȝ be thin appélloure, wete it weel,　　77

I've often warnd you to be ready.

Synderesis will accuse you.

(12)

" Aneinptes me, that alway wold thi prowe ;　　78
　fful folili thu hast thi self mystake :
for thu behetest—this knowist weȝ I-nowe—
　þat alle thin foli woldest thu for-sake,
　And woldest thi-self very clenë make,　　82
　　Puttyng [thi] flesch vnder subieccioun,
　　To be gouérned after thi reason).　　84

You promist me to forsake your folly,

(13)

" But sekerly she euery deel reuerse　　85
　vsurped hath hire ownë ladi riȝt,
By here delites and lustës fuȝ dyuers
　Oppressyng her' with alle hir' mayn & myȝt.

but you never have.

A fool is he (as semitħ in my sigħt) 89
That be no lore ne wiħ his freend[is] knowe
Tiħ þat he be in myschief ouerthrowe. 91

(14)

[leaf 19]
Now put
away your
sloth, for me

the Star of
Truth.

Remember
my sweet
songs.

" But now I rede, take good entent & hepe, 92
Puttyng awey thi slombre & [thi] slouthe.
A fool he is, that leitħ him self to slepe,
To whom I springe, the veray sterre of trewthe.
How ofte hast thu refused, for thi yowthe, 96
To herë me? and sone hast thu for-yete
Myn lusty songës veary hony-swete. 98

(15)

Are you
spotless?

" Now sey me, be thi feitħ, whethir þou were he 99
Alone of woman in this world I-bore,
So clene of wemme, that no thing is in the
To weylë ne to wepe thi synnës sore.

No. You're
full of sin,

Nay, sekerly—and þat me for-thinke sore— 103
That thu ne canst [nat] se thi wrechidnesse,
Thi synne, thi surfeet, and thin vnthriftynesse,

(16)

" And hard conflicte of bataile, the withinne. 106
Thu felë mygħt (but if thu be vnwys),
How þat þⁱ sowle assailed is witħ synne,
And vnder-cast þou art of hye malice,

and subject
to vice.

And subiecte, thu madist thi selfe, to vice, 110
Wicħ þat of god, the Juge omnipotent,
Condempned is witħ-owt[en] iugëment. 112

(17)

At chess, it's
a shame for
a pawn to
checkmate
the king.
So, it's a
shame when
your Spirit
obeys your
Flesh.

" Shamë hatħ he þat at the cheker pleitħ, 113
Whan þat a powne saitħ to the kyng 'chek mate;'
And shame it is, whan that thi gost obeitħ
Vnto thi flessħ, þat schuld obeye algate
Vnto thi goost. And now, thowe it be late, 117
Yilte helpe thi self, and cast her' vnder' fote,
Or elles þou art lost: þere is now other bote. 119

(18)

It's no shame
for a strong
man to fall
in battle,

" In bataylë, as it hatħ ofte be-tydde 120
a mygħti man to falle, it is no schame,
The first[ë] tyme, the secunde, and the thridde,

And rysith weel—this holde I but a game ;—
But gretly, me thinkith, is he to blame,   124   but he's a
   And worthi as [a] fool to be reproeved,   fool who doesn't seek aid.
That not enforsith him to be releuyd.   126   [leaf 19, back]

(19)

"Now youthë may no lengere the excuse,   127   Youth can't excuse you. You're old.
   for age is come, and calengith his plase.
Yeld thi promyse ! þou mygħt it not refuse.   Fulfil your promise !
   A fool is he þat desobëytħ grace,
     And is to meward fallë in trespace,   131
     And castitħ him nougħt ámendis to make :
Suche one, what wondir is, thougħ I forsake ? 133

(20)

"Ful long I haue a-beden and susteyned   134
   to haue amendës for thi forfeture ;
And or this tyme I haue me not compleyned.
   I may no more the wrechidnesse endure :
   I rede the do[1] thi besynesse and cure ;   138
     Amende thi self ; it is anow to me,   Amend yourself.
     That is the amendës þat I askë the.   140

(21)

"Now chese thin port, at wicħ thu wilt aryve ;   141   Choose one of two ports,
   But to there beꝺ, of solace and distresse :
At one, thow mygħt thi self[en] kepe a lyve,
   And euere abide in ioye and lustynesse ;   either Joy,
   That othir, is but care and wrechidnesse ;   145   or Wretched-ness.
     here comë detħ ; and if þat he [schal] smyte   Death comes.
     Thi liffe, there is noꝺ leche that [may] respite. 147

(22)

"Se now thi self, that hauest no defence !   148
   A-bove thin heed the swerd is redy drawe ;   The Sword's over your head.
I redë the to look thi conscïence,
   How þou hauest lyved a-geyn thi lorde-is lawe ;
   And after this, a-nothir wey thu drawe,   152   Turn and mend !
     þat alle thi tyme in foly so dispended,
     yit at the last[ë], lat it be amendyd.   154

[1] MS. to do.

(23)

"How oftë tyme have I the tolde & taughͭ   155
      The worthynesse of vertue, and the mede!

I've often rescued you from Satan's clutches.

how ofte haue I the from the clowches caughͭ
      Of sathanas! yitte takist thu now heed.

But now be ware, and noughͭ withͤowt[ë] nede; 159
      ffor sekirly the bowe is bent ful sore

[leaf 20]
The bow is bent to slay you.

      To smytë the: than may I do no more.   161

(24)

"The birde that syngith on a braunche on hye, 162
      And schewith him self a lusty Jolyvet,

Vnto the dethͤ is sinet sude*in*gly
      Or he be ware, and takë with a net.

Death besieges you.

I have the said, how dethͤ hath the be-sette; 166
      And almost vnder-myned is thi waH;

      But thu be ware, ful grevous is thi faH.   168

(25)

What will you say to the Judge at the Day of Doom?

"Allas! what thinkest thu? what wilt þou sayn, 169
      In þat ilke day of anger' and of dreed,

Vn-to the heighë Iugë souereyne?
      What dost þou, man? whi takist thu now hede?

If þou wilt be releuyd in thi nede,   173
      What helpith it, thus [for] to preche and teche?

Confess thy sin to me,

But schewe thi soore, to me þat am thi leche, 175

(26)

"And [than] I schal a-voyde the of thi fylthe, 176
      receyvyng the anon vnder my cure.

and I will cure thee,

I schal the bringe in redynesse of tylthe,
      So that [thu] schalt thi selff[e] weel assure,

þat whan thi fleschͤ is laid in sepulture,   180

and bring thee into heaven's bliss.

      Thu schalt be haved up in-to heven blisse;
      EternaH myrthës schalt þou neu*er*e mysse."   182

---

(2) **The chartre of pardon'.**

[14 stanzas of 7 lines each, *ababb, cc.*]

(1)

[leaf 26]
Jesus, to St. Michael

I hesu, kyng of hie heuen a-bove,   1
      Vnto Michael my chief lieu-tenaunt,

And alle thin ássessourës wich I love,
   That in my seruice be persêueraunt
have euermore, and to me ful pleasaunt—   5
    My gretyng;—and, upon the peyne of dreed,
    Vnto this present chartre take[th] heed.   7

and all Angels, greeting!

(2)

Me hath be-sought, this present ladi here,   8
   Misericorde; and at hire gret instaunce,
And also eek myn ownë modier dere—
   That alway redi is, at hire pleasaunce,
ffor synful men to makë purueaunce   12
    Above thei have me bede; wich, of my grace,
    Graunted hath, hire prayer have his place.   14

Mary and My Mother have

[leaf 26, back]

prayd me to help sinners, and I've agreed to do so.

(3)

Ther be pilgrymës (as thei certifie)   15
   That to meward hire weiës had [i]take,
Wich have mysgon, and erred folily
   Be steryng of the foulë bestis blake,
That som of hem hire iourney had forsake,   19
    And efte hire iourney have a-geyn be-gunne,
    But sudei[n]gly hath failed him the sonne.   21

Some Pilgrims to Me have gone wrong.

(4)

Some have be lettid be foule temptacïoun   22
   And steryng of hire fleschly wrechidnesse;
So, be disease and tribulacïoun
   Thei have [i]falle in-to huge hevynesse;
And somme also to this worldes besynesse   26
    So greuously hire hertës ouersette,
    So þat thei have of hire iournéy be lette.   28

Some have been stopt by temptation and disease.

(5)

But thei haue[n] repented wondir sore,   29
   Some of hem, but at hirë lyvës ende;
& somme of hem, a litel what be-fore
   Be-gan him selfë somwhat to amende,
In wil theraftir neuer to offende,   33
    But schreven hem of alle hire olde trespace,
    And put them self[ë] only in my grace.   35

But they have repented,

and begun to amend.

(6)

I, urged by
Mary and
Mercy,

At the instaunce of myn̄ owne modier swete—   36
 To whom I may no maner' thing denye,
And mercy also may I nought for-gete ;
 But vnto hir' bone I wil myself applie :—

grant these
Pilgrims
My peace,
and release
from Hell.

This grace I graunte them of my Regalye,   40
 That I schal hem receyve vnto my peas ;
 Of hellë peyne I graunte hem ful relees.   42

(7)

These who
have cried
[leaf 27]
to Me,

So thei that han̄ me, Ihesu, mercy cried   43
 Or *that* the breeth out of the body yeed,
And alle hire wrechid lustys have defied
 In veray faith (as techith hem the crede)

ye shall not
condemn to
Hell,

So þat ye schal not a-geyn hem procede   47
 As to iuge hem to hellë [bittre] peyne,
 But that in this, your' rygoure ye restreyne.   49

(8)

tho' their ill
deeds out-
weigh their
good ones.

And thow þat hir' wikked[1] workis counterpeise   50
 hire good[ë] dedës whan thei schul be weye,
So þat the beter' part hem selfë reyse
 As for defawte of weighte, yit thus I seye
And wiħ, þat [to] this chartre ye obeye,   54
 Wich I have graunted for my modier sake :
 To mercy also her' have I [i-]take.   56

(9)

Out of the
treasure of
My suffering

Of tresour' of my bitter passïoun̄,   57
 And of the merite of my modier' der—
To whom now̄ othir hath comparysoun̄—

and My
Saints' merit,

 With merite of myn̄ seintës alle in fer',
 That to my biddyng ful obeysaunt were,   61

put a weight
in the scale

 Of plente and of superhábundaunce
 A forcet ful, wich puttith in the balaunce,   63

(10)

to counter-
poise the
Devil's,

The countirpeis a-geyn the fendis part,   64
 So that he faile of his entencïoun̄

so that he
may not
bring em to
Damnation.

To bringë hem, so with his subtile art,
 To be iuged [vn-]to dampnacïoun̄
 Withowt ony comfort of saluacïoun̄,   68

[1] ? wikke.

With cursidnesse of alle the synnës sevene,
Syn̄ the[1] that he was chased owt of hevene.　　70

(11)

And nought for-thi,—this is not myn̄ entent,—　71
　Ne for this cause my blood ne shadde I nought,
That ony wight in mysgouérnëment
　A-bidë schulde, and trust[en] in his thought
That this chart[r]e schulde [him] a-vaile[n] ought 75
　As of this pardon̄ to be partenere,
　Or of this grace þat I haue graunted her'.　　77

But I don't mean

that continuers in sin shall share this Pardon.

(12)

Therfore, owt of this chartre I excepte　　78
　To allë which, vnto hir' lyvës ende,
Have euermore in cursed synnës slepte,
　Purposyng nowt hire lyvës to amende,
Vpon trust here-of, hem selfë to defende　　82
　ffrom hellë peynë, be this present grace,
　Alle tho þat schal be exiled fro my face ;　84

[leaf 27, back] I except out of this Charter all who sind till they died,

(13)

And this also, wich that be obstynat,　　85
　and never wil [vn]to my lawe obeye ;
This also þat be veray desperat,
　That wil no gracë ne no mercy pray,
But right so in hire cursed synnës deye :　89
　To them is due the hotë fier of helle,
　With Sathanas eternally to dwelle.　　91

all who don't obey Me,

and all who won't pray for mercy.

They must go to Hell.

(14)

Wherfore, no man so boldë ne so hardy be,　92
　Trustyng upon this present pardonaunce,
To surfeet or to synne in no degre,
　Vpon the trust of fynal répentaunce,
Wich is my gifte ; and aftir my pleasaunce　96
　I geve it him þat schul myn̄ mercy crave,
　withxowt[en] wich, no wight [ne] wil I save.[2]　98

Let no man sin, trusting

to repentance at his end.

---

[1] Since that, since the time.　　　[2] MS. crave.

[leaf 29]

(3) **Cantus peregrino**rum.

[5 stanzas of 7 lines each, *ababb, cc.*]

(1)

Honourd be
Jesus

Honowred be thu, blissed lord on hye,   1
   That of the blisful maydë were I-bore,
That with thi deth us boughtist myght[i]ly :
   Thin ownë flesch and blood, þou gaue us fore,
   And for us suffred peynës wonder sore,   5

who shed His
heart's blood
for us!

      Bothe foot and hand [i]nayled to the rode,
      And bledest alle thin veray hert[es] bloode !   7

(2)

Honourd be
God the
Father,

Honowred be thu, fadir souereigne,   8
   That vowchedsaff suche raunsom [us] to sende
Thin ownë lovëd sone to suffre peyne,
   Oure mysease & myschief [for] to amende !

and God the
Holy Ghost!

   Thu holigost, þat art withowt[en] ende,   12
      With fadier & sone, one god in trinite,
      ffor euere honured be thi maieste !   14

(3)

Honourd be
Mary, Queen
of Heaven!

And thu, [o] blisful maide & modier mylde,   15
   Thu lady, qween of heven), emperice,
Whom Ihesu chees ; and as thi ownë childe
   Thow bare, his veray modiere & noryce,
   Thu floure of vertue, modiere of delice,   19
      Thu toure of trist, and [trew] tresoure of grace,
      honowred mote thu be in euery place !   21

(4)

Honourd be
Jesus, who
has so
helpt us in
Purgatory!

Honowred be þou, blissed lord Ihesu,   22
   Suche grace and mercy have we found in the ;
Suche godlihede, suche myght & suche vertue,
   Whil þat we in purgátory haue be !
   Of alle oure peynes, relesed now be we,   26

Tho' we've
sind

      Wich long[ë] tyme we have a-byden) inne,
      But wonder schort, in régard of oure synne,   28

(5)

and offended
[leaf 29, back]

With whiche we have the souereyn blisfulheed   29
fful grevously displeasyd & offended,

4. *The Angels' Song. We bring Thee back Thy Pilgrims.* xxxiii

In word & werk, & with vnthryfty dede;
  But thanked be thu, lord, it is amended;
  But now is alle oure noyows laboure ended ; 33
  To the we come, as fyne of oure labour,
  Whom willeth eueri trewë trauayloure. 35

yet, thanks to Christ, we're come to him as the end of all our toil.

---

(4) **What tyme þat the pilgrymes had songyne in this wise, hire aungeles wiche þat led them, ansuerid a-nothir song ful swete & ful delicious, as it sewith :**

Cantus angelorum.

[5 stanzas of 7 lines each, *ababb, cc.*]

(1)

Al-myghti lord, oure blisful lord Ihesu,
  Thu myroure of the fadier in maieste,
In whom is seyn his myght and his vertue,
  The welle of witte &[1] wisdaum is in the,
  To whom-is[2] presence now retourned we be 5
  With this pylgrymës which to the we bringe ;
  To thin honoure ful ioyefully we synge. 7

Jesu, we bring Thee these Pilgrims.

(2)

Towardës the, ful longe thei haue trauayled ; 8
  Thu wost thi selfe, how thei han be distressed.
The falsë feend so sorë hem asseyled,
  And greuously diseased & oppressed ;
  But be thi grace, his malice was repressed, 12
  And thrughe thy[3] mercy weel th[e]i be releved,
  And hire entent, fully thei han acheved. 14

They have journeyd long and been sore distrest.

(3)

What laboure & what anguysch have we had, 15
  Sithe þat we took them in oure gouernaunce,
Thu wost Ihesu ; and now, [lord,] we be gladde
  Of alle þat we have don to thi pleasaunce ;
  Wherfore thu wilt with reward us auaunce 19
  Suche as the list a-bove[n] in thi blisse ;
  Eternal Ioye, we schul it neuere mysse. 21

We have had great trouble with them.
Thou wilt raise us to Thy bliss.

(4)

Lo, we presente in-to thin hand a-geyn, 22
  alle-myghty lord, þat to vs þou hast betake,

We give Thee back the folk thou handedst us.

[1] MS. & of. [2] whos. [3] MS. his.
REGEMENT. *c*

honured be thu, Ihesu souereyn),
   Of that we have labóurëd for thi sake,
   Of this labourë, now an ende thu make!   26

[leaf 30]   Thi crëaturës, vnto thi presence,

Receive them well!   Receyve hem of thin heighe benevolence!   28

(5)

They erd, but sufferd. F or thow [that] thei[1] han erred or myswent,   29
   Thei have it a-bought with woundës hard & sore,
And purgeid with grete peyne & [with] torment,
   And duely to hem was Iugëd therfore,
   Alle-thow thei hadde deserued muchë more,   33

Thou wilt put them in Heaven. The remenaunt is relessed, of thi grace;
   In heven) is assigned hirë place.   35

[leaf 30]   (5) **The aungelys song within.**

[7 stanzas of 7 lines each, *ababb, cc.*]

(1)

All honour and thanks to Thee, Lord, in Trinity! A l worshippe, wisdam, welthe and worthinesse, 1
   All bounte, beawte, ioye and blisfulheed,
All honure, vertue, and alle myghtynesse,
   All grace & thankyng, vnto thin godheede,
   ffrom whom alle grace & mercy doth procede!   5
   Ay praised be thu, lord, in Trinite,
   And euere honured be thi maieste!   7

(2)

These Pilgrims join us as Angels. T hat be mankynde oure nombre is encreased, 8
   Of this that longe have be in pilgrymage;
And now is alle hire noyows laboure cessed,
   That was be-gonne here first[ë] dayës age.
   Here is the port of sekire áryuáge   12

[leaf 30, back] Welcome be . you, Honured be thu, blissed lord on hye,
   And wolcome be ye to owre companye!   14

(3)

N ow passed be youre perilous auentures, 15
   and alle youre Auenture hath an endë take.

blessed creatures Right wolcome be ye, blissed crëatures!
   Tyme it is, þat scrippe & burdon) ye forsake,
   ffor now ye schal no longere iourne make;   19

[1] MS. thine.

and aftir laboure, tyme is of quiete ;   Rest ye here!
Alle hevinesse & Anguysch is for-gete.   21

(4)

For ye have don̄ a nobiłł victory,   22   Ye've won a
   And youre labourë nobly díspended,   noble victory.
That so ageyn youre treble enemye
   Youre selffë mygħtely haue défendid ;
   And þat ye have mysdon̄, it is amended   26
     Be sustenaunce of purgatory peyne ;
   Thanked be thu, [o] Ihesu souereyne !   28   Thanks be to
                                                   Christ!

(5)

In heven̄ blisse, here schul ye be witħ vs   29   Ye shall stay
   Vnto the day of fynałł iugëment,   with us till
To wichë day ye schul a-bydë thus,   Judgment-
   And preisë god witħ al youre hool entent,   Day,
   While þat youre bodi, be assignëment   33   tho' your
     Of god, is turned to correpcïoun,   bodies rot.
   And fully schal haue hire purgacioun.   35

(6)

For Reasoun [sayeth] wele, & god-is lawe,   36
   That he þat hatħ don alle his besynesse
(ffor god-is will) youre lustës to witħdrawe—
   Encombryng yow witħ muche vnthryftynesse,—
   That from þat fowle and wofułł wrechidnesse   40
     I-clensid be, and alle renewyd clene
   That manere weye, youre flesċħ is, þat I mene. 42

(7)

So at the last[ë] day thei schal a-ryse,   43   They shall
   And come be-fore that Iugë souereyn̄,   then rise,
To yow conioyned in a wondere wise   and join your
   In a good áccorde witħowt ony peyne,   souls,
   And in this ioye eternally remayne.   47   [leaf 31]
     What ioye is here, ye schul assaye & see,   and stay in
   Honured be the hey[ë] maieste !   49   Heaven.

(6) [The Angels' Song.   Honour to Jesus.]

[5 stanzas of 7 lines each, *ababb, cc.*]

(1)

[leaf 31]
Honourd be
Jesus, !

Honured be thu, blisful lord Ihesu,   1
    and preysed mote thu be in eueri place,
So full of myght, [of] mercy and vertue,
    Of blisse, of bounte, of piete and of grace!
    Who is honurë, may no thing deface ;   5
        Who is [ther] that withstondë may thi myght ?

whom all
must serve!

        But servë the, of fors mote eueri wight.   7

(2)

Honúred be thu, Ihesu, heven̄ kyng,   8

[leaf 31, back]
He has com-
mitted to me
a man
obeying and
loving Him,

    That hast be-taken to my gouernaunce
Suche one that hath, a-bove al othire thing,
    Abowed to the with lowely obeysaunce,
    And loued the with sadde perséueraunce,—   12
        Thi counseil and thin hey comaundëment
        Obseruyng with his hertely hool entent.   14

(3)

who has kept

He hath nought walked be the wey[ë]s large,   15
    That to the worlde so lusty be, & grene ;
But he hath be ententif to thi charge,

himself pure,

    ffrom dedly synne to kepe him selfë clene,

and walkt
the way of
toil;

    And gon̄ to the wey of trauayle & of tene,   19
        Of penaunce and of tribulacïoun,
        In grevous formës of temptacïoun.   21

(4)

who sufferd
Purgatory on
earth.

So hath he had in erthe his purgatórye,   22
    wich þat he hath susteyned wilfully ;

Take him
then, Lord, to
Thy glory!

Wherforë, now receyve him to thi glorye,
    And take him up in[to] thi blisse an hye,
    with the to be in ioye eternally,   26
        In what degre that to him is condigne,
        Right as thi selffë liketh to assigne.   28

(5)

Honourd be
Thou,

Honoured be thu, Ihesu graciows,   29
    That man became thi selfe, for mannës nede ;

who taught
us virtue,

And man thu taughtist to be vertuows,
    To servë the be veray love & dreed,

Rewardyng hem with blisse for hirë mede   33   and rewarded
That doꝛ hire devoire as thei may & kan :   us with bliss !
Thanked be thu, [o] Ihesu, god and man !   35

---

(7) A lamentacioun of the grene tree, complaynyng of the losyng of hire appiɫ.

[40 stanzas of 7 lines each, *ababb, cc.*]

(1)

O fader god, how fers & how cruel,   1   [leaf 63]
   In whom the list or wilt, canst þou the make!   O God! how
Whom wilt thu spare? ne wot I neuere a deel,   cruel art Thou,
Sithe thu thi sone hast to the deth be-take,   for sending
That the offended neuere, ne dide wrake,   5 Thy Son to death!
   Or mystook him to the, or disobeyde,
   Ne to non othere dide he harm, or seide.   7

(2)

I had ioye éntiere, & also gladnesse,   8   [leaf 63, back]
   Whan þou be-took him me to clothe & wrappe   I rejoist when you let
In mannes flesch.   I wend, in sothfastnesse,   me clothe Him in man's
   Have had for euere Ioyë be the lappe ;   flesh.
   But now hath sorwe caught me with his trappe ; 12
   Mi ioye hath made a permutacioun   Now I
   With wepyng & eek lamentacioun.   14 lament.

(3)

O holy gost, þat art alle comfortoure   15   O holy Ghost,
Of woful hertës that wofullë be,   help of the
And art hire veray helpe & counceyloure,   woeful,
   That [eke] of hey vertue shadówist me
   Whan þat the clernesse of thi diuinite   19
   So shynyng in my feerful gost alight,
   Which that me sore agasted & affright,—   21

(4)

Whi hast thu me not in thi rémembraunce   22   why dost
   Now at this tymë, right as thu had tho?   thou not overshade me,
O whi is it noght [vn-]to thin pleasaunce
   Now for to schadwe me as weel also,
   That hid from me myght be my sonës woo? 26 and hide
   Wherof, if þat I may no counfort haue,   my Son's woe from me?
   ffrom deth-is strok there may no thing me save. 28

(5)

O Gabriel,
O gaubriel, whan þat thu come a place, 29

 And madest vnto me thi salewyng,

 And seidist thus : " heil, Mary, ful of grace ! "

why didst
thou not
warn me that
grace would
fail ?
Whi ne had thu govë [to] me warnyng

Of þat gracë that veyn is and faylyng ? 33

 As thu now seest, & sey it weel beforne,

 Sitħ my ioye is me rafte, my grace is lorne. 35

(6)

O Elizabeth,
thy words
end otherwise
than thou in-
tendedst.
O thu elizabeth, my cosyn dere, 36

 The word[ës] þat thu spak in the mountayne

Be ended al in á-nothére manere

 Than thu had wened ; my blissyng in-to peyne

My joy is
gone.
Retorned is ; of ioye am I bareyne ; 40

 I song to sone ; for I sang be the morwe,

[leaf 64]
 And now at evene I wepe and makë sorwe. 42

(7) [See *Minor Poems I*, p. 1—8.]

O Woman,
who saidst
that Blest
was my womb
and teats,
O woman, þat among the poepil speke, 43

 how that the wombë blissed was þat bere,

And the tetýs þat gave to sowkë eek

 The sone of god, the whicħ þat hongitħ hire,

What seist þou now ? whi comest þou not nere ? 47

why can you
not see my
woe ?
 Whi art thu not here ? a, woman ! where art thu,

 That nogħt ne seest my woful body nowe ? 49

(8)

O Symeon,
you said truly
that the
stroke should
pierce my
heart.
O Symeon, þou seidist me ful sothe, 50

 " the strook þat perchë schal my sones herte,

Myn sowle eek thirle it schal " ; & so it dotħ ;

 The wonde of detħ [ne] may I not astirte ;

There may no martirdam me makë smerte 54

 So sore as this martírdam smertitħ me :

 So schuld he sey, þat myght myɴ hurtë see. 56

(9)

O father and
mother, Joa-
chim and
Anne,
why did you
beget me to
such grief ?
O Ioachim, a, derë fadir myɴ, 57

 And thu seint anne, my dere modire also,

To what entent, or to what ende or[1] fyne [1 MS. of]

 Engendred ye, me þat am greved soo ?

 Mirthe to me is become a veray foo : 61

Youre fadire dauid, þat an harpowre was,
Conforted men þat stod in hevy cas.　　　　63

(10)

Me thinkiþ ye do not to me ariȝt,　　　　64
　that were his súccessoures, siþ instrument
Have ye now left, wherwiþ to hauë liȝt,
　And me counfort in my woful turment.
Me to [doon] esë, have ye no talent,　　　68
　And knowë my counfort[e]les distresse :
Ye auȝt to wepë for myn hevynesse.　　　70

You've no harp, like your father David, where-with to comfort me.

(11)

O blissed sone, on the wil I owt-throwe　　71
　My salt[ë] teres ; for singulerly on the
My loke is sette.　o, thinke how many a throwe
　Thu on myn armës lay, and on my knee
Thu sat, & had many a cusse of me ;　　　75
　Also, the to sowke, of my brestis yaf I,
Thé norissching [right] faire & tenderly.　77

O Christ, my Son,

think how I dandled, kist

[leaf 64, back] and suckled Thee.

(12)

Now the, from me, withdrawiþ bitter deþ,　78
　And makiþ a wrong[ful] disseueraunce.
Think þou not, sone, in me þat ony breþ
　Endurë may, þat fele al this greuaunce.
Mi martirdom, me haþ at vtteraunce ;　　82
　I nedës stervë mot, siþ I the see
Shamefully naked, streit upon this tree.　84

Now Death divides us.

I must die. I see Thee naked on the Cross,

(13)

And this me sleth, that in the open day　　85
　Thin hertis wondë schewiþ him so wide,
That allë men see and be-holde it may,
　So largëly, lo, openèd is thi side ;
O, wo is me, þat siþ I may not hide !　　89
　And, among other of my smert[ë] grevës,
Thu art now put also among [the] thevës,　91

and Thy wounds wide open.

Thou art put among thieves ;

(14)

As thowe, my sone, had be a wiked wiȝt.　92
And lest þat som men also, perauenture,

No knowleche had of thi *per*sone a-riḡht,

Pilate hath̄ put up th*i* name in scripture,

That knowë it may eueri crëature, 96

ffor þat thi pena*u*nce schuld[ë] not be hid.

O, wo is me, þat see alle this beted! 98

(15)

H̄ow may my eynë [þat] be-holde alle this, 99

Refreynë hem to schewë by wepyng

My*n* hert[es] greef? mot I not wepe? o, yis.

Sone, if thu hadist her*e*, fadir*e* lievyng,

þat woldë wepe and makë weymentyng 103

ffor cause he had[de] part in thi persone,

That wer*e* [a] gret abreggyng of my mone. 105

(16)

B̄ut thu, in erthë, fadir had[dist] neu*ere*; 106

No wiḡht for the, suche cause hath̄ for to wepe,

As now haue I. schalt thu fro me disseuere,

That art al̄l hooly my*n*? my sorwes deepe

Have al̄l my*n* hert-is ioyës leyd to slepe. 110

No wiḡht with̄ me, in the, my sone, hath̄ part;

Alle holy of my blod, der*e* child, þou art. 112

(17)

T̄hat dowbleth̄ al my torment & my greef; 113

Vn-to my*n* hert it is confusïc*n*,

Thi harme to see, þ*a*t art to me so leef.

Myḡht not this raunsom*n* or redempcïo*n*

Of man, have be w*ith*owt effusyo*n* 117

Of thi blood? Yis, if it had be thi lust;

But what þ*a*t it be do, suffre the must. 119

(18)

O deth̄, þat so kithest thi bittirnesse, 120

ffirst on my sone, and afterward on me,

Bitter*e* art thu, and ful of crabydnesse,

That thus my sone hast slayne w*ith* cruelte,

And noḡht me slest! certayn I wil not flee. 124

Come of, come [of], and slee me her*e*, as blyff;[1]

ffro him depar*t*ë wil I not a-lyffe. [1 MS. be lyff] 126

(19)

O mones, o sterrës, and thou[1] firmament, [¹ MS. the] 127   O Moon and Stars,
how may ye nowe from wepyng yow restreyne,
And see youre crëature in suche torment?
  Ye owgħt, tourbled to be in euery veyne,   weep for my Son's death!
  And his dispietows detħ witħ me compleyne. 131
    Wepitħ and crietħ as lowde as euere ye may!
    Oure crëature witħ wrong is slayn this day! 133

(20)

O Sonnë, witħ thi cleerë bemys brigħt, 134   o Sun,
That seest my child nakéd this now-is tyde,
Whi suffrist him [thou] in the open sigħt   why leav'st thou my Child naked here,
Here of this men, vncovered to abide?
  Thu art, as muche or more, holde him to hide, 138   and dost not cover Him as Shem coverd Noah?.
  Than[2] Sem þat heled his fadir Noe   [² MS. Tham]
  Whan he aspyed þat naked so was he. 140

(21)

If thu his sonë be, do like there-to! 141   Withdraw thy light, and hide my Son's nakedness.]
let see witħ-drawe thi bemës brigħt[e]nesse:
þou art to blame, but if þat thu so do.
  ffor schame, hide my sones nakidnesse!   [leaf 65, back]
  Is there in the no droppe of kendënesse? 145
    Remembre, he is thi lord & crëature;
    Now covere him for thi worshippe and honoure!

(22)

O erthe, what lust hast thu, so to susteyne 148   O Earth, why bear'st thou His Cross?
The crosse on whicħ he þat the made, and it,
Is hongëd, and adornëd the witħ grene
  Whicħ þat thu on weredist? how hast thu the qwitte
  Vnto thi lord? o, do this for him yitte! 152
    Now qwakë yow for dool, & clevë thu in two,   Cleave in two, and swallow His blood,
    And alle þat blood, restorë thu me to, 154

(23)

Which þou hast drunken: it is myn, & not thin. 155   which is mine, not thine;
Or elles thus, witħ owt[en] tarieng,
Tho bodies deed[ë] whicħ þat in the lyne,   [³ MS. tasted]   or cast up thy dead.
  Cast owt: for thei be taste[3] of sucħ dewyng
  hem owt to clothe[4] a-geyn in hire clothing. 159
    Thu Caluary, art holdë, namëly   [⁴ MS. calle hem]
    So for to do: parde, to the speke I. 161

(24)

O derë sone, my detħ now neigħitħ fast, 162
　　Sitħ to a-nothere thu hast goven me,
Than vnto the; And how may my liffe last,
　　þat me gevest to ony othere than to the,
　　Thow [it] so be that he a virgyne bee? 166
　　　if thu, be Iuste Balaunce, woldest wey aħ,
　　　The weigħt of him & the is not egaħ. 168

(25)

He a disciple is; thu art his lord; 169
　　Thu alwey art gretterë than he is;
Be-twyꝏ youre mygħt*is* is there gret discorde.
　　My woful turnement[1] dowblyd is be this; [1 torment]
　　I nedës mornë must, & fare a-mysse. 173

　　it semitħ þat thu makist départyng
　　Of the & me, for ay witħowt endyng; 175

(26)

A*nd*,[2] namely, sitħ thu me but "woman" callest, 176
　　As I to the were straunge & al vnknowe; [2 ? MS.]
There-throw, my sone, my Ioyës thu appallest;
　　Weel fele I thát detħ hís vengeábiħ bowe
　　hatħ bent, & me *pur*pósitħ douꝏ to throwe; 180
　　　Of sorwe, takë may I not Inowe,
　　　Sitħ [that] my namë douꝏ awey is nowe: 182

(27)

Wel may men calle or namë me "marra" 183
　　Fro[3] hen[ne]s forth; and so men may me calle.

How schuld I longere be called 'Mária,'
　　Sitħ 'I,' which is Ih*esus*,[4] is fro me falle
　　This day, and my swetnesse [is] in-to galle 187
　　　Turned, sitħ 'I'[5] which was the bëawte,
　　　Lo, of my name, this day beraft is me. 189

(28)

O Ioħn, my derë frende, thu hast receyved 190
　　A woful modier'; & an hevi sone
have I of the. detħ hatħ mynꝏ other' veyued:

[3] MS. For.　　[4] MS. Sith he the which is called Ihc.　　[5] MS. he.

How may we two the detħ eschewe or schone ?
We drery wiȝħtës two, where may we wone ?   194
 Thu art of counfort destitute, I se,
 And so am I ! o, carefull now be we !   196

We are full of care

(29)

Un-to oure hertës, detħ hatħ sent his wonde ;   197
Now of vs may allegen othir-is peyne ;
So many sorwis in vs two abounde,   [1 MS. for]
We haue no myȝħt fro[1] sorwe vs to restreyne.
 I se non othir², but deyë mot we tweyne ;   201
 Now let vs stervë here be companye :
 Stervë thu there, & riȝħt here I wil dye.   203

and sorrow.
Let us both die!

(30)

O Aungeles, theï² ye mornë, wayle & wepe,   204
Ye do no wrong ; for slayn is youre créatoure,
Be the poepil þat ye were wont to kepe,   [2 though]
To gide & lede : thei to the dedës³ schowre   [3 death's]
have put him.   thow ye have wo & langoure,   208
 No wonder is it : who may blamë yowe ?
 And most chier² he had, of hem þat him slowe. 210

O Angels who weep, your Creator is slain.

(31)

O special love, which þat me ioyned hast   211
Vnto my sone, ful strong is thi knettyng !
This day, there-inne fynde I a bitter tast ;
ffor now I tast & felë the streynyng
Of detħ, be thi detħ : detħ fele I me styng.   215
 O purë modier², what schalt thu now seye ?
 Pore Maryë ! thi witte is now awey.   217

O Love, who bound me to [leaf 66, back] my Son,
I feel the sting of Death.
Poor Mary !

(32)

Maria, nay, but 'marred' I the call ;   218
So may I weel ; for þou art, weel I wot,
Vessel of care & woo, & sorwes alle.
 Now þou art frosty coold ; now fery hoot ;
 And riȝħt as þat a schippe, or barge or boot,   222
 Among the wawës dryvetħ sternëles,
 So dost thu, woful woman counfortles.   224

'Marred,' not 'Mary,' I call thee.
Thou drivest rudderless among the waves.

(33)

And also of modier² hast þou lost the style ;   225
No more may thu be called by that name.

Thou hast lost the name of Mother.

O sones of Adam, al to long[ë] while
Ye tarie hens! hastitħ hedir for schame!

See how my sonë, for youre gilt and blame,   229
lo, hangitħ here, bibléd upon the crosse!
Bymenetħ him in hert, in chiere & voysse!   231

(34)

His blody stremës, se now, & be-holde!   232
if ye to him have [any] affeccïoun,
Now, for his woo, youre hertës owt[en] colde;
Schewytħ youre kendnesse & youre dileccioun,
ffor youre gilt makitħ he correccioun,   236

And ámenditħ right be his ownë detħ:
That ye nogħt rewe on him, myn) hert it sletħ. 238

(35)

A, modier', þat so sone hire cotë tare   239
Or rentë! say ye neuere none or this,
ffor child [the] whicħ [she] of hire body bare,
To yeve hire tete.   and my child þat here is,
his cote hatħ torne, for youre gilt, not for his,   243

[&] hatħ of his blood spilt in gret foysoun;
And alle his, lo, for youre redempcïoun!   245

(36)

My derë childe, my fruyt þat on [me] growed,   246
Myn) lusty appil, blisful faire and sweet,
Now detħ hatħ him be-clapped witħ his clowde,
That him perced [vn]to the hertë rote.

Go to, thow man, þere thu mygħt haue thi bote! 250
Go suke the Iuce! the is no thing so sweet;
Go take thin part! I rede the not for-gete.   252

(37)

Go nere, & see how þat he is for-bete,   253
And alle for-persed sore and pietously!

See how there rennë fyvë stremës grete,
That yelde[n] owt the Iuce habundauntly!

Go sowke therof! I say you faithfully,   257

In good tyme was he bore, þat hatħ þat grace,
In tho woundes to make his duellyng place.   259

(38)

O Aduersari, [t]how cruel dryë tree,   260   O cruel Cross,
  To the speke I! nowe hast þou thi entent;
My sweet[ë] fruyt þou hast be-reved me   thou hast
  A-geyn) my wiH, nothing of myne assent.   ta'en my
    I se how al to-Raced and to-rent   264   Fruyt;
      On the he hongitħ : is this weel I-doo?   he's rent and
      I bare him monethis nyne, but no thing so. 266   torn on thee.

(39)

O cruel tree, sitħ thu hast thi desire,   267   Why hast
  Whi wilt þou not, to my fruyt[1] be fauorábiH,   thou
To saue it hool? but feruentere than the fiere
  he fyndetħ, & nothing [in thee] agrëáble.   not kept Him
    It is to me but alle discountfortáble   271   whole?
      To se myn) herte attached the vpon),
      ffor he & I, oure hert[ë] is but one.   273

(40)

Now witħ my fruyt art þou here openly,   274   All the world
  That alle the world it may be-holde & see   is here to see
Restored, whicħ (I sey the sekerly)   my Fruit
Is more of vertue and of dignyte   restored.
Than was the fruyt þat spoyled was from the.   278
    Thu hast thi wiH; thin honoure schal suffise   Give it me in
    To the: yelde me my fruyt in goodly wise! 280   goodly wise!
                                                                [leaf 67, back]

---

(8) The recordyng of aungeles song of the   [leaf 95, back]
Natiuite of oure lady.

[7 stanzas of 7 lines each, ababb, cc.]

(1)

HOnured be thu, blisseful lord benigne,   1   Honour to
  That now vntó man wil be merciáble   God,
As he may se apertly be a signe,   who's given
  A braunche, þat sprongen is ful profitable,   man
  fful frescħ & faire, & heily commendable   5
    Of Iesse-is Rote, þat called is marie,   a branch
    That schal the blisseful appil fructifie.   7   of Jesse's
                                                                root, Mary,

[1] Scan "to my fruyt" as one measure.

(2)

A blisful flour', owt of this spray schal springe;   8

whose fruit   The fruyt þer-of schal be ful precïous;

A causë haue [we] for to ioye & synge,

In honure of þat maidë gracïous,

shall comfort
us,   That gret comfort schal cause[n] vnto vs;   12

and make
peace 'tween
God and man.   ffor now schal faste oure company encrees,

And god with man schal makë smallë pees.   14

(3)

She shall
be mother of
Christ,   Now be we glad, in honure of this maide,   15

That schal be modier' of the kyng eterne,

Be whom the raunsom fully schal be paid

who shall
fetch man
from Hell.   ffor man, þat loken is in hellë herne.

Now schal we haue no power' for to warne   19

Man for [to] entre in-to paradise;

The lord wil sette him at so highe a price.   21

(4)

Thu, lucifer', þat list in helle I-bounde,   22

[leaf 96]
She shall
confound
Lucifer,   That whylom were one of oure companye,

This maidë schal the vtterly confounde,

And do the muchë schame & vilanye,

who deceivd
Eve.   Which Eua hast deceyuëd traytouresly,   26

And made hire trust[en] on thi fals behest,

Wherby thu hast hire lynage alle arest.   28

(5)

Thu cursed caitiff! mawgre thi malice[1]!   29

Man shall
be regiven
Paradise.   fful sone he schal be sette owt of thin hande;

Reseised schal he be with paradise;

Thu schalt not be of powire to with-stande;

But, as an hound þat tied is with a bande,   33

Lucifer shal
be bound in
pain.   So schalt thu eternally lyn) in thi peyne;

Ne no counfort getist thu, thow þou pleyne.]   35

(6)

He deceivd
Eve.   To gret distresse & gret desólacioun   36

A maidë first was déceyvëd be the:

Mary shall
shame him.   Vnto thi schame and [thi] confusïoun,

A blissed maidë schal thi ladi be.

But weel is him þat schal þat maidë see,   40

[1] MS. malace.

And schal be schent to salue hir*e*, & grete,

And say "heil, mary, maidë faire & sweet!"   42   Blest is he who shall hail her.

(7)

Who euer*e* it be, þat schal do this messáge,   43

fful weel is him that fyndë may that grace :

It schal him weel suffisë for his wage,   The sight of her shall reward him.

To see þat blissed sweet[ë] lady face.

Now witħ alle ioyës, myrthë & soláce,   47

ffor loue of hire honure, we [synge] this day

Witħ alle the songes & myrthës þat we may.   49

---

(9) The aungeles song.   [leaf 97]

[2 stanzas of 7 lines each, *ababb, cc.*]

(1)

Honured be thu, blisful heuen*e* queen*e*,   1   Honour Mary,

And worschepid mot þou be in eueri place,

That modier' art, and veari maidë clene !   mother and maid,

Of god, oure lord, thu geten hast þat grace.

Thu, cause of Ioyës art, and alle soláce,   5   source of joy!

Be merite of thi gret humilite,

And by the flour*e* of thi virginite.   7   [leaf 97, back]

(2)

Honured be thu blissed ladi bright !   8   Honour her!

Be thi persone, embasshëd is natúre ;

Of heuene blisse, augmented is the ligħt,

Be presence of so fare a crëature ;

Thi worthinessë pasitħ aħ mesúre ;   12

ffor vnto thin astate imperiaħ,   No praise can equal her.

No praisyng is, þat may be peregaħ.   14

---

(10) The aungeles songe in the feste of the   [leaf 99]
Epiph*a*nie of our*e* lord.

[4 stanzas of 7 lines each, *ababb, cc.*]

(1)

HOnured be this blissed holy festë day   1   Honour this Feast-day,

In worshipp*e* of the sweet[ë] welle of liffe,

With alle the ioyes & mirthë þat we may,

for Christ
has wed the
Church.

for Crist, the kirke hatħ chosë to his wiffe ;

And fynally abated is þat striffe,   5

þat him betwyn), & man, hatħ longë be ;

Honured be this blessed Trinite !   7

(2)

Owt of this welle, so noble licoure ran),   8

So faire, so fressħ, so lusty, hony-sweet,

That sitħ this first day þat the world be-gan),

With suche a wellë migħt[ë] no man mete.

Man is for-
given.

Alle heuynesse & malice is for-gete   12

As toward man ; excused clene is hee ;

Honour the
Trinity !

honured be the blissed Trinite !   14

(3)

On this day
Christ turnd
water into
wine ;

This day, so lowe he wold him self incline,   15

The thrid[dë] festë witħ his higħe persone

To honure, turnyng watir in-to wynne.

and was
baptized by
John.

This day was Ihesu baptised of seint Iohn ;

The fadir-is voice was herd owt of his trone :   19

" This is my loued sone, þat liketħ me."

honured be the souereyn Trinite !   21

(4)

The Holy
Ghost
lighted on
Him as a
Dove.

And þat he schuld haue recorde Autentyk,   22

The thrid[dë] persone, on oure lord a-ligħt,

The holy gost, vn-to a dowe I-lyk,

[leaf 99, back]

That pleyn[ë]ly was seyn) of eueri wigħt.

Thus blissed hatħ he watir, god al-mygħt,   26

In honure of this [higħe] solemnite.

Honour the
Trinity !

Honured be the blissed Trinite !   28

---

(11) the aungeles song on pask day.

[5 stanzas of 7 lines each, *ababb, cc.*]

(1)

[leaf 100]
Honour to
Jesus,

HOnurèd be thu, Ihesu saueour',   1

þat for mankendë were do on the rode ;

And þerto woldest do vs þat honure,

who fed us
with His flesh
and blood !

To fede vs witħ thi flesche & witħ thi bloode.

was neuere to vs fleschë halfe so goode ;   5

ffor wonderly oure ioyes it doth renewe.
honured be thu, blissed lord Ihesu !   7

(2)

Whan thu were died, to hellë þou descended,   8   He descended
   And fette hem owt þat [longe] lay there in peyne ;   into Hell,
ffor be thi deth, oure mis was alle a-mended.   and brought
                              out those in
                              pain.
   The thrid day, thu a-roos to lyffe a-geyne   He rose again
   With highe tryumphe, & ioyë souereyn) :   12   the third day.
   As champioun [the chef] of hie vertue,
   Honured be þou, blissed lord Ihesu !   14

(3)

The grevous iourney þat thu took on hande,   15   His pain paid
   hath clerly maad, to eueri wight appere,
In sothfastnesse to see & vnderstonde,—
   To þat only was thi talent & thi chiere
So suffisaunt, lo,—that oure raunsoum were   19   more than
   Superhabundaunt over þat was due ;   our ransom.
   Honured be thu, blisseful lord Ihesu !   21

(4)

On thursday, a noble soper þou made,   22   He ordaind
   Where thu ordeyned first thi sacrament ;   the Sacra-
                                ment at
But muchë more it doth oure hertës glade,   supper on
                                Thursday.
   The worthi dyner' of this day present,   He shows
                                Himself al-
   In which þou schewest thi self omnipotent,   26   mighty in to-
                                day's dinner.
   Rising from deth to lyve, it is ful trewe :
   Honured be thu, blisful lord Ihesu !   28

(5)

Now for this festë schal we say the graces,   29   Let us say
   And worthi is, with alle oure diligence,   grace for this
                                feast,
And thank the here, & [eke] in allë places,   and thank our
                                Lord Jesus !
   Of thi ful bountevous benevolence,
   Thi myght, thi grace, thi souereyn excellence :   33
   Thu art the ground & welle of alle vertue :
   Honured be thu, blisfull lord Ihesu !   35   [leaf 100, bk.]

REGEMENT.   *d*

(12) The song of graces of alle seintes upon Paske day.

[4 stanzas of 7 lines each, *ababb, cc.*]

(1)

Honourd be
Christ,

HOnured be thu, blisfull lord a-bove,   1
    That vowchidsaffë this iourny to take,
Man to become, only for man-is love,

who sufferd
death for our
sins.

    And deth to suffre, for my synnës sake ;
    So hast thu vs owt of the bondë schake,   5
        Of Sathanas, þat held us longe in peyne :
        Honured be thu, Ihesu souereyne !   7

(2)

When Adam
took the
apple,

Full evele I dede, whan I the appil took ;   8
    I wend to haue had *ther*bi prosperite ;
It satte so ny my sidës, þat thei ooke ;

he fell,
and his issue
too.

    To greet myschief I fill from hey degre,
    And alle my issue, for be-cause of me ;   12
Now Christ
has set all
right.
        Now hast þou, lord, restored all a-geyn) :
        Honured be thu, Ihesu souereyne !   14

(3)

So richëly þou hast refresshëd vs,   15
    And vs counfórted with thi feste riall ;
So swet a fruyt, & so delicïows,
    So faire it is, and so celestiall,

Our mishap is
all forgotten.

    That oure disease now is forgotten all,   19
        This fruyt hath so visíted eueri veyne :
        Honured be thu, Ihesu souereyne !   21

(4)

This may be called weel the fruyt of liff.   22
    The fruyt of deth, was wherof I asaide ;

4000 years we
lay in Hell,
till Christ
rescued us.

That, be thi Iugëment diffinitiffe,
    ffoure thowsande yer*e* I was ful ille araide,
    Til þat this fruyt, þat born) was of a maide,   26
Honour
Him !
        haddë reformed : therefor lat vs seyn),
        Honured be thu, Ihesu souereyn) !   28

(13) The aungeles song & alle othir seintes in the feste of Pentecost.

[leaf 102]

[3 stanzas of 7 lines each, *ababb, cc.*]

(1)

HOnured be thu, holy gost in hie,   1   Honour the Holy Ghost,
That vn-to poeple of so pore astate
hast youe thi grace, to stondë myghtely   who's given us grace
Ageyn tyrauntës fiers & obstynate,
ffor to endwe them with thi principate   5
  To leve hire erroure, & hire liffe to amende :   to leave sin, and amend.
honured be thu, lord, with-owt[en] ende !   7

(2)

Thu gave hem wete & cunnyng [for] to preche,   8   He gave knowledge
And corage for to stand[ë] be the lawe,
Alle maner' poepil, to wisshe & to teche,   to teach folk to quit their vices,
ffrom vices alle hir' lustës to with-drawe,
And of hire lord [&] god to stande in awe,   12   and fear God.
  To his pleasaunce hire hertës to intende :
Honured be thu, lord, with-owt[en] ende !   14   [leaf 102, bk.]

(3)

This ffischeres alle be ávoyded of slowthe :   15   The Martyrs
ffor blaundisshing, for manasyng, ne for drede,
Thei spared nought, but stodë by the trowthe ;
Of peynës & tormént toke thei non) heed,   took no heed of tortures,
But fayne to see hire heed & hire sides blede,   19
  [aferd] fful myghtly thi lawys to offende :   but stood by the Truth.
Honured be thu, lord, with-owt[en] ende !   21

---

(14) The pietous complainte of the Soule.

[leaf 8]

[52 stanzas of 7 lines each, *ababb, cc.*]

(1)

Blisful lord on heigh, what schall I do,   1
  or in what place may I my selfë hide ?   Where can I hide my-self?
Refute ne wot i non) to drawë to.
no doute I must my Iugëment a-byde ;
my foo is alwei redy be my side,   5   My foe is beside me.
  me schapyng to appelë and accuse ;
I can no worde myn selffë to excuse.   7

14. *The piteous Complaint of the Soul.*

(2)

I am aryved to a peꞃilous port,   8
  ne knowe I nougꞓt to whom I may retourne ;
I am arrest ; now kaꝺ I noꝺ confort ;
  mawgre my selfe, rigꞓt here mot I soiourne ;
  For my mysshappe, A cause haue I to mourne ;   12

And in my skrippe now fynde I no vetayle,
  ne my burdonë dotꞓ me nought avayle.   14

(3)

Burdone ne skrippe may I no lengere bere,   15

  Myne enemy so sore assailetꞓ me ;
I holde it best to cast awey this gere,
  And shape my selfe preuély for to flee.
O blisful lord, I wis it wele nougꞓt be,   19
  And weel þou woot, how þat me hath bywiled
  Myne enemy that hatꞓ now me defiled.   21

(4)

Wherfore now I am brougꞓt to iugëment,   22
Sithe I am falle in myschieff and porcert,
Ne I ne may, to myn accusëment,
Ne can nougꞓt say but aftir my desert,
And my trespace, that knowë is apert,   26
If þat I shaꞟ myne[1] réwarde vnderfonge :
Allas ! whi have I be synfuꞟ so longe.   [1] MS. alle   28
           myne

(5)

But best it is, if reasoꝺ say me trowthe,   29
  That of some helpe I make me puꞃveaunce ;
Parde, some wigꞓt on me wil havë rewthe ;
  Asay I shal ; but, for my sustenaunce,
  My burdone must I bere for suffisaunce,   33
   For, mygꞓt wiꞇhowt[en] it [ne] haue I none ;
   I bere it nougꞓt ; it beritꞓ my persone.   35

(6)

Allas, but I haue now experience   36
  Off wis[ë]dam, my selffë to demeane,
To éxcuse me have I none audience,
  And alle my witte availetꞓ not a beane ;
  Thus is myne hope alle discounfórted clene,   40

I kan nougħt do but cryë & compleyne,
That charite nougħt rekkitħ of my peyne. 42

But I can only cry, that Charity cares not for me.

(7)

Whi saitħ Powle, that othere yiftes alle 43
Schul failë here, but only charite
A-bydyng is, for he kowdë nougħt falle.
Whethir this be sotħ? but nay, as it semitħ me,
He wold[ë] than myne [good] aduócat be, 47
And somwhat say¹ to helpë in myne cause,
For I kan nother spekë word ne clause. ¹ MS. say I

[leaf 9]

(8)

I am adred that charite is deed, 50
And slayne in erthe, of wikked[ë] men there,
Withowt[en] eyre or issue of hire seed,
Left here on higħë :—lo, this is my fere ;
And if I wiste that sche on lyvë were, 54
I wold not spare to callë and [to] crie,
If I hire, in oný place mygħt a-spie. 56

I fear Charity is dead.

(9)

O charite, so good & so gracious ! 57
Thu hast be euere to tho þat have nede !
I that am in this brikë perilous,—
That, in myne schippe, my self[ë] for to fede
Haue I no bred now of thin almësdede,— 61
Somwhat thu helpe, myn hunger to abate,
Havyng reward vnto my pouer astate. 63

But I appeal to her.

(10)

I meanë thus : if oný part of grace 64
Reserued be, in tresoure or ellës where,
That thu, for me purveyë and purchase
Wolde vouchësaff, gret wondere but there were
I-nowgħ for me : nougħt ellës I require ; 68
Do somwhat, than, aftir thi propirte,
And schewe whi thu art cleped charite. 70

If any grace is left,

let me have it !

(11)

But now, allas, ful weel I may recorde, 71
Whil I had mygħt and space of tyme I-nowgħ,
Of this mattere, towchid I no word,
Ne, to seint, I tho my self[ë] drowgħ,

I know that in youth I never sought it,

That in myne nede for me may spekë now,   75
As for no service that I have to him do :
Wot I not, whom to make my monë to.   77

(12)

and never
servd any
saint;

If I, to ony seint in special   78
Had ony thing [i]forsed myne entent
Witñ ony service, othir' gret or smaħ,

[leaf 9, back]

I wold me have avaylèd in present ;
But thus have I be slowe and necligent,   82
That I no freend have made, ne no seint pleased ;
Wherfore, as now, am I [right iħ] disseased.   84

(13)

To hem am I a straunger' and vnknowe ;   85
I knowe nougħt, to whom I shal my selffe dresse
To askë helpe, as I suppose and trowe,
Ther is none that wold done that besynesse ;
And nougħt for this, I be-hotë expresse,   89

but yet I'll
cry to them.

Vnto hem I wiħ [both] compleyne and crye,
To make my causë knowenɔ openly.   91

(14)

Jesu, I

To the, Ihesu, the sone of god above,   92
That were of mary, verray maidë, borne
In very flesch and blood, for mannës love,

appeal to
Thee !

To the, will I now áppelë beforne,
Synɔ thu art man, and forthermore   96
Oure brothir', and a part of ourë kynde :
Good is to us that we thi fauoure fynde.   98

(15)

This dare I say, sithe that thu wilfully   99
Where done to detħ, only for mannës sake,
And of thi selfe whas none encheasoun whi,

Thou wilt not
forsake one
who seeks
Thy grace.

This knowe I weel, þou wilt it nougħt forsake,
To alle that wiħ vnto thi grace him take,   103
And askë it : as oftë I haue lerned,
Was neuere yitte none, to whom it was warned.

(16)

I have sorely
offended
Thee,

This woot I weel, I haue ful sore offendid   106
Thi maiestes ; wherof I me repente.
Ful late it was, or I my selfe amended,

But yitte ne come it neuere in myne entente
To disallowë thi gouérnëmente ; 110

 That 'lord and kyng' I have callëd the euere ;
 Thi lawës also ne forsoke I neuere. 112

but I never
denied Thee.

(17)

My scrippe of feithë, haue I nougħt for-lete, 113
 but hool, rigħt as it was [i]takë me,
I have it kepte ; but that no thinges gret[e]
(This knowe I weel) susteigned I for the,
 Nor do that I was bound of duëte.

I have kept
my Faith.

[leaf 10]

     ¹ MS. the witħinne.

 Yitte wote I weel, so gret is nougħt my synne,
 as grace & mercy is, Ihesu witħinne.¹ 119

(18)

Away, yit nougħt, eueri deel that grace 120
 Dispendid is, that tho in thi persone
was plentevous whan, witħ so pale a face,
For me thu hengë on the crosse alone ;
 But, for we beggyng wrecchis euerychone 124
  Be procuryng alway for our purveaunce,
  Thi grace thu woldest hiden) now purchaunce.

The Grace
Thou hadst
on the Cross
is not all
gone.

(19)

Yitte may we, by the persëd holës weħ, 127
 And be tho also that large be, & wide,
Behalde and see, that certeyn) euerideħ
Now spended is, though that thu woldest it hide ;
 For thowe there ran) a Rever' from thi side, 131
  That alle the world hatħ fully ouerflowen)
  Thi grace is hool, as euery man may knowen. 133

Thou hast it
all still.

(20)

Sithe yitte thi grace is nougħt dispendid aħ, 134
 Witħ that thu hast me schewid to the tyme present,
And² come, and with the thus argue I schaħ,
 "Sithe it alway hatħ ben) [so] affluent,
 Discreasyng nougħt, ne none appeyrëment 138
  Be-fallitħ it, thougħe neuere so largëly
  Thou yeve it where thu list habundauntly, 140

² ? Now

And since it
is so full,

(21)

Thu owist to defendë me this day, 141
 kepyng my cause, that stonditħ al in dowte

Thou
oughtest to
take up my
cause.

A-geyn my foo, with all that euere he may.
  Thi grace, me to be-revyn) is a-bowte,
    And, me for to passen al with-out ;   145
      Ful ofte he hath grevèd me here-be-fore,
      And hopith now that all I haue forlore.   147

(22)

[leaf 10, back] Though þat my speche be sownyng to foly,   148
  Yitte, blissed Lord, displease it nought to the,
    That to haue spokë of aduócacie,
Be my advocate, Thou, the Judge!   So that thu schuldest myn aduócat be :
    Thu Art the souereigne iuge of equite,   152
      And nought for-thi, to hem that to the truste,
      Here aduocat thu art, whan that the liste.   154

(23)

For, sothe it is, where synne and wrechidnesse   155
  A-boundeth most, there nedeth most[ë] grace,
    To tho that askë thë for-gevënesse,
Turn not Thy face from me!   It sittith the nought to wrye awey thin face ;
    Thi charite will cleyme there is a place :   159
      But this were southe, gret peril must redounde,
      Al mortal men with mischief to confounde."   161

(24)

Mary, mother and maid, Now maide & modier', of this worlde Princesse,   162
  So ful of gracë fulfilled thu were
Whan gaubriel his massage gan expresse,
  And ' Aue' was resownyng in thin ere,
    By wich oure lord, blissed saueoure thu bere,   166
I appeal to thee.   And of thi blood he took his humanite,—
    My cause also I áppele vnto the,   168

(25)

As aduocate for man, & procuresse   169
  Approovid oftë be experience,
Be my help against my foe!   So be myne helpe to ávoide and represse
  Myne enemy, wich that be violence
    Wold schend[ë] me, but if[1] thi résistence, [1 ? for] 173
    Now be myne helpe, o blisful qwene !   [2 ? some]
      So lat somwhat[2] of thi grace on me be sene !   175

(26)

Sith that thi sone and thu of one accorde   176
    Be vearili, (as reason is that ye be),
I, that for dreed vnnethe kan) speke a worde,
    But tremble as doth a leef vpon) a tree,
      Thu, ladi ful of merci and piete,   180   Succour me in this troublous time!
       Now must thu be myne helpe and myne socoure
       Of refute, in this áuentóurës howre!   182   [leaf 11]

(27)

For, but thu wilt my causë [now] defende   183   But thou helpest,
    A-geyn[ës] him wich is thyne enemy,
that redi is, to greve and to offende
    Bothe the, and allë that wolde hertely
      The servë, and thi blisful sone also,   187
       he will hem castë in-to hellë dike,   the Devil 'll cast us into
       And berith me an hande þat I am him like.   189   Hell.

(28)

I ám like, now that I haue done a-mys,   190
    Eternal deth deserued with my dede;
But, gracïous queen[ë] of heuene blisse,   I deserve endless death; but, Queen of Heaven, help me!
    Thu be myne helpe and counfort in this nede,
      But I recordë—and this is my dreed,—   194
       That wonder sympillë[1] I have the served,
       So that I haue no thing of the deserved.   1 ? synfullye

(29)

And nought for-thi, thes burdon is my trest,   197
    In wich I have my solace & my disport;
Of[2] this pomel will I my self[ë] rest,   2 ? On
    That specially to me geuith gret counfort;
      My febill gost it helpith to support,   201
       That is, thi selfë, moder', maide and wiffe,   Thou art the solace of my
       The sustenaunce and solace of my liffe.   203   life.

(30)

And I schal neuere trowë ne suppose,   204
    Sithe he, the wich of merci is the welle,
Within thi sidës wold him selfë close,
    Right as thi childe, in veari flesch & falle,   Thy Son will not let Satan
      That he schuld lete the foulë feend of helle   208

take those
who seek
thee.

To execute malice, or elles vengeaunce,
On hem þat the besekë witħ instaunce.   210

(31)

No beast is
so fierce that

Theᵣe is no lyonꝯ, ne cruel lyonesse,   211
So fiers ne so dispietous of corage,
That hire malice attempren¹ and oppresse   ¹ ? nil tempren
Ne witħ cessynꝯ of hirë felle corage

it 'll not obey
thee.
[leaf 11, back]

To the, that lowëly hem selfe witħ wage   215
Witħ mekë hertë to the ground obeye :
Such is the nature, as this clerkës say.   217

(32)

I am the same that heighli hath mys-wrougħt   218
A-geyn thi childe Iheſu, and also the ;

Christ is no
lion, thou no
lioness ;

Yit knowe I wel that " lyon " is he nougħt,
Nor thu no " lyonessë " [fiers] may be.
In you there is no malice ne cruelte ;   222

but mercy
and grace.

But mercie, pite, goodnessë & grace,
In you thei have hire veray propirꝰ place.   224

(33)

Wherfore I schal the pray[ë] and be-seke,   225
That thu, a-geyn me, nothing be amoeved,
With lowely hertë sitħ I my-self meke.
Thougħ þat I have thi sone and the agreved,
Be the is alle my trust to be releuyd,   229

Take up,
then, my
case !

And that thu schalt my quareħ take an hande,
This foulë wightës malice withstande.   231

(34)

For weel I wottë, thu wold[est] renome,   232

Thou wilt not
refuse me.

As for mynᵉ causë, wilt thu nougħt refuse,
Ne that thi grace thu wilt nougħt warnë me,
But that thu wilt thin ownë manerꝰ vse,
My quareħ now to helpë and excuse,   236

Chase off the
evil spirit !

And be my socourꝰ in this perilows day,
Chasyng this foulë gost from me a-way.   238

(35)

For alwey hath he be mynꝯ enemy   239
Sitħ I was child, and [eke] tendre in yowthe.
Me think thu schuldest let[të] him for-thi
To prócede in his acciʒonꝯ as nowthe,

Or suffre him accusë, thow he cowthe;   243   Let him not
  Thu schuldest¹ nougħt berë no fals witnesse,   bring his
    action now
  That is him-self conuicte of cursidnesse.   245   against me!

(36)   [¹ ? He scholdë]

For sekirly this is the comon lawe,   246
  That he ne schulde non accion) procede,
That onës owt of courte hath be with-drawe   [leaf 12]
  Convicte as fals,—now here-to takith hede!   He is guilty,
This knoweth wel euery wigħt (it is no dreed),   250
  Thi sone him banysshed from heuen) blisse,   and was
    driven out of
  as for enfamed; he and allë his.   252   heaven.

(37)

Michael, prouost, on the I take recorde!   253   Provost Mi-
  Thi selffe dedist this execucion).   chael, I ap-
    peal to you.
Thow I my selff wolde lyen ony worde,
  Yit am I nought of this oppinïon),
  To couere so be excusacïon)   257
    Of this infame, the malise of my synne: 259
    This were a folës purpoce to be-gynne.   259

(38)

But this put I in thi discreacïoñ,   260   I submit to
  That suche a fals deformèd one as he,   you
I may refusë be excepcïon),
  That this quarel schal nougħt receyued be   that this
    Fiend should
Here in this courte; ne to accusë me   264   not be heard
    in Court,
  He schuld not be admitted, as be righ̄t,
  But I-put away, this foulë fals[ë] wigħt.   266   but should be
    turnd out.

(39)

For whi, sere prouost Michael gracïows,   267   You and all
  And alle the Aungeles of thi company   the Angels
That him enfamed, hath foriuged thus,   have judgd
    him,
  And fals convictë cleere and openly,
And him [sente] into peyne eternally,   271   and sentenst
    him to Hell.
  In hellë to be [kepte] without[en] ende,
  With tho that so be déformed in kende.   273

(40)

Ful mek[ë]ly at onës I reclayme   274   I claim
  you alle to do your devere in this case:
This cursed gost, whom malice doth enflame,

that this
Fiend has no
place in this
Court.

Here in this court, his malice haue no place :
This aske I you of right, and also of grace,   278
That ye, his cry & [eke] his bost abate,
þat he neuére more bere aftir estate.   280

(41)

St. Michael,
if þou fail me,
I am ruind.

Seint Michael, if þou rekkest nought at alle,   281
Ne nought rewardest [on] myne heuynesse,

[leaf 12, back]

Alle manere of hope awey from me is falle,
So am I than) encombred with distresse ;

Daniel says
you alone
helpt him.

For Danyell the prophete seith expresse,   285
That in his myschief and suche aduersite
He fonde none othir helpe but only the.[1]   287

(42)

Wherfore, if I haue the displeased ought,   288
So that of me thu takest now none heed,

Henceforth
I'll do my
best to please
you.

Aftir this oure, I mote with alle my thought
The done pleasaunce, for betere I schal spede ;

Placebo must
come first,
as in the Cris-
cross book.

For who þat well be holpen at his nede,   292
Ful sekere, Placebo mvst go before,
As doth the Crosse in the litel childes lore.   294

(43)

John the
Baptist,
Prophets and
Evangelists,

Baptist, an holy man, martir, seint Iohn,   295
and alle prophetës of oure lord on heighe,
And ye euaungelistës euerichon),
And also aposteles, alle the company,
With alle myne herte I pray you humb[le]ly,   299

give me
some of your
merits!

Of youre meritës superhábundaunce,
As grauntith me of almesse some pietaunce.   301

(44)

You have so
much of em,

In youre tresoure suche plente is bestowe,   302
Of wich you nedith nought a deel I-wis,
And lorne it may not be—this weel I knowe,—
Discreasyn) may it nought—the sothe it is—
For whi, of almesse-dede (I pray you this)   306

[1] Dan. x. 13 : but lo, Michael, one of the chief princes
[angels], came to help me. x. 21 : And there is none that
holdeth with me in these things, but Michael your prince.
xii. 1 : And at that time shall Michael stand up, the great
prince which standeth for the children of thy people.

That I some manere of porcïon) may haue,
Where-witħ I may my self[ë] helpe and saue. 308 give me a
share!

(45)

Ye that haue suffird hard and grevous peyne 309
Of martirdam, for ihesu crist-is love,
Wicħ, weel I wottë, was not done in veyne,
Yit merite is youre medë muche a-bove;
I that am pore, and gret[e]ly be-hove, 313 I'm so poor.
Of helpe I pray you, and [of] almës-dede, Help me!
Of youre meriteis, helpitħ at this nede! 315

(46)

And sithë thei schul endëles endure, 316 [leaf 13]
Thei wastë nougħt be dymynucïon) :
To me, that am so pore a crëature,
Of almesse grauntitħ now a porcïon),
I you require, witħ hool affeccïon), 320 Appeal to God in Heaven for me!
That blisful that sittitħ an higħe in trone,
Appelitħ him as töward my persone. 322

(47)

Ye cónfessourës, and ye othir seintes, 323 Confessors, Saints and Virgins,
And uirginës þat to Crist be so dere,
Entenditħ to my pietous complayntes, pity me!
Be moevid [now] witħ rewthe vpon) my chiere ;
For woman none, the wicħ that is ful nere 327 No woman in childbirth is fuller of dread than I.
To childe-beryng, so of her' peynës dredetħ,
As I woot that my iugëment procedeth. 329

(48)

And if that ye, of youre meriteis grete, 330 If you'll help me,
Somwhat departen) to so pouere a wigħt,
ye wil vouchesaff such gracë me to gete,
This foulë gost to putte owt of my sigħt,
Yitte wolde I hope to Ihesu ful of mygħt, 334 Christ will conquer my foe.
Of malice wicħ he hatħ a-geyn me spoke,
He schuld be¹ atteynt, & alle his barrës broke.

(49)

I have not whom, my selff to turnë to, 337 I have no one to turn to.
In spécial to speke, or elles compleyne,

¹ Scan "He schuld be" as one measure.

That may me ony helpe and socoure do,
My symple cause to forthere or susteyne :
That doth me sorë¹ grevë and constreyne.   341

O, Court of
Saints, I trust
to you.

The holy Court of Seintës I appele,
Betakyng you my quarell eueridell. [¹ MS. me sore doth]

(50)

You know my
wants.

Ye knowë weel [right] now what is my nede   344
Ageyn the malice of myne enemy,
þat is a-bowte to noyë and mysbede
Me, nedi wrecchë : help[ë] me forthþthi !

Hear my
piteous cry !
Reconcile me
to God !

Geve audience vnto my pietows cry,   348
And to my Kyng now reconsilë me,
Schewyng the feruoure of youre charite !   350

(51)

[leaf 13, back]
Saints, relieve
me from the
Devil's blame
that,

The relieff of youre excellent merites,   351
Ye preciows seintës chosen euerichonÞ,
A-geyn the malice of this perilous wites
Wich þat the feend [now] puttith me upon,

while I was
young,
I followd
him.

þat whil I was levyng in flesch and bonÞ,   355
With his disceiptës and his fraudës fele
He drowe me to, & now me doth appele.   357

(52)

St. Paul says
that Charity
is enough for
many folk
(? 1 Cor. xiii.).

Seint Poule him-selff[ë] writith in this wise,   358
And saith that " veray parfight charite
Is a thing þat may to muche poepil suffice " ;
Sche aboundith nought in propirte.

Since then
it is to be
shared,
let me have
some of it !

Sithe it behouith, than, in communalte   362
Among the nedi to be dispended,
Let myne estate somwhat be ámendid !   364

Minor Poems, I, 38/417. Le Sire de Fournivall
Tresourer, was appointed of Henry IV's Council on 27
Nov., 8 Hen. IV, 1406.—*Proc. Privy Council*, i. 295
(ed. Nicolas, 1834).   See also *Rot. Parl.* iii. 572 *b*.

SOME WORDS AND MEANINGS.

appélloure, *n.*, xxv/77, accuser.

bywiled, lii/20, beguiled.

checkmate, xxvi/114.

dewyng, xli/158, dewing, moistening with Christ's blood.

embash, *v.t.*, xlvii/9, abash.

forcet, *n.*, xxx/63, forcer, chest.

fructify, *v.t.*, xlv/7.

guideress, *n.*, xxiii/3.

herne, *n.*, xlvi/18, corner.

infame, *n.*, lix/258, rascal.

jollyvet, *n.*, xxviii/163. '*Joliveté* as *Joliete ; f.* Jollitie, iollinesse
. . . iocondnesse, mirth.'—Cotgrave.

kirke, *n.*, xlviii/4, church.

Mary and Marah, xlii/183.

mistake, *v.t.*, xxxvii/6, misbehave. '*Mesprendre*, to err, mistake ;
transgresse, offende.'—Cotgrave.

ooke, *vb.*, l/10, ached.

owten, *vb.*, xliv/232, ought.

perche, *v.t.*, xxxviii/51, pierce.

phlebotomy, *n.*, xxiv/28, bleeding.

principate, *n.*, li/5, power.

reseise with, *v.t.*, xlvi/31, re-give possession of.

steltles, 66/1809, stealthless.

sterneless, *a.*, xliii/221, rudderless.

streit, *p.p.*, xxxix/84, stretcht.

style, *n.*, xliii/223, title, name.

sweat, *n.*, xxiv/41.

Synderesis, *n.*, xxv/76.
> Sinderesis, to speke in pleyn,
> Ys as muchë for to seyn
> (By notable descripcíon)
> The hiher party of Resoñ,
> Wherby a man shal best discerne
> His consciencë to govérne.
> > 1426. Lydgate, in Stow MS. 952, leaf 91. His *Pilgrimage
> > of the Lyf of Man,* englisht from De Guilleville.

thei, *conj.*, xliii/202, though.

this, xxxiv/9, xli/137, these.

tilth, *n.*, xxviii/178, training, culture.

veyued, xlii/190, waived, removed.

The Regement of Princes.

By THOMAS HOCCLEVE.

[Harl. MS. 4866.   Leaf 1 in a hand about 1700 A.D.]

Heere begynnyth the Book how ⎱
Pryncys sholden be governyd. ⎰

[leaf 1 *a*] [1]

Oxford. [2]

B. H.

(1)

Mvsyng vpon the restles bisynesse　　　　　　1
　Which that this troubly[3] world hath ay on honde,
That othir thyng than fruyt of byttirnesse
Ne yeldeth nought, as I can vndirstonde,
At Chestre ynnë,[4] right fast[5] be the stronde,　　5
　As I lay in my bed vp-on a nyght,
Thought me bereft of sleep with[6] force and myght.

Thinking of the worry of this world,

I lay awake one night at Chester Inn, Strand.

(2)

And many a day and nyght that wykked hyne　　8
　Haddë[7] beforn vexid my poorë goost
So grevously, that of anguysh and pyne
No richere man was nougher[8] in no coost;
　This dar I seyn, may no wight make his boost　12
　That he with thought was bettir[9] than I aqveynted,
For to the deth it wel nigh hath me feynted.　14

Oft before had I been harast with anxiety:

no one worse.

---

[1] The first leaf has been torn out of Harl. 4866, but the first 8 stanzas have been copied on another leaf of parchment by a later hand about 1700 A.D.

[2] Signature of Edward Harley, 2nd Earl of Oxford, who made the collection of Harleian MSS. If the 'B H' is not the pressmark, I don't know what it is.   On the fly-leaf is "See another copy of this book in this [Harley] Library marked 35 A. 17."

[3] troubly Reg. 17 D vi, *om.* H.   [4] Chestres Inne R.   [5] fast R H.
[6] the R.　[7] hadde R, had H.　[8] neu*er* R.　[9] bette R.

(3)

I ponderd
on the uncer-
tainty of
Fortune,

Bysily in my mynde I gan revolue   15
    The welthe onsure of everye creature,
How lightly that ffortune it can dissolue,
    Whan that hir lyst that it no lenger[1] dure ;
And of the brotylnesse of hyre nature,   19
    My tremlyng hert so gretë[2] gastnesse hadde,
    That my spiritis were of my lyfë[2] sadde.   21

(4)

and remem-
berd Richard
II.'s fall.

Me fel to mynde[3] how that, not long ago,   22
    ffortunës strok doun threst estaat royal
Into myscheef[4] ; and I took heed also
    Of many anothir lord that had a fall ;
In mene[5] estaat eek sikernesse[6] at all   26
    Ne saw I noon ; but I sey attë laste,
    Wher sëwrte, for to abyde,[7] hir caste.   28

(5)

[leaf 1b][8]

Yn poore[9] estaat sche pyght hir paviloun,   29
    To covere hire from the storm[10] of descendyng ;
For [that] sche kneew no lowere discencion,
    Save oonly deth, fro which no wight lyvyng
Defendyn[11] hym may ; and thus, in my musyng,   33
I was bare
of Joy and
Hope.
    I destitut was of[12] joye and good hope,
    And to myn esë no thyng koude I groope.   35

(6)

I thought
I might lose
the little I
had.

For right as blyvë ran it in my thought,   36
    Though I be poore, yet som what leese I may ;
Than deemed I that seurëte[13] would nought
    With me abyde, it is nought to hir pay,
Ther to soiurne as sche descendë may ;   40
    And thus vnsikir of my smal lyfloode,
    Thought leyd on me full[14] many an hevy loode.

---

[1] no lenger R, not long H.   [2] grete . . lyfe R, gret . . lyf H.
                [3] mynde R, my mynde H.
[4] The deposition of Richard II, A.D. 1399.   [5] mene R, many H.
[6] sikirnesse R, siknnesse H.   [7] sewete for to abide R, tabyde H.
    [8] This page is in a later hand than the rest of the MS.
[9] In pou*e*re R, Yn the poore H.   [10] To kever hir fro the stroke.
        [11] Defende R.   [12] of R, for H.   [13] seurtee R.
                [14] full R, *om.* H.

(7)

I thought eek, if I in-to povert creepe,   43   Tho poverty
is fixedness,
I should be-
wail it:
  Than am I entred in-to sykirnesse ;
But swich seurete myght I ay wayle and weepe,
  ffor poverte breedeth but[1] hevynesse.
Allas ! wher is this worldis stabilnesse ?   47
  Heer vp, heer doun ; heer honour, heer repreef ;
  Now hool, now seek ; now bounte, now myscheef.

(8)

¶ Boecius de[1]
consolatione
Philosophiæ;
maximum
genus infor-
tunii est,
fuisse felicem
&c.[4] And whan I haddë rolled vp and doun   50
  This worldës[2] stormy wawës in my mynde,
I seey weel povert was exclusïon[3]   it shuts out
well-being.
  Of all weelfarë regnyng in mankynde ;
And how in bookës thus I wryten fynde,   54   Boece says,
"The worst
misery, is
after pros-
perity."
  " The werstë kynde of wrecchednessë is,
  A man to havë been weelfull or this."   56

(9)

¶ [5]" Allas ! " þoghte I, " what sykirnesse ys þat   57   [leaf 2 a]
  To lyue ay seur of greef and of nuisaunce ?
What schal I do ? best is I stryuë nat   I'd better not
strive against
Fortune :
  Agayne þe pays[6] of fortunës balaunce ;
ffor wele I wote, þat hir brotel constaunce,   61
  A wyght no whilë suffer can soiourne
  In a plyt ; þus nat wiste[7] I how to torne.   63

(10)

¶ ffor whan a man weneþ stond most constant,   64
  þan is he nextë to his ouer throwyng ;
So flyttyng is sche, and so wariant,   she cannot be
trusted.
  Ther is no trust vp-on hir fair lawhyng ;
After glad loue[8] sche schapiþ hir to styng ;   68
  I was a-drad so of hir gerynesse,
  That my lif was but a dedly gladnesse."   70

---

[1] but R, nought but H.   [2] worldes R, world H.
[3] pouertee was conclusion) R.   [4] felicem &c. R, homines H.
[5] *The old writing, c. 1430-40, of Harl. 4866 begins here.*
[6] peys R.   [7] o plite / thus I wist nat R.   [8] looke R.

(11)

¶ Thus ilkë nyught I walwyd to and fro,   71

    Sekyng restë ; but, certeynly sche
Appeerid nogħt, for þoght, my crewel fo,
    Chaced hadde hir & slepe a-way fro me ;
    And for I schuldë not a-lonë be,   75
      Agayn my luste, Wach profrid his seruise,
      And I admittid hym in heuy wyse.   77

(12)

¶ So long a nyught ne felde I neuer non,   78
    As was þat samë to my iugëment ;

Who so þat thoghty is, is wo-be-gon ;
    þe þoghtful wight is vessel of turment,
    þer nys no greef to him equipolent ;   82
      He graueþ deppest of seekenesses[1] alle ;
      fful wo is him þat in swich thoght[2] is falle. 84

(13)

¶ What whyght þat inly pensif is, I trowe,   85
    His moste desire is to be solitarie ;
þat þis is soþ, in my persone I knowe,[3]
    ffor euere whil þat fretynge aduersarie
    Myn hert[e] madë to hym tributarie,   89
      In sowkynge of þe fresschest of my blod,
      To sorwe soule,[4] me thoght it dide me good. 91

(14)

¶ ffor þe nature of heuynesse is þis :   92
    If it haboundë gretly in a wight,

þe place eschewit he where as ioye is,
    ffor ioye & he not mowe accorde a-ryght ;
    As discordant as day is vn-to nyught,   96
      And honur, aduersarie is vn-to schame,
      Is heuynessë[5] so to ioye and game.   98

---

[1] sikenesses R, seekenesse H.   [2] caas R.   [3] knawe H.
[4] soole R (alone).   [5] heuynes H, So heuyncsse is R.

(15)

¶ Whan to þe þoghtful whiȝt is tolde a tale,   99 The anxious man heeds no tale told to him.
  He heeriþ it as þogh he þennës were;
Hys heuy thoghtës hym so plukke & hale
  Hyder and þedir, and hym greue & dere,
  þat hys erës auayle hym nat a pere;   103
    He vnderstondeþ no þing what men seye,
    So ben his wyttës fer gon hem to pleye.   105

(16)

¶ þe smert of þoght, I by experience   106 I know the pain of Anxiety; its chill and heat.
  knowe as wel as any man doþ lyuynge;
His frosty swoot & fyry hote feruence,
  And troubly dremës, drempt al in wakynge,
  My mayzed heed sleeplees han of konnynge,   110
    And wyt dispoylyd, & so me be-iapyd,
    þat after deþ ful often haue I gapid.   112

[HOCCLEVE'S MEETING AND DIALOGUE WITH AN OLD BEGGAR.]

(17)

¶ Passe ouer whanne þis stormy nyght was gon,   113 [leaf 3 *a*]
  And day gan at my wyndowe in to prye,   Next morning
I roos me vp, for bootë fonde I non
  In myn vnresty bed lenger to lye;
  In-to þe feld I dressed me in hye,   117 I walkt in the fields.
    And in my wo, y herte-depe[1] gan wade,
    As he þat was bareyne of þoghtës glade.   119

(18)

¶ By þat I walkyd hadde a certeine tyme,   120
  Were it an houre, I not or more or lesse,
A poore olde horë[2] man cam walkyng by me,   A poor old Beggar soon greeted me;
  And seydë, "good day, syre, & god yow blysse!"
  But I no word; for my seekly distresse   124 but I didn't answer.
    ffor-bad myn eres vsen hire office,
    ffor which þis[3] olde man helde me lewed & nyce,

---

[1] in my wofull hert deepe R.   [2] hore R, *om.* H.
[3] this R, þus H.

(19)

The old Beggar	¶ Tyl he tooke hedë to my drery chere,	127

¶ Tyl he tooke hedë to my drery chere,   127
  And to my deedly colour pale & wan ;
Thanne thoghte he þus :—þis man þat I se here,
  Al wrong is wrestid, by oght þat[1] I se can :
  He sterte vp to[2] me, & seyde, " scleepys þou, man ?
shook me.   Awake ! " & gan me schakë wonder faste,
  And wi*th* a sigh I answerde attë laste.   133

(20.   *Hoccleve and Beggar.*)

¶ " A ! who is þer ? "   " I," qu*od* þis oldë greye,   134
  " Am heer," & he me toldë the[3] manere
How he spak to me, as ye herd me seye ;
  " O man," quoþ I, " for cristës louë dere,
  ¶ If þat þou wolt aght don*e* at my preyere,   138
I prayd him   As go þi way, talkë to me no more,
to go away.   þi wordës al annoyen me ful sore ;   140

(21.   *Hoccleve and Beggar.*)

[leaf 3 b]   ¶ " Voydë fro me ; me list no compaignye ;   141
  Encressë noght my grife ; I haue I-now."
¶ " My sone, hast þou good lust þi sorwe drye,
  And mayst releuëd be ? what man art þou ?
He told me   Wirke after me ! it schal be for þi prow ;   145
to follow his
lead.   þou nart but ȝong, and hast but litel seen,
I was but
young.   And ful seelde is, þat ȝong folk wysë been.   147

(22.   *Hoccleve and Beggar.*)

¶ " If þat þe likë to ben esyd wel,   148
  As[4] suffre me wi*th* þe to talke a whyle.
Art þou aght lettred ? "   " ya," qu*od* I, " som dele."
He was glad   " Blissed be god ! þan hope I, by seint Gyle,
I was a let-
terd man,   þat god to þe þi wit schal reconsyle,   152
  Which þat me þinkeþ is fer fro þe went,
  þorgh þe assent of þi greuouse tu*r*ment.   154

---

[1] wrest by ought that R, wrestid by oght H.   [2] vnto R.
[3] the R, *om.* H.   [4] Then R.

(23. *Beggar.*)

¶ " Lettered[1] folk han gretter discreciou*n*,   155 because let-
      And bet conceyuë konne a mannes saw,   terd folk will
And ra*þ*er wole applië to resou*n*   listen to
And from folyë[2] soner hem w*ith*-draw,   Reason.
   *þ*an he *þ*at no*þ*er reson can, ne law,   159
      Ne lerned ha*þ* no man*er* of[3] lettrure :   He hoped to
      Plukke vp *þ*in herte ! I hope I schal *þ*e cure." cure me.

(24. *Hoccleve.*)

¶ " Curë, good man? ya, *þ*ow arte a fayre leche ! 162
      Curë *þ*i self, *þ*at tremblest as *þ*ou gost,   I advis'd him
ffor al *þ*in art wole enden[4] in *þ*i speche ;   to cure him-
   It li*þ* not in *þ*i power, porë gost,   self:
   To helë me ; *þ*ou art as seek almost   166 he was as
      As I ; first on *þ*i self ky*þ*ë *þ*in art ;   badly off as I
      And if aght leue, late me *þ*anne hauë part. 168 am.

(25. *Hoccleve.*)

¶ " Go forth *þ*i way, I *þ*e preye, or be stylle ; 169 [leaf 4 *a*]
      *þ*ou dost me more annoy *þ*an *þ*at *þ*ou wenest ; I again askt
*þ*ou art as ful of clap as is a mylle ;   him to go
   *þ*ou dost nought[5] heer, but greuest me & tenest. away.
Good man, *þ*ou woste but lytyl what *þ*ou menest ; 173
      In *þ*e, li*þ*e not redressë my nuysance,[6]
      And ȝit *þ*ou mayste be wele willéd p*er*chaunce.

(26. *Hoccleve and Beggar.*)

¶ " It mostë be a greter[7] man of myght   176
*þ*an *þ*at *þ*ou art, *þ*at scholdë me releue."

¶ " What, sone myn ! *þ*ou felist not a-right !   He said
   To herkene me, what schal it harme or greue?" "Listen to
   " Peter ![8] good man, *þ*ogh we talke here tyl eue, me."
      Al is in veyne ; *þ*i myght may nat atteyne
      To helë me, swich is my woful peyne."   182

---

[1] Lettred R, Letterd H.   [2] folye R, foly H.   [3] of *om.* R H.
[4] enden R, ende H.   [5] nought R, not H.   [6] noiaunce R.
[7] moste be a gretter R, most be a grete H.
[8] *In the* 17*th cent. hand :* " Peter Goodman was perhaps som
olde man w*t.* whom hee consulted concerning his pension &c."
Peter = by St. Peter.

(27.   *Beggar and Hoccleve.*)

¶ " What þat I may or can, ne wost þou noght ;   183
    Hardyly, sonë, telle on how it is ! "

Hoccleve says
his trouble is
Anxiety.
¶ " Man, at a word, it is encombrous þoght
    þat causeþ me þis sorowe & fare[1] amys."

¶ " Now, sone, & if þer no þing be but þis,   187
The Beggar
undertakes to
cure him,
    Do as I schal þe seye, & þin estat
    Amende I schal, but þou be obstinat,   189

(28.   *Beggar.*)

if he'll do as
he's told.
¶ " And wilfully rebelle & dissobeye,   190
    And liste not to my lorë the conforme ;
ffor in swiche cas, what scholde I speke or seye,
    Or in my bestë wysë þe enforme ?
    If þow it wayue, & take an oþer forme   194
    After þi childissh mysrulëd conceyt,
    þou dost vn-to þi self, harm & deceit.   196

(29.   *Beggar.*)

[leaf 4 b]
Hoccleve
must give up
his solitari-
ness.
¶ " O þing seye I, if þou go feërlees[2]   197
    Al solytarie, & counsel lakke, & rede,
As me þinkeþ, þi gyse is douteles,
    þou likly art to bere a dotyd[3] heed.
    Whil þou art soulë,[4] þoght is wastyng seed,   201
    Swich in þe, & þat in grete foysoun,
    And þou redeles, nat canst[5] voyde his poysoun.

(30.   *Beggar.*)

Ecclesiastes
says, Woe to
him that is
alone, when
he falleth !
iv. 10.
¶ " The boke seiþ þus,—I redde it yore agon,—   204
    ' Wo be to hym þat list to ben allone !
ffor if he fallë, helpe ne haþ he non
    To rysë ' ; þis seye I by þi persone ;
    I fonde þe soul, & þi wyttës echone   208
    ffer fro þe fled, & disparpled ful wyde ;
    Wherefore it semeþ, þe nediþ a gyde,   210

¶ Ve soli !
quia, si cadat,
non habet
subleuantem.

---

[1] fare R.   [2] without a 'fere' or companion, felaweles H.
[3] fonned R.   [4] soole R, soul H.   [5] kanst not R.

(31. *Beggar.*)

¶ "Which þat þe may vnto þi wyttës lede ;   211   Hoccleve
    þou[1] graspist heer & þere, as doþ þe blynde,   needs a guide:
And ay mys-gost ; & ȝit haue I no drede,
If þou receyuë wold in-to þi mynde   if he'll follow
                                       the Beggar,
My lore, & execute it, þou schalt fynde   215   he'll get re-
                                         lief.
    þere-in swiche esë, þat þi maladye
A-bregge it schal, & þi maléncolye.   217

(32. *Beggar.*)

¶ "fful holsum were it, stynten of þi wo,   218   He must stop
                                         sorrowing,
¶ *Prouerbia.*   And take vnto þe, spirit of gladnesse ;   and be glad.
Animus gau-
dens etatem   What profyt fyndest þou to mournë so ?
floridam fa-
cit; spiritus   Salamon seiþ, þat sorowe & heuynesse,
autem tristis
desiccat ossa.   Bonës of man dryeþ by his duresse,   222
       And hertë glad makiþ florissching age ;
    þerfore I redë þou þi wo a-swage.   224

(33. *Beggar.*)

¶ "He seiþ, 'as motthës to a cloþe annoyen,   225   [leaf 5 *a*]
    And of his wollë maken it al bare,
And also as wormës a tre destruen
¶ *Item sicut*   þorogh hir percyng, riȝt so sorowe and care   Sorrow
tinea vesti-
mento, & ver-   By-reuen man his helþe & his welfare,   229   makes men
mis ligno, &c.   ill, and
       And his dayës a-bregge, & schorte his lyf ;   shortens their
                                         life.
    lo ! what profyt is for to be pensyf ?   231

(34. *Beggar.*)

¶ "Now, godë sonë, telle on þi greuaunce ;   232   The Beggar
                                         bids Hoccleve
    What is þi cause of þoght in special ?   disclose his
                                         grief.
Hast þou of worldly goodës hábundaunce,
And carist how þat it i-kept be schal ?
Or art þou nedy, & hast nouȝt but smal,   236
    And thristist sore[2] a rychë man to be ?
Or louest herë þat not loueþ þe ?[3]   238

---

[1] That R.   [2] trustest sone R.
[3] Or elles lovest thou hir that loveth not the R.

(35.   *Beggar.*)

¶ " I haue herd seyn, in kepyng of richesse   239
   Is thoȝt and wo, & besy a-wayte al-way ;

The pore & nedy ek haþ heuynesse,
   ffor to his purpos not atteyne he may ;

þe lou*er* also seen men day by day,   243
    Prolle after þat, þat he schal neu*er* fynde ;
    þus þoȝt turmentiþ folk in sondry kynde.   245

(36.   *Beggar.*)

¶ " If þou þe fele in any of þese i-greued,   246
   Or elles what, tell on, in goddës name.

þou seest al day, þe begg*er* is releued,
   þat sitte and beggeþ, blynd, crokyd & lame ;

And whi ? for he ne lettiþ, for no schame,   250
    his harmës & his pou*er*t to by-wreye
    To folk, as þey gon by hym in þe weye.   252

(37.   *Beggar.*)

¶ " ffor, and he kepe hym cloos, & holde his pees, 253
   And noght out schewe how seek he inward is,
He may al day so sytten helpëlees ;[1]
   And, sonë myn, alþogȟ he faire[2] a-mys
   þat hydith so, god wot þe wyt is his ;   257
    But þis begg*er* his hurtës wol not stele,
    He wele tell*e* al and more ; he can nouȝt hele.

(38.   *Beggar.*)

¶ " Ryȟt so, if þe liste haue a remedye   260
   Of þyn annoy þat prikkeþ þe so smerte,
The verray cause of þin hyd maladye

þou[3] most discou*er*, & telle oute al þin herte.
If þou it hydë, þou schalt not astarte   264
    þat þou ne fallë schalt in som myschau*n*ce ;
    ffor-þi amendë þou þi gou*er*naunce.   266

---

[1] helpeles R, helplees H.   [2] fare R.
[3] Thow R, þe H.

(39.   *Beggar.*)

¶ " Be war of þoȝht, for it is perillous ;   267
    He þe streight wey to discomfórt men ledeþ ;
His violence is ful outragëous ;
    Vnwise is he þat besy þoȝht ne dredeþ.   *Dread busy*
    In whom þat he his mortel venym schedeþ,   271 *Thought :*
                                                              it may lead
        But if a vomyt after folwe blyue,   *to Despair.*
    At þe port of despeir he may arryue.   273

(40.   *Beggar.*)

¶ " Sonë, swych thoghtë lurkynge þe with-ynne,   274
    þat huntith after þi confusioun,
Hy tyme it is to voyde & late hym twynne,
    And walke at largë out of þi prisoun.
    Be war' þe fendës sly conclusioun,   278 *Beware of the*
                                                              Fiend !
        ffor if he may þe vnto déspeir brynge,
    þou mornë schalt, & lawȝh he wol, & synge.   280

(41.   *Beggar.*)

¶ " Som man, for lak of occupacioun,   281 [leaf 6 *a*]
                                                              Some stretch
    Museþ forþer þanne his wyt may strecche,   their wit to
                                                              Damnable
And, at þe fendës instigacioun,   Error,
                                                              like the
    Dampnable errour holdeþ, & can not flecche   Lollard Jn.
                                                              Badby, who
    ffor no counseil ne reed, as dide a wrecche   285 was burnt on
                                                              1 March,
        Not fern agoo, whiche þat of heresye   1410, at
                                                              Smithfield.
    Conuyct, and brent was vn-to ashen drye.   287

[1](42.   *Beggar.*)

¶ " The precious body of oure lorde ihesu   288 He said the
                                                              Sacramental
    In forme of brede, he leued no[t][2] at al ;   Bread was
                                                              not Christ's
He was in no þing abassht, ne eschu   body, but
                                                              simple bread,
    To seye it was but brede material ;   and that a
                                                              Priest
    He seyde, a prestës power was as smal   292 couldn't
                                                              make it God's-
        As a Rakérs, or swiche an oþer wiȝte,   body.
    And to mak it, hadde no gretter myȝt.   294

---

[1] This stanza has been crossed out with the pen.
[2] not R, no H.

(43. *Beggar.*)

Henry,
Prince of
Wales, was
at Badby's
burning,

¶ " My lorde þe prince—god him saue & blesse !— 295
    Was at his deedly castigacioun,
And of his soulë hadde grete tendernesse,
    Thristyngë sorë his sauacioun :
    Grete was his pitous lamentacioun,   299
        Whan þat þis renegat not woldë blynne
        Of þe stynkyng errour þat he was inne.   301

(44. *Beggar.*)

and promist
him his life,
and a liveli-
hood, if he'd
renounce his
errors.

¶ " This good lorde hiȝte hym to be sweche a mene 302
    To his fader, oure ligë lorde souereyne,
If he renouncë wolde his errour clene,
    And come vn-to oure good byleue ageyne,
    He schulde of his lif seure ben & certeyne,   306
        And sufficiant lyflode eek scholde he haue,
        Vn-to þe day he clad were in his graue.   308

¹(45. *Beggar.*)

[leaf 6 b]
Prince Henry

¶ " Also þis nobyl prince & worþy knyght—   309
    God quyte hym his charitable labour !—
Or any stikkë kyndled were or light,

also had the
Sacrament
brought to
Badby ;

    The sacrement, oure blissed saueoure,
    With reuerencë grete & hye honoure   313
        He fecchë leet, þis wrecchë to conuerte,
        And make oure feiþe to synkyn in his herte. 315

(46. *Beggar.*)

but that
Heretic stuck
to his Damn-
able opinion.

¶ " But al for noght, it woldë not bytyde ;   316
    He heeld forþ his oppynyoun dampnáble,
And cast oure holy cristen feiþ a-syde,
    As he þat was to þe fende acceptáble.
    By any outward tokyn resonáble,   320
        If he inward hadde any repentaunce,
        þat wote he, þat of no þing haþ doutaunce.   322

¹ The three following stanzas are all crossed out with the pen.

(47. *Beggar.*)

¶ " Lat þe diuinës of hym speke & muse 323
   Where his soule is by-come, or whider gon ;
Myn vnkonyng[1] of þat me schal excuse,
   Of whiche materë knowleche haue I non.
But woldë[1] god, tho cristes foos echon, 327
   þat as he heeldë[2] were I-seruëd soo,
ffor I am seur þat þer ben many moo, 329

(48. *Beggar.*)

¶ " The more ruthe is : allas ! what men ben þey 330
   þat hem delyten in swiche surquidrie ?
ffor mannës reson may not preue ourë fey,
   þat þey wole it dispreuen or denye.
To oure lorde god þat sytte in heuenes hyë, 334
   Schal þey desyre for to ben egal ?
Nay, þat was neuer, certes, ne be schal. 336

(49. *Beggar.*)

¶ " þát oure lord god seiþ in holy scripture 337
   May not be fals ; þis knawit euery whiȝt,
But he be mad ; & þogh a creature
   In his goddës werk[3] feelë not a-ryght,
Schal he rebelle ageyn his lordës myght, 341
   Which þat þis wydë world haþ made of noght,
ffor reson may not knytte it in his thoght ? 343

(50. *Beggar.*)

¶ " Was it not eek a moustre as in nature 344
   þat god I-borë was of a virgine ?
Ȝit is it soþ, þogh man be[4] cóniecture
   Of reson, or what he can ýmagine,
Not sauoure it, ne can it détermyne. 348
     He þat al myghty is, doþ as hym lyste ;
     He wole his konnynge hydde be, & nat wyste. 350

---

[1] wolde R, wold H.   [2] helde R, held H.
[3] werkes R.   [4] by R.

(51.   *Beggar.*)

If Faith
could be
prov'd, hold-
ing it would
not be meri-
torious.

¶ "Oure feiþ not were vnto vs meritórie   351   [R] Fides non
habet meri-
tum ubi hu-
mana ratio
præbet ex-
perimentum.
　　If þat we myghten by reson it preue ;
Lat vs not fro god twynnen[1] & his glorie ;
　　As holy chirche vs byt, lat vs be-leue ;—
But we þere-to obeye, it schal vs greue   355
　　Importably ; lat vs do as sche byt,
　　Oure goedë fadres olde[2] han folwyd it.   357

(52.   *Beggar.*)

¶ "Presumpcïoun, a ! benedicite !   358
　　Why vexest þou folk with þi franesie ?
þogh no þing ellës were, I seye for me,

To the
Prelates and
learned
Clergy

But se how þat þe worþi prelacie,
　　And vnder hem þe suffissant clergye,   362
　　Endowyd of profound intelligence,
　　Of al þis land werreyen þi sentence ;   364

(53.   *Beggar.*)

[leaf 7 b]

¶ "That seluë samë to me were a bridel,   365

I submit,

　　By whiche wolde I gouérned[3] ben & gyed,
And ellis al my labour were in ydel.

and to Holy
Church.

By holy churche I wole be iustified ;
　　To þat, al holly is myn herte applied,   369
　　And euer schal ; I truste in goddës grace,
　　Swiche surquidrie in me schal haue no place. 371

(54.   *Beggar and Hoccleve.*)

¶ "Sone, if god wolë, þou art non of þo   372
þat wrapped ben in þis dampnacïoun ?"
¶ "I ?[4] criste forbede it, sire !" seyde I þo ;

Hoccleve says
he doesn't
want to
search into
God's Mys-
teries.

　　"I þanke it god, non inclinacïoun
Haue I to labour in probacïoun   376
　　Of his hy knowleche & his myghty werkys,
ffor swiche mater, vn-to my wit to[5] derk is.   378

---

[1] twynne R.   [2] For our faders aħ R.
[3] gouerned R, gouernend H.   [4] Ey R.   [5] fuħ R.

(55. *Hoccleve.*)

¶ " Of oure feiþ wol I not despute at all ;　　379 Hoccleve be-
　　But, at a¹ word, I in þe sacrament　　　　　　lieves in the
Of þe auter fully bileue,² & schal,　　　　　　　Sacrament
　　With goddës helpe, while life is to me lent ;　of the Altar
And, in despyt of þe fendës talent,　　　　383 and the other
　　In al oþer articles of þe feiþ　　　　　　　Articles of
　　Byleue, as fer as þat holy writ³ seiþ."　　385 the Faith.

(56. *Beggar.*)

¶ " Now good thrifte come vn-to þe, sonë dere !　386 The Beggar
　　þi gost is now a-wakyd, wel I se,　　　　　　thinks he's
And som-what eke amendid is þi chere ;　　　　done Hoc-
　　And firste I was ful sore a-gast of þe,　　　cleve some
　　Lest þat þou thorgh thogͪt-ful aduersyte,　390 good,
　　Not haddest standen in þi feyþe a-rygͪt ;
　　Now is myn hertë⁴ waxen glad & lygͪt.　　392

(57. *Beggar and Hoccleve.*)

¶ " Hast þou in me ony gretter sauour　　　393 [leaf 8 a]
　　þan þat þou haddest first whan þou me sy,
Whan I opposyd þe of þi langour ?
　　¶ Seye on þe soþë."　" Ya, somdele," quod I.
　　¶ " My sone, in fayth, þat is seyde ful feyntly ;　397
　　Thi sauour yit ful smal is, as I trowe ;　　tho' not
　　But or ogͪt longe, I schal þe soþë knowe.　399 much.

(58. *Beggar.*⁵)

¶ " I wote wel, sone, of me þus wold þou þinke :— 400 He fancies
　　þis oldë dotyd Grisel holte him wyse,　　　that Hoccleve
He weneþ maken in myn heed to synke　　　　scorns him.
　　His lewed clap, of which set I no pryse ;
　　He is a nobil prechour at deuyse ;　　　　404
　　Gret noyse haþ þorgͪ hys chynnëd⁶ lippës drye
　　þis day out past, þe deuel in his eye.　　406

---

¹ o R.　　² beleue R, I bileue H.
³ I beleeue as holy writte R.　　⁴ hert H.
⁵ This and the 15 following stanzas occur as a separate poem
in Laud 735, lf. 67, &c. (Bodl. Lib.), and I so printed em in my
Queene Elizabethes Achademy (E. E. T. Soc.), p. 105.
⁶ thynne R.

(59. *Beggar.*)

¶ " But þogħ I olde & hore be, sonë myin,   407
    And porë be my clethyng & aray,
And not so wyde a gowne haue, as is þin,
    So smal I-pynchid, ne so fresche and gay,
Mi redde, in happë,[1] ʒit the *perfet*[2] may ;   411
    And likly, þat þou demest for folye,[3]
    Is gretter wysdom þan þou canste espye.   413

(60. *Beggar.*)

¶ " Vndir an old pore habyt, regneþ oft   414
    Grete *vertu*, þogħ it moustre porëly ;
And where as gret array is vp on loft,
    Vice is but seelden hid ; þat wel wote I.
But not report, I pray þe, inwardly,   418
    þat fresch array I *generally* depraue ;
    þis worþi men mowe it wel vse & haue.   420

(61. *Beggar.*)

¶ " But þis me þinkiþ an abusïou*n*,   421
    To se on[4] walke in gownës of scarlet,
xij ʒerdës wyd, wit[5] pendant sleues downe
    On þe grounde, & þe furrour þer-in set
Amountyng vnto *twenty*[6] pound or bet ;   425
    And if he for it payde haue, he no good
    Haþ lefte him where-wit for to bye an hood.   427

(62. *Beggar.*)

¶ " ffor þogħ he iettë[7] forth a-mong þe prees,   428
    And oue*r* lokë euerey porë wigħt,
His cofre and eke his purs ben penylees,
    He haþ no morë þan he goþ in rygħt.
ffor lond, rent, or catel, he may go ligħt ;   432
    þe wegħt of hem schal not so mochë peyse
    As doþ his gowne : is swiche array to preyse ? 434

---

[1] happe R, hap H.   [2] profite R.   [3] folie R, foly H.
[4] one R.   [5] with R.   [6] MS. xx^ti   [7] gode R.

(63. *Beggar.*)

¶ " Nay sothely, sone, it is al a-mys me þinkyþ ;   435

So pore a wight his lord to counterfete

In his array, in my conceyit it stynkith.

Certes to blamë ben þe lordës grete,

If þat I durstë seyn, þat hir men lete   439

Vsurpë swiche a lordly apparaille,

Is[1] not worþ, my childe, with-outen fayle.   441

(64. *Beggar.*)

¶ " Som tyme, afer men myghten lordës knowe   442

By *there* array, from oþer folke ; but now

A man schal study and musen a long[2] throwe

Whiche is whiche : o lordes, it sit to yowe

Amendë þis, for it is for youre prowe.   446

If twixt yow and youre men no difference

Be in array, lesse is youre reuerence.   448

(65. *Beggar.*)

¶ " Also ther is another newë get,   449

A foul wast of cloth and an excessyf ;

Ther goth no lesse in a mannës tipet

Than of brood cloth a yerdë, by my lif ;

Me thynkyth this a verray inductif   453

Vnto stelthe : ware hem of hempen lane !

ffor stelthe is medid with a chekelew bane.   455

(66. *Beggar.*)

¶ " Let euere lord, his ownë men deffende   456

Swiche gret array, and þan, on my peryl,

This land within a whilë schal amende.

In goddys namë, putte it in exyl !

It is synnë outragïous and vyl ;   460

Lordës, if ye your éstat and honour

Louen, fleemyth this vicius errour !   462

---

[1] It is R.   Cp. our modern slang "it is not good enough."
      [2] muse a longe throwe R.

REGEMENT.   C

(67. *Beggar.*)

¶ " What is a lord withouten his meynee ?   463
    I puttë cas, þat his foos hym assaille

How can a
man with
wide sleeves
defend his
Lord ?
Sodenly in þe stret,—What help schal he,
    Wos sleeuës encombrous so sydë traille,
    Do to his lord ? he may hym nat auaille ;   467
        In swych a cas he nys but a womman ;
        He may nat stand hym in steed of a man.   469

(68. *Beggar.*)

His arms can
only hold up
his own
sleeves.
¶ " His armys two han ryght y-now to done,   470
    And sumwhat more, his sleeuës vp to holde ;
The taillours, trow I, moot heer-after soone
    Shape in þe feeld ; thay shal nat sprede and folde
    On hir bord, thogh þei neuer só fayn wolde,   474
        The cloth þat shal ben in a gownë wroght ;
        Take an hool cloth is best, for lesse is noght. 476

(69. *Beggar.*)

[leaf 9 b]
¶ " The skynner vn-to þe feeld moot also,   477
    His hous in london is to streyt & scars
To doon his craft ; sum tyme it was nat so.
    O lordës, yeue vnto your men hir pars
    That so doon, and aqwente hem bet with mars, 481
        God of bataile ; he loueth non array
        That hurtyth manhode at preef or assay.   483

(70. *Beggar.*)

The most
lavish dresser
is praisd;
¶ " Who now moost may bere on his bak at ones 484
    Of cloth and furrour, hath a fresscħ renoun ;
He is ' a lusty man ' clept for þe nones ;
but he doesn't
pay.
    But drapers & eek skynners in þe toun,
    ffor swich folk han a special orisoun[1]   488
        That troppid is with curses heere & there,
        And ay schal, til þei paid be for hir gere.   490

---

[1] orisoune R, orsoun H.

(71. *Beggar.*)

¶ " In dayës oldë, whan smal apparaille 491
Suffisid vn-to hy estat or mene,
Was gret houshold wel stuffid of victaille ;
But now housholdes ben ful sclender & lene, Household-
ffor al þe good þat men may repe or glene, 495 ers' money
goes in ex-
travagant
Wasted is in outragëous array, Dress.
So that housholdës men nat holdë may. 497

(72. *Beggar.*)

¶ " Pryde hath wel leuer bere an hungry mawe 498 Folk 'ud
To beddë, than lakke of array outrage ; sooner go
He no prys settith[1] be mesurës lawe, hungry than
Ne takith of hym cloth[ë], mete, ne wage : shabby.
Mesure is out of londe on pylgrymage ; 502
But I suppose he schal resorte as blyue,
ffor verray needë wol[2] vs ther-to dryue. 504

(73. *Beggar.*)

¶ " Ther may no lord tak vp no[3] newë gyse 505 [leaf 10 *a*]
But þat a knauë shal þe same vp take. Lords' new
If lordës wolden in þis wyse, fashions are
ffor to do swichë gownës to hem make copied by
As men did in old tyme, I vndertake 509 Workmen.
The samë get[4] sholde vp be take and vsid,
And al þis costelew[5] outrage refusid. 511

(74. *Beggar.*)

This was
John of
Gaunt, father
to Henry *the*
fourth, and
Grandfather
to Henry *the*
fyuth. hee
dyed an*n*o
1399.
(*In the* 1700
hand.)
¶ " Of lancastre duk Iohn, whos soule in heuene 512 John of
I fully deme, And trustë sit ful hye— Gaunt was
A noble prince I may allegge & neuene, the best
(Other may no man of hym testifye)— Model of
I neu*er* sy a lord that cowde hym gye 516 Conduct.
Bet like his éstat ; al knyghtly prowesse
Was to hym girt : o god ! his soulë blisse ! 518

---

[1] setteth R, setthit H.   [2] wole R, wel H.   [3] a R.
[4] jette R.   [5] costeleue R, costlew H.

(75. *Beggar.*)

¶ " His garnamentës weren noght ful wyde,　　519
　　And yit þei hym becam wondérly wel.

May Waste
and Pride
be banisht!

Now wold[ë] god þe waast of cloth & pryde
　　Y-put were in exyl perpetuel,
　　ffor þe good and profet[1] vniuersel.　　523
　　　And lordes myght helpe[2] al this, if þei wolde
　　　The olde get take, and it furth vse & holde.[3]　525

(76. *Beggar.*)

Then there'd
be more
Money about.

¶ " Than myghtë[4] siluer walkë morë thikke　　526
　　Among þe peple þan þat it doþ now ;
　Ther wold I fayne þat were y-set þe prikke,—
　　Nat for my self ; I schal doo wel ynow,—
　　But, sonë, for þat swichë men as thow　　530
　　　That with þe world wrastlen, myght han plente
　　　Of coyn, where as ye han now scarsetee.　　532

(77. *Beggar.*)

[leaf 10 *b*]
Long Sleeves,
not Brooms,
sweep the
streets.

¶ " Now hath þis lord[5] but litil neede of broomes　533
　　To swepe a-way þe filthe out of þe street,
　Syn sydë sleuës of penýlees gromes
　　Wile it vp likkë, be it drye or weet.
　　O engelond ! stande vp-ryght on thy feet !　　537
　　　So foul a wast in so symple degree
　　　Bannysshe ! or sore it schal repentë the.　　539

hos versus Io.
Stow citat in
Chronicae
sua, fol. 559
sub nomine
Tho. Hoc-
clive.
(*In the* 1700
hand.)

(78. *Beggar.*)

Folk with
tight clothes
are scornd.

¶ " If a wiȝt vertuous, but narwe clothid[6],　　540
　　To lordës curtës now of[7] dayës go,
　His compaignye is vn-to folkës lothid ;
　　Men passen by hym bothë to and fro,
　　And scorne hym, for he is arrayed so ;　　544
　　　To hir conceit is no wight vertuous,
　　　But he þat of array is outrageous.　　546

---

[1] profite R.　　[2] do R.
[3] jette vp take, and it forth holde R.　　[4] myght H R.
[5] thise lordes R.　　[6] with narwe clothes R.
[7] courtes now a R.

(79. *Beggar.*)

¶ " But he that flater can, or be a baude, 547
  And by tho tweynë, fressch array him gete,
It holden is to him honur & laude.[1]
Trouth and clennessë musten men for-gete
In lordës courtës, for they hertës frete ; 551
  They hyndren folk : fy vpon tongës trewe !
  They displesaunce in lordës courtës breewe. 553

Flattery and new Clothes are preferd to Truth and Purity.

(80. *Beggar.*)

¶ " Lo, sonë myn, þat[2] tale is at an eende : 554
  Now, goodë sone, haue of me no desdeyn,
Thogh I be old, and myn array vntheende ;
ffor many a yong man, wot I wel certeyn,
Of corage is so prowde and so hauteyn, 558
  That to þe poore and old mannës doctrine,
  fful seelde him deyneth bowen or enclyne. 560

Son Hoccleve, don't disdain me, tho I'm, old.

(81. *Beggar.*)

¶ Seneca ad Lucillum.

¶ " Senek seiþ, ' age is an infirmitee 561
  þat lechë non can curë, ne it hele,
ffor to þe deþ next neghëburgħ is he ;

¶ Nil cercius morte *etc.*

Ther may no wight þe chartre of lyf ensele,
  The ende is deþ of male & of femele ; 565
  No thyng is morë certein þan deþ is,
  Ne more vncertein þan þe tyme I-wis.' 567

[leaf 11 *a*]
Age is next to Death,

(82. *Beggar.*)

¶ Exod*us.* honora pa-trem & ma-trem, vt sis longeuus su-*per* terram.

¶ " As touchyng agë, god in holy writ 568
  Rygħt þus seiþ : ' fader & moder honure,[3]
þat þou mayste be longlyued :' þus he byt.
þan moot it folwen vpon þis scripture,
Age is a guerdoun to a crëature, 572
  And longlyuëd is non *with*-outen age ;
  Where-for I seye, in eld is auauntage. 574

and a Benefit to any man.

---

[1] laude R, laue H.   [2] this R.
[3] Non-Chaucerian ryme -*oure* with -*ure*, as in the " Mother of God," &c. See Forewords to Hoccleve's *Minor Poems*, Part I, p. xxxix.

(83. *Beggar.*)

¶ " And þe reuard of god may not be smal,   575
  His ȝiftës ben ful noble & profitabil ;
ffor-þi ne lakkë þou not age at al ;
  Whan youþe is past, is agë sesonable.

Age knows
how unstable
this world is,
Age haþ in-sigĥte how vnsure & vnstable   579
  þis worldës cours is, by lengthe of his yeeres,
  And can deffende hym from his scharpë breres.

(84. *Beggar.*)

¶ " Lord, wheþer it be maystrie to knowe   582
  Whan a man ofte haþ sundry weyës ride
Which is þe bestë ? nay, for soþe I trowe ;
  Rigĥt so he þat haþ many a world abyde
and can see
the faults of
its Youth.
þer he in youþë wrogĥtë mis or dyde,   586
  His age it seeþ, & byt him it eschue,
  And seekiþ weyës couenable & due.   588

(85. *Beggar.*)

[leaf 11 b]
When you,
Hoccleve,
grow old,
¶ " Whan þat þou hast assaydë boþë two,   589
  Sad age, I seye, after þi skittisĥ youþe,
As þou must nedys atteynë ther-to,
you'll heed
my advice.
  Or steruë ȝong, þan trowe I þou wolt bowe þe
  To swichë conceytës as I haue nowþe [1] ;   593
  And þankë god deuoutly in þin herte
  þat he haþ suffred þe þi youthe asterte.   595

(86. *Beggar.*)

¶ " Youthë [2] ful smal [3] reward hath to goodnesse,   596
  And peril dredith he non, wot I wel ;
Youth de-
votes itself to
the Tavern.
Al his deuocioun and holynesse
  At tauerne is, as for þe mostë [4] del ;
  To Bachus signe & to þe leuësel   600
  His youþe him haliþ ; & whan it him happiþ
  To chirchë gon, of nycetë he clappiþ.   602

---

[1] youeþe R.   [2] your H.   [3] smaĦ R, smal H.   [4] most H R.

(87. *Beggar.*)

¶ " The cause̤ why men oghten þider gon, 603 <small>Youth can't see why it should go to Church.</small>
 Nat conceyue[1] can his wyldë steerissħ heed
To folwen it. Also bote is it non
 To telle it him, for thogh men sowen seed
Of *ver*tu in a yong man, it is deed 607
  As blyue, his rebel goost it mortifieþ ;
  Al þing sauf folye in a yong man dieþ. 609

(88. *Beggar.*)

¶ " Whan I was yong I was ful rechëlees, 610 <small>When I was young,</small>
 Prowde, nyce, and riotous for þe maystrie,
And, among oþer, consciencëlees ;
 By þat sette I naght þe worþ of a flye ;
 And of hem haunted I þe compaignie 614 <small>I went to the Tavern, the Lantern to Waste.</small>
  þat went on pylgrymagë to tau*er*ne,
  Which be-for vnthrift beriþ þe lant*er*ne. 616

(89. *Beggar.*)

¶ " There offryd I wel morë þan my type, 617 <small>[leaf 12 *a*] I paid it my Church-tithes, and more.</small>
 And wit-drowe holy chirche his[2] duëtee ;
My frendës me cou*n*seylëd often siþe,
 þat I, w*ith* lownesse & humylitee,
 To my curat go scholde, & make his gree ; 621
  But straw vnto hir reed ! wolde I nat bowe
  ffor aght þey kouden preyen aħ, or wowe. 623

(90. *Beggar.*)

¶ " Whan folk wel rulyd dressyd hem to bedde, 624 <small>When good folk went to bed, I playd all night at the Tavern,</small>
 In tymë due by redë of nature,
To þe tau*er*në quykly I me spedde,
 And pleyde at dees while þe nyghte wolde endure.
 þere, þe former of eu*er*y creature 628
  Dismembred y w*ith* oþës grete, & rente <small>and swore great oaths.</small>
  Lyme for lyme, or þat I þennës wente. 630

---

   [1] conceyue R, cause H.   [2] holy chirches R.

(91. *Beggar.*)

I used to take false oaths for gain.

¶ " And ofte it fals was þat I swoer or spak,   631
   ffor þe desire feruént of couetyse
   ffonde[1] in periúrie no defaute or lak,
    But euer entyced me þat in al wyse
    Myn oþës gretë I scholde excercyse;   635
     And specially for lucre, in al manere
     Swere and for-swere with boldë face & chere. 637

(92. *Beggar.*)

¶ " But þis condicïoun, lo, hadde I euere :   638
   þogh I prowde were in wordës or in speche,

But when fighting began, off I went.

Whan strokës cam a[2] place, I gan disseuere
   ffro[3] my felawës ; soghte I neuere leeche
   ffor hurt which I there[4] toke ; what scholde I seche
    A saluë, whan I þer-of hadde no nede ?
    I hurtlees was ay, þurgh impressyd drede.   644

(93. *Beggar.*)

[leaf 12 *b*]
I'd spend 100 marks a year,

¶ " Tho myghte I spende an *hundred*[5] mark by ȝere,
   Al thyng deduct,[6] my sone, I gabbë noght ;
I was so prowde, I helde no man my pere ;
   In pryde & leccherye was al my þoght ;

and defoul wives, girls, and nuns.

No more I haddë set þerby or roght,   649
    A wif or mayde or nunë to deffoule,
    Than scheete, or pleyën[7] at þe bal or boule. 651

(94. *Beggar.*)

I had a heap of girls and wives at my will.

¶ " Ryght nycë girlës at my retenue   652
   Hadde I an heep, wyuës & oþere mo ;
What so þey werë, I wolde non eschue :
   And yeerës felë I contynued so ;
   Allas ! I no þing was war of þe wo   656
    þat folwyd me ; I lookyd nat behynde ;
    Conceytës yongë[8] ben ful derke & blynde. 658

---

[1] Fonde I R.   [2] in R.   [3] Fro R, For H.
[4] there R, *om.* H.   [5] a C, H.   [6] quytta R.
[7] pleyn H, pleye R.   [8] yonge R, yong H.

(95. *Beggar.*)

¶ " An office also hadde I lucratyf,   659 I had a lucra-
   An wan y-nowgĥ, god wot, & mochel more ;   tive post,
But neuer þoght I, in al my yongë[1] lyf,
   What I iniustly gat, for to restore ;
   Wherefore I now repentë wonder sore ;   663
     As yt mysgoten was, mys was despendid,   and spent
     Of whiche oure lord god gretly was offendid. 665 what I got
                                                          wrongly.

(96. *Beggar.*)

¶ " He sy I nolde absteenë for no good   666
   Of myn outragëous iniquitee ;
And whan þat his lust was, *with*-drow þe flood
   Of welþe, & at grounde ebbë sette he me ;   Then I ran
   With pouert for my gylt me feffed he,   670 dry.
     Swiche[2] wrechë toke he for my cursyd synne ;
     No morë good haue I þan I stond inne.   672

(97. *Beggar.*)

¶ " Gold, siluer, iewel, cloþ, beddẏng, array,   673 [leaf 13 *a*]
   Ne haue I non, oþir þan þou mayste se.   Now I've
Parde ! þis bare olde[3] russet is nat gay,   nothing but
   And in my purs so gretë sommës be,   this old rus-
   þat þere nys countour in al cristente   677 set suit.
     Which þat hem can at any noumbre sette ;
     þat schaltow se ; my purs I wole vnschete.   679

(98. *Beggar.*)

¶ " Come hider to me, sone, & look whedir   680 See ! no-
   In þis purs þer be any croyse or crouche,   thing's in
Sauf nedel and þrede, & themel of leþer ;   my Purse
   Here seest þow nagĥt þat man may handil or touche ; but a needle
   þe feend, men seyn, may hoppen in a pouche   684 and thread,
     Whan þat no croys þere-innë may a-pere ;   and a leather
     And by my purs, þe same I may seye here.   686 thimble.

---

[1] yonge R, yong H.   [2] Such R.
           [3] this olde R.

(99. *Beggar.*)

¶ " O wher is now al þe wantoun moneye   687
That I was maister of, and gou*er*nour,
Whan I knewe nat what pou*er*t was to sey ?

Now is pou*er*t þe glas and þe merour
In whiche I se my god, my sauyour.   691
Or[1] pou*er*t cam, wiste I nat what god was ;
But now I knowe, & se hym in þis glas.   693

(100. *Beggar.*)

¶ " And wherë be my gounës of scarlét,   694
Sanguyn, m*ur*reye, & blewës sadde & ligħte,
Grenës also, ánd þe fayre violet,
Hors and harneys, fresche and lusty in sygħte ?
My wykked lyf haþ put al þis to fligħte ;   698

But certes ȝit me greueþ most of al,
My frendschipe is al clenë fro me fal.   700

(101. *Beggar.*)

¶ " O while I stode in wele, I was honoured,   701
And many on, of my compáignie glad,
And now I am mys-lokyd on & loured ;
þere rekkeþ non how wo[2] I be bystad.
O lord ! þis world[3] vnstabyl is, & vnsad,   705
þis world hunuriþ[4] nat mannës p*er*sone
ffor him self, sonë, but for good[5] allone.   707

(102. *Beggar.*)

¶ " fful soþ fynde I þe word of salomon,   708
þat to moneie obeien allë[6] þinges ;[7]

ffor þat my coyn & coynworþ is a-gon,
Contrarien þei my wille & my byddynges ;
þat in my welþë w*ith* here flaterynges   712
Helden w*ith* me what þat I wroght or seyde,
Now disobeien þey þat þanne obeyde.   714

---

[1] or R, of H.   [2] harde R.   [3] world' R, wold H.
[4] honoureth R, hunriþ H.   [5] God' R.   [6] aħ R, al H.
[7] Salamon. Omnia pecunie obediunt : (R. in margin, not in H).

(103. *Beggar.*)

¶ " Now seyn þey þus—' I wistë wel al-way   715 My former
friends taunt
me.
    þat him destroyë wolde his fool largesse ;
I tolde hym so ; & eu*er* he seydë nay : '
    And ȝit þey lyen, also[1] god me blisse ;
      þey me comforted ay in myn excesse,   719
       And seyde I was a manly man w*ith*-alle :
       Hire hony wordys tornen me to galle.   721

(104. *Beggar.*)

¶ " God, whiche of his benyngnë curteseye   722 But God has
    And of his cheerë[2] louyng tendirnesse,
He of his synful haþ nat wele[3] he die,[4]
      But lyuë for tamende his wykkednesse ;   let me live
to mend,
      Hym thanke I, and his infynyt goodnesse ;   726
       His gracë likiþ þat, þorȝht[5] worldly peyne,   and escape
the Fiend.
       My soule eschapë may þe fendës cheyne.   728

(105. *Beggar.*)

¶ " Iob hadde an heuyer fal þan I, pardee !   729 [leaf 14 *a*]
Job fell more
heavily.
    ffor he was clumben hyer in rychesse ;
And paciently he his adu*er*site
      Took, as þe bybleberë can wytnesse ;
      And after-ward, god al his heuynesse   733
       Torned to ioye ; and so may he do myne,   God may give
me joy again.
       Whan þat it lykiþ to his myȝht dyuyne.   735

(106. *Beggar.*)

¶ " Lord, as þe lyst,[6] ryȝht so þou to me do,   736
    But eu*er* I hopë seur ben of þat place
Whiche þat þi m*er*cy boȝht vs haþ vnto,
    If þat vs list for to suë þi grace.
      A ! lord almyghty, in my lyuës space,   740 Lord, grant
me repent-
ance !
       Of my gylt grauntë þou me répentau*n*ce,
       And þi strook take in greable[7] souffrau*n*ce.   742

---

[1] als H, as R.   [2] chere R, cheer H.
[3] wille R, ' wele ' is H's often spelling of ' will ' : see l. 749.
[4] Scriptum est : Nolo mortem peccatoris, &c. (R. in margin,
not in H).   [5] thurȝh R.   [6] thow lust R.   [7] charitable R.

(107. *Beggar.*)

¶ " I coude of youþe han talkyd more & tolde   743
  þan I haue done, but þe day passiþ swiþe,

But, son Hoccleve, tell me all your trouble.
And eke me leu*er* is by many folde¹
  þy greef to knowë, whiche þat sit so ny þe.
Telle on anon, my goodë sone,² and I the   747
  Schal³ herken, as þou [so longe] hast don*e* me ;
And, as I can, wele I conseylë þe."   749

(108. *Hoccleve.*)

¶ " Graunt m*er*cy, derë fadir, of youre speche ;   750
  Ye han ryght wel me comforted & esyd ;

Hoccleve begs the Beggar's pardon for not answering him at first.
And hertily I praye yowe, and byseche,
  What I firste to yow spak be nat displesyd ;
It rewiþ me if I yow haue disesyd,   754
  And mekely yow byseche I of p*ar*doun,
Me súbmittyng vn-to⁴ correccïoun.   756

(109. *Hoccleve.*)

[leaf 14 *b*]
¶ " I wot wel, first whan þat I w*ith* yow mette,   757
  I was ful mad, and spak ful rudëly,
þogh I nat sleptë, yit my spirit mette

He was anxious and troubled,
  fful angry dremës ; þogĥt ful bysily
Vexid my goost, so þat no þing wyste I   761
  What þat I to yow spak, or what I þogĥte,
But here & þerë I my seluen soghte.   763

(110. *Hoccleve.*)

but didn't despise the Beggar.
¶ " I preye yow demeth nogĥt þat in dispyit   764
  I haddë yow, for age or poueretee ;
I mente it nogĥt ; but I stode in swiche plyit
  þat it was noþing likly vn-to me,
þogĥ ye had knowen al my pryuete,   768
  þat ye myghten my greef þus han abregged
As ye han don*e* ; so sore I was aggregged.   770

---

¹ folde R, flode H.   ² sone R, *om.* H.
³ ShaꝈ R, And schal H.   ⁴ vnto your R.

(111.   *Hoccleve.*)

¶ " ffadir, as wisly god me saue and spede,   771
   Ye ben not he whom þat I wende han founde ;
Ye ben to me ful welcome in þis nede ;   Hoccleve
   I wot wel ye in hy vertu habounde.   welcomes the
                                                              Beggar,
Your wys reed, hope I, helë schal my wounde ;   775
   My day of helþe is present, as me þinkiþ ;
   Youre confort deepe in-to myn hertë synketh. 777

(112.   *Hoccleve.*)

¶ " Myn hertë seiþ¹ þat youre beneuolence,   778   thanks him
   Of reuthë meeuëd, & verray pytee   for his kind-
                                                            ness,
Of my wo, doþ his peyne & diligence
   Me to releue of myn infirmytee.
O goodë² fadir, blissed mote ye be,   782
   þat han swich reuthe of my woful estat,
   Which wel ny was of helpë desperat.   784

(113.   *Hoccleve.*)

¶ " But, fadir, thogh ther be dyuersitee   785   [leaf 15 a]
   fful gret betwixt your excellent prudénce
And þe folyë þat regneth in me,
   Yit god it wot, ful litil differénce
Is ther betwixt þe hete and þe feruénce   789   says he
   Of louë wich to agid folk ye haue,   (Hoccleve)
                                                            loves aged
   And myn, al-thogh ye deeme I hem depraue. 791   folk, and

(114.   *Hoccleve and Beggar.*)

¶ " ffor if þat I þe sothë schal confesse,   792
   The lak of oldë mennës cherisshynge   suffers from
Is cause and ground [eke]³ of myn heuynesse,   lack of their
                                                            support.
   And éncheson of my wofúl murnynge ;
That schal ye knowe, if it be your lykynge,   796
   þe causë wite of myn aduersitee."
   " þis telle on, in þe name of crist," seyde he ; 798

---

¹ secth R.   ² goode R, good H.
³ cause of the ground R.

(115. *Beggar and Hoccleve.*)

¶ " Sauf first, or þow any forthér preceede,[1] 799
  On tyng[2] of þe, wite wold I, my sone ;

Hoccleve has been 24 years in the Privy-Seal Office. Wher dwelles[3] þow ?" [*Hoc.*] " fadir, wi*th*-outen drede, Nota Hee was an officer of yᵉ Privie Seale ; yᵉ Clerke, i trow. (*In the* 1700 *hand.*)
  In þe office of þe priue seal I wone ;
  And wrytë þer, is my custume and wone 803
    Vn-to þe seel, and hauë xx^{ti} yeer
    And iiij,[4] come estren, and that is neer." 805

(116. *Beggar.*)

¶ " Now sekir, sonë, that is a fair tyme ; 806
  The token is goode of thy continuance.
Come hidir, goode,[5] and sitte a-doun heer by me,
  ffor I mot rest awhile, it is my penance ;
  To me thus longë walke, it doth nusance 810
    Vnto my crookid feeble lymës olde,
    That ben so stif, vnnethe I may hem folde." 812

(117. *Beggar and Hoccleve.*)

[leaf 15 *b*] ¶ Whan I was set adon, as he me prayede, 813
  " Telle on," seyde he, " how is it wi*th* þe, how ?"[6]
An[7] I began my tale, and þus I seyde :—

Henry IV has " My ligë lord, þe kyng wich þat is now, Henricus iiijᵘˢ [R.]
    I fyndë to me gracious ynow ; 817
      God yelde him ! he haþ for my long se*r*uise
given him   Guer-douned[8] me in couenable wyse. 819

(118. *Hoccleve.*)

an Annuity of 20 Marks, or £13 6*s.* 8*d.* ; ¶ " In thé schequér, he of his special grace, 820
  Hath to me grauntid an annuitee
Of xx^{ti} mark, while I haue lyuës space. His annuitee of xx^{ti} marks. (*In the* 1700 *hand.*)
  Mighte I ay paid ben of þat duëtee,
  It schuldë[9] stondë wel ynow wi*th* me ; 824
but he can hardly get it paid.   But paiëment is hard to gete adayes ;
    And þat me put in many foule affrayes. 826

---

[1] procede R. [2] O thyng R. [3] dwellest R.
[4] foure R (read 'fourë'). [5] R. leaves out 'goode.'
[6] now R. [7] And R. [8] Guerdouned? R, Euer douned H.
[9] shulde R, schuld H.

(119. *Hoccleve.*)

¶ " It goht[1] ful streite and scharp or I it haue ;   827
   If I seur were of it be satisfiëd
ffro yeer to yeer, than, so god me saue,
   My deepë[2] rootid grief were remediëd
Souffissantly ; but how I schal be gyëd   831
     Heer-after, whan þat I no lenger serue,
     This heuyeth me, so þat I wel ny sterue.   833

If his Annuity were paid yearly, Hoccleve 'ud be happy.

(120. *Hoccleve.*)

¶ " ffor syn þat I now, in myn agë grene,   834
   And beyng in court, w*ith* gretë[3] peyne vnneth
Am paid ; in elde, and out of court, I weene
   My purs for þat may be a ferthyng shethe.
Lo, fader myn, þis dullith me to deth ;   838
     Now god helpe al ! for but he me socoure,
     My futur yeerës lik ben to be soure.   840

But as he can hardly get it now, he'll not get it all when he's old : hence his grief.

(121. *Hoccleve.*)

¶ " Seruyse, I wot wel, is non heritage ;   841   [leaf 16 *a*]
   Whan I am out of court an oþer day,
As I mot, whan vpon me hastiþ age,
   And þat no leng*er*e I labourë[4] may,
Vn-to my porë cote, it is no nay,   [see l. 940]   845
     I mote me drawe, & my fortune abyde,
     And suffre storm after þe mery tyde.   847

When he can't work, he'll have to suffer,

(122. *Hoccleve.*)

¶ " þere preue I schal þe mutabilitee   848
   Of þis wrechéd worldës affeccioun,
Which, whan þat youthe is past, begynneþ flee.
   ffrendchipe, a dieu ! farwel, dileccïoun !
Age is put out of youre proteccioun ;   852
     His loke vnlusty, & his impotence,
     Qwenchiþ youre loue & youre beneuolence.   854

and lose his friends and pleasure.

---

[1] goth R.   [2] depe R, deep H.   [3] grete, R, gret H.
[4] laboure R, labour H.

(123. *Hoccleve.*)

¶ " That after-clap, in my myndë so deepe   855
  Y-fycched is, & haþ swich roote y-cagħt,
þat al my ioye & myrthe is leyde to slepe ;

My schip is wel ney *with* dispeir y-fragħt.
þey þat nat konnë lerned be ne tagħt   859
  By swiche ensaumples, smerte as þey han seen,
  Me þinkeþ, certes, ouer blyndë been.   861

(124. *Hoccleve.*)

¶ " Allas ! I se reuthe & pitée exiled   862
  Out of þis land ; allas, compassïoun !
Whan schol ye þre to vs be reconsiled ?
  Youre absence is my greuous passïoun ;
Resorte, I preye yow, to þis regioun ;   866
  O, come ageyn ! þe lak of your *presénce*
  Manaceþ me to sterue[1] in indigence.   868

(125. *Hoccleve.*)

¶ " O fekil world ! allas, þi variaunce !   869

  How many a gentilman may men nowe se,
þat whilom in þe werrës olde of fraunce,
  Honured were, & holde in grete cheerte
ffor hire prowesse in armës, & plente   873
  Of frendës hadde in youþe, & now, for schame,

  Allas ! hir frendeschipe is crokéd & lame.   875

(126. *Hoccleve.*)

¶ " Now age vnourne a-wey puttéþ fauoúr,   876
  þat floury youþe in his seson conquerde ;

Now al forgete is þe manly labour
  þorgħ whiche ful oftë þey hire foos afferde ;

Now be þo worþi men bet *with* þe yerde   880
  Of nede, allas ! & non haþ of hem routhe ;

  Pyte, I trowe, is beried, by my trouþe.   882

---

[1] sterue R, streue H (compare H.'s 'flode' for 'folde,' l. 745,
p. 28 ; 'triste' for 'thirste,' l. 901, p. 33).

(127. *Hoccleve.*)

¶ " If sche be deed, god haue hire soule, I preye ; 883

And so schal mo hereafter preye, I trowe.

He þat pretendiþ him of most nobley,

  If he hire lakkë,[1] schal wel wyte & knowe

þat crueltee, hire foo, may but a throwe 887

    Hym suffre for to lyue in any welþe ;

    Hertë petous, to body & soule is helþe.[2] 889

If Nobles are not pitiful, they'll be ruind.

(128. *Hoccleve.*)

¶ " Ye oldë men of armës þat han knowe 890

  By syghte & by report hire worþynesse,

Lat nat mescheef tho men thus ou*er*-throwe !

  Kythe vp-on hem youre manly gentillesse !

Ye yongë men þat entre in-to prowesse 894

    Of armes, eek youre fadres olde hunurith[3] ;

    Helpe hem your self, or sum good hem pr*o*curith ![4]

Hoccleve appeals to old Men of Arms to help their poor fellows.

(129. *Hoccleve.*)

¶ " Knyghthode, awakë ! þou slepist to longe ; 897

  Thy brothir, se, ny dyeth for myschief ;

A-wake, and rewe vp-on his peynës stronge !

  If þou heer-after come vn-to swych pref,[5]

Thow wolt ful sorë triste[6] after releef ; 901

    þou art nat seur what that ye schal be-faH :

    Welth is ful slipir, be ware lest þou faH ! 903

[leaf 17 a]

He calls on Knights to aid the old fighters against the French.

(130. *Hoccleve.*)

¶ " þou þat yclomben art in hy[7] honoures, 904

  And hast þis worldës welth at thy deuys,

And bathist now in youthës lusty floures,

  Be war, rede I ! þou standist on þe ys :

It hath ben seen, as weleful[8] and as wys 908

    As þou, han slide : and þou þat no pitee

    On othir folk hast, who schal rewe on þe ? 910

He warns the Young, that they stand on ice,

and will fall unless they show Pity.

---

[1] lak H R.   [2] But ever after in sorwe and vnwelthe R.
   [3] honoure R, hunrith H (as in l. 706, p. 26).
   [4] self with some gode of youre R.   [5] myschief R.
 [6] thurst R (Compare H.'s 'streve' for 'sterve,' l. 868, p. 32).
       [7] hye R.   [8] wilfuH R.

(131. *Hoccleve.*)

Every man's
wealth may
fail:

¶ " Leeuë me wel, þer is non erthly man   911
    þat hath so stable a welth, but þat it
May failë, do he what þat he do kan :
    God, as hym list, visitith folk, & smyt.

let the rich
then relieve
the unfor-
tunate,

Wher-fore I deme and hold it *grace* & wit,   915
    In hy estat, man, god and himself knowe,
And releeue hem þat myscheef hath doun throwe.   917

(132. *Hoccleve.*)

¶ " God willë þat þe nedy be releeued ;   918
    It is on of þe werkës of mercy ;

and specially
the tried
Soldiers who
are poor.

And syn tho men þat ben in armës preeued,
    Ben in-to pouert fallë, trewëly
    Ye[1] men of armës oghten specialy   922
      Helpe hem : allas ! han ye no pitous blood
      That may yow stirë for to do hem good ?   924

(133. *Hoccleve.*)

[leaf 17 *b*]

These re-
duced Sol-
diers show
Hoccleve
what he may
soon be.

¶ " O now in ernest, derë fadir myn   925
    This worthi men to me þe[2] mirour shewe
Of sliper frenchipe, and vn-to what fyn
    I drawë[3] schal with-in a yeerës fewe,
    Vp-on þis woful thoght I hakke & hewe,   929
      And musë so, that vn-to lite I madde,
      And leuer dyë þan lyuén I hadde.   931

(134. *Hoccleve.*)

His income
(besides his
Annuity) is
but 6 Marks,
£4.

¶ " In faith, fadir, my lyflodë, by-side   932
    Thainuittee of which aboue I tolde,
May nat exceedë yeerly in no tyde
    Vj mark ; þat sittiþ[4] to myn herte so colde,   *Nota hoc.*
    Whan þat I look abouten, and byholde   936 *(In the* 1700
                                          hand.)
      How scars it is, if þat that othir faille,
      That I nat gladdë can,[5] but murne & waille.   938

---

[1] Ye R, þe H.   [2] Thise . . . a R.   [3] drawe R, draw H.
[4] sitte R, sit H.   [5] glad kan be R, glad can H.

(135. *Hoccleve.*)

¶ " And as ferforth, as I[1] can deeme or gesse,   939
  Whan I at home dwell in my poore cote,
I fynde[2] schal as frendly slipirnesse
  As tho men now doon, whos frendeschipe is rote.
Nat wold I rekke as mochel as a mote,   943
    Thogh I no more hadde of yeerly encrees,
    So that I myght ay païed be doutlees.   945

When Hoccleve retires poor, his friends 'll leave him.

(136. *Hoccleve.*)

¶ " Two partes of my lif, & mochil more,   946
  I seur am, past ben ; I ne doute it noght ;
And if þat I schold in my yeerës hore
  ffor-go my duëtee,[3] that I haue boght
With my flessh and my blode, þat heuy thoght   950
    Which I drede ay, schal fal, as I it thynke ;
    Me hasteth blyue vn-to my pittës brynke.   952

Half his life is gone;

and if he can't get his dues when old,

he'll be ruind.

(137. *Hoccleve.*)

¶ " ffaylyng, fadir, myn annuite,   953
  ffoot hoot in me crepith disese and wo ;
ffor þei þat han by-forë knowen me,
  ffaillyngë good, me failë wole also.
Who no good hath, is fer his frendës fro ;   957
    In muk is al þis worldës frendlyhede ;
    My goost is wrappëd in an heuy drede.   959

[leaf 18 a]
If his Annuity fails, his friends 'll fail.

(138. *Hoccleve.*)

¶ " If þat I hadde of custume, or þis tyme,   960
  lyued in indigences wrechednesse,
The lesse heerafter schuld it sit[4] by me ;
  But in myn agë wrastle with hardenesse,
That with hym stroglid[5] neuere in grennesse   964
    Of youthë, þat mutacïon and chaunge
    An othir day me seemë shulde al straunge.   966

Had he livd niggardly, he'd not care;

but having been comfortable, the change 'll be hard.

---

[1] I R, *om.* H.   [2] fynde R, fynd H.   [3] duetee R, deutee H.
    [4] sette R.   [5] stroglede R, stroglid H.

(139. *Hoccleve.*)

¶ " He þat neu*e*re knewe þe swetnesse of wele,   967
   Thogh he it lakke ay, lesse hym greue it schal,
Than hym þat hath ben weleful yeerës fele,
   And in effect hath felt no greef at al.

Hoccleve would sooner die than live a pauper's life.

O pouert! god me sheldë fro thy fal!   971
   O deth! thy strok yit is more agreáble
   To me, þan lyue a lyf so miseráble.   973

(140. *Hoccleve.*)

£4 a year is too little for him,

¶ " VI marc, yeerly, and no more þan þat,   974
   ffadir, to me, me thynkyth is ful lyte,
Consideryng, how þat I am nat[1]
   In housbondryë, lerned worth a myte;

who can hardly scare the kite that 'ud steal his poultry.

Scarsely cowde I[2] charre a-way þe kyte   978
   That me bireuë woldë my pullaille;
   And more axith housbondly[3] gouernaylle.   980

(141. *Hoccleve.*)

[leaf 18 *b*]
He can't plough, or fill a barrow:

¶ " With plow can I nat medlen, ne with harwe,   981
   Ne wot nat what lond, good is for what corne;
And for to lade a cart or fille a barwe,—
   To which I neu*e*r vsed vas[4] to-forne,—

his stooping, too, spoils him.

My bak vnbuxum hath swich thyng forsworne,   985
   At instance of writyng, his Werreyour,
   That stowpyng hath hym spilt with his labour.

(142. *Hoccleve.*)

Writing is

¶ " Many men, fadir, wenen þat writynge   988
   No trauaile is; þei hold it but a game:
Aart hath no foo but swich folk vnkonynge: ¶ Ars non habet inimi-cum nisi ignorantem.
   But who so list disport hym in þat same,
   Let hym continue, and he schal fynd it grame;   992

such hard work.

   It is wel gretter labour þan it seemeth;
   þe blyndë man of coloures al wrong deemeth.   994 ¶ Cecus non iúdicat[5] &c.

---

[1] I suppose this line to be deliberately made of 9 syllables,—
'how' serving, with a pause, for the usual 2,—to correspond
with the 9-syllable line 974 which it rymes with, and in which
'Six,' with a pause, represents a measure or 'foot.'

[2] knowe I to R.   [3] husbonderye R.   [4] was R.

[5] R. continues: de colorib*us*; et nota hic de scriptorib*us*.

(143. *Hoccleve.*)

¶ " A writer mot thre thyngës to hym knytte,   995 A writer's mind, eye
   And in tho may be no disseuerance ;   and hand, must all work
Mynde, ee, and hand, non may fro othir flitte,   together:
   But in hem mot be ioynt continuance.
The mynde al hoole with-outen variance   999
   On þe ee[1] and hand awaytë moot alway,
   And þei two eek on hym ; it is no nay.   1001

(144. *Hoccleve.*)

¶ " Who so schal wrytë, may nat holde a tale   1002 he can't talk or sing.
   With hym and hym, ne syngë[2] this ne that ;
But al his wittës hoolë, grete and smale,
   Ther must appere, and halden hem ther-at ;
And syn, he spekë may, ne syngë[2] nat,   1006
   But bothë[3] two he nedës moot forbere,
   Hir labour to hym is þe alengere.[4]   1008

(145. *Hoccleve.*)

¶ " This artificers, se I day be day,   1009 [leaf 19 *a*] But workmen
   In þe hotteste of al hir bysynesse   can sing and joke at their work.
Talken and syng, and makë game and play,
   And forth[5] hir labour passith with gladnesse ;
But we labour in trauaillous stilnesse ;   1013 Writers must stick to their sheepskin,
   We stowpe and stare vp-on þe shepës skyn,
   And keepë muste our song and wordës in.   1015

(146. *Hoccleve.*)

¶ " Wrytyng also doth grete annoyës thre,   1016
   Of which ful fewë folkës taken heede
Sauf we oure self ; and thisë, lo, þei be :
   Stomak is on,[6] whom stowpyng out of dreede   and get pains in their
Annoyeth soore ; and to our bakkës, neede   1020 stomachs, backs, and eyes.
   Mot it be[7] greuous ; and þe thrid, our yen,
   Vp-on þe whytë mochel sorwe[8] dryen.   1022

---

[1] On eye R.   [2] syng H R.   [3] bothe R, both H.
   [4] elengere R.   [5] forth R, for H.   [6] one R.
      [7] be R, *om.* H.   [8] for to H.

(147.   *Hoccleve.*)

¶ " What man þat *thre & twenti*[1] yeere and more   1023
  In wryting hath continued, as haue I,
I dar wel seyn it smerteth[2] hym ful sore
  In euere veyne and place of his body ;

And yen[3] moost it greeueth trewëly[4]   1027
  Of any crafte þat man can ymagyne :
ffadir, in feth, it spilt[5] hath wel ny myne.   1029

(148.   *Hoccleve.*)

¶ " Lo, fadir, tolde haue I yow þe substance   1030
  Of al my greef, so as þat I can telle ;

But wel I wot it hath bene gret penance
  To yow with me so longë for to dwelle ;
I am riȝt sikir it hath ben an helle,   1034
  Yow for to herken me þus iangle & clappe,
  So lewdly in my termës I me wrappe.   1036

(149.   *Hoccleve.*)

¶ " But nathëlees, truste I, your pacïence   1037
  Receyuë wole in gree my wordës aH ;
And what mys-seyd I haue, of negligence,
  Ye wole it lete asidë slippe and faH.
My fadir dere, vn-to your grace I caH ;   1041

  Ye wote my grief ; now redeth me[6] þe best,
  With-outen whom my goost can han no reste."

(150.   *Beggar and Hoccleve.*)

¶ " Now, sonë myn, hast þou al seid and spoke   1044
  þat þé good likyth ? "   [*Hoccl.*] " ya, fadir, as now."
[*Beg.*] " Sone, if oght in þin herte elles be loke,
  Vnlokke it blyue ! com of[7] ; what seist þou ? "

[*Hoccl.*] " ffadir, I can no morë tellë yow   1048
  þan I beforë spoken haue and sayd."
[*Beg.*] " A goddes half, sone, I am wel appayd.

---

[1] xx^tiiij H.   [2] smerteth R, smerth H.
[3] yen R, than H (the same mistake occurs in the *Minor
Poems*, I).   [4] trewly H, truly R.
[5] feith it sate R.   [6] rede me for R.   [7] forth R.

(151. *Beggar.*)

¶ "Conceyued haue I, þat þou gret fere haast
   Of pouert, for to fallen in þe snare ;
Thow haast þer-innë[1] caght so deep a taast,
   þat of al ioyë þou art voide & bare ;
   þou ny dispeirëd art of al wele-fare,
     And þe strook of pouert art þou fer fro ;
     ffor shamë ! why makest þou al this wo ?

1051 Just for fear
of Poverty,

you're de-
spairing.
1055

1057 For shame !

(152. *Beggar.*)

¶ "I put cas,—as god þer-fro þe keepe ! —
   þou were y-fall in indigent pouert ;
Suldest þou grucche, and thyn annoy by-weepe ?
   Nay ! be þou riche or poore, or seke or quert,
   God thank alway, of thyn ese and þi smert ;
     Prydë þe noght for no prosperitee,
     Ne heuye þe for non aduersite.

1058 Even if
you were a
Pauper,

1062 you ought to
thank God.

1064

(153. *Beggar.*)

¶ "Pouert hath in himself ynow greuance,
   With-outen þat that man more him purcháce ;
Who-so it taketh in pacient suffraunce,
   It is ful plesant beforn cristës face ;
   And whoso gruchith, forfetith þat grace
     That he schuld han, if þat his pacience
     Withstoode þe grief, and made it résistence.

1065 [leaf 20 *a*]
Don't make
more trouble
for yourself.

1069

1071

(154. *Beggar.*)

¶ "My sone, as witnessith holy scripture,
   Discreet and honest pouert manyfold
Commendid is ; crist himself, I þe insure,
   To loue and teche and prechen it hath wold.
   He did al þis ; be þou neuer so bold,
     A-gayn pouert heer-after grucche, I rede ;
     ffor forther-more in holy wryt I rede ;

1072

Christ
preacht Pov-
erty.

1076

1078

---

[1] inne R, in H.

(155. *Beggar.*)

Christ was poor all His life.

¶ " Beholde þe lyf [eek][1] of our sauëour, 1079
    Right fro the tyme of his natiuite
Vn-to his deth, as þat seith myn Auctour,
    And tokne in it schal þou non fynde or se,
    Bot of pouert, with which content was he. 1083
        Is man better than god ? schal man eschewe
        Swych lyf, syn god þat samë wolde ay swe ? 1085

(156. *Beggar.*)

It's an Abuse for man to want Riches.

¶ " ffy ! it is to gret an abusioun, 1086
    To seen a man, þat is but wormës mete,
Desire richés,[2] and gret possessioun,
    Wher as our lord god wold hym entremete
    Of no richés ; he deynëd it nat gete ; 1090
        He lyued poorëly, and pouert chees,
        þat myghte han ben ful riche ; it is no lees. 1092

(157. *Beggar.*)

[leaf 20 b]
The poor sleeps with open doors :

¶ " The poorë man slepith ful sikirly 1093
    On nyghtës, thogh his dorë be noght shit,
Where-as þe riche, a-beddë bisily
    Casteth and ymagineth in his wit,

the rich needs locks and bars ;

    That necessarie vnto him is it 1097
        Barrës and lokkës strongë[3] for to haue,
        His goed[4] from theeuës for to keep & saue. 1099

(158. *Beggar.*)

and when he sleeps, he dreams of Thieves.

¶ " And when þe deed sleep fallith attë laste 1100
    On hym, he dremeth theeuës comen in,
And on his cofres knokke, & leye on faste,
    And some hem pykë[5] with a sotil gyn,
    And vp is broken, lok, hasp, barre & pyn ; 1104
        And in, þe hande goth, and þe bagge out takiþ ;

He wakes,

        ffor sorwe of which, out of his slepe he wakiþ ;

---

[1] lyfe R.   [2] richesse R, riche H.   [3] stronge R, strong H.   [4] goods R.   [5] of hem vnpyke R.

(159. *Beggar.*)

¶ " And vp he rysith, foot and hand tremblyng,   1107
   As þat assailed hym þe parlësye[1];
And at a stirt, withouten tarying,   *and rushes to his chest,*
   Vn-to his cofre he dressitħ hym in hye;
    Or he there come, he is in poynte to dye;   1111
     He it vndoth, and opneth, for to se   *to see if his money is*
     If þat his falsë[2] goddës ther-in be :   1113 *safe.*

(160. *Beggar.*)

¶ " He dredith fynde it as þat he hath drempt. 1114 *The rich are always in*
¶ Idem Sene-   This worldës power ánd riche hábundance, *fear.*
ca: Saeculi[3]
autem potes- Of drede of peryl neuere ben exempt;
tas sine ti-
more periculi But in pouert is ay[4] sikir constance : *The poor, if content, have*
nunquam est, Who holdith hym content, hath sufficiance. 1118 *enough.*
sed pauper-
tas semper   And sonë, by my rede þou schalt do so,
secura est.
     And by desir of good nat sette a slo.   1120

(161. *Beggar.*)

¶ " Wilful pouért in princes ancïen   1121 [leaf 21 *a*]
   So ferforth was, þat þey desired more
Good loos þan[5] good; bot now-of-dayes, men *Now, men care more for Cash than*
   Yerne[6] and desiren after muk so sore, *Fame.*
    þat they good fame han leyd a watir yore,[7] 1125
    And rekken neuer how longe it þer stipe,[8]
    Or thogh it drenchë, so þei good may grype.[9] 1127

(162. *Beggar.*)

¶ " Of Siȝilë whilom[10] þer was a kyng   1128 *A King of Sicily had*
   With erthen wessel serued at his table ; *earthen ves-sels on his*
Nota And men, wondryng faste[11] vpon this thyng *table.*
   Seyd vn-to hym, it was nat honurable
    To his estat, ne nothyng comendable,   1132
     Axynge hym why hym list be serued so ;
     To which demandë he answerdë tho :   1134

---

[1] As that hym shoke the palsye R.   [2] fals H R.
[3] Simili R.   [4] ay R, an H.   [5] than R, that H.   [6] Renne R.
[7] That her gode fame is leid a water thore R.   [8] slepe R.
[9] kepe R.   [10] Cesile somtyme R.   [11] fast wondrede R.

(163. *Beggar.*)

¶ " He seyd : 'thogh I kyng be of siȝilë,   1135
      A potter was my fadir, is no nay ;
      How long I schal induren, or what while
      In my prosperitee, nat knowe I may :

      ffortunës variance I drede alway ;   1139
          Ryght as sche madë me to clymbe on highte
          Sodenly, so sche may me make alighte.   1141

(164.   *Beggar.*)

¶ " 'I thynke alway of my natiuitee,   1142
      And of my poorë lenage & my blode ;

  Erthen vessél, to swich a man as me
      fful sittyng is, and acceptable & good.'
      O, fewë ben ther now left of þe brood   1146
          That he cam of ; he loued bet profyt
          Commun, than his a-vantage or delyte.   1148

(165.   *Beggar.*)

¶ " How seystow by affrýcan Scipion ?—   1149
      Affrican clept, for þat he affryk wan ;—
  To pouert hadde he swych affeccïoun,
      Of his ownë free wil & lust, þat whan

  He dyed, no good had þis worthy man,   1153
      Wher-with his body in the[1] erthë brynge,
      But þe común cost made his enterynge.   1155

(166.   *Beggar.*)

¶ " Be-forn þe senat was he bore on honde   1156
      Ones, after he affrik wonnen hadde,
  That he was riche, as þey cowde vnderstonde,
      Of gold :· to which, with wordes sobre and sadde,
      Answerde he þus : 'thogh I be feble & badde, 1160

      The sooth is, vnto youre subieccïoun
      I gat Affrik ; of þat haue I renoun.   1162

---

[1] in the érthe to R, vp on erth H.

(167. *Beggar.*)

¶ " ' My namë was al þat I therë¹ gat;
　To wynne hono*ur* was only þe purpos
Whiche þat I took, or þat I cam ther-at;
　Othir good hadde I non þan richë² loos;
　　ffor al þe good there was, opne or cloos,
　　Myn hertë myghtë³ nat so wel content,
　　As þe renou*n* only, þat I ther hent.'

1163　Scipio wisht only to win Honour.

1167

1169

(168. *Beggar.*)

¶ " Of coueytise he was no þing coupáble,
He settë⁴ nat þ*er* by, þ*o*u mayst wel se.
ffy on þe! gredynes insaciable,
　Of many a man, þat can nat content be
　Of muk, al thogh neu*er* so moch haue he!
　　The kynde is euere of wreched couetyse,
　　To coueyte ay, and haue, and nat suffyse.

1170　He was not covetous.

1174　Many folk are insatiable of money.

1176

(169. *Beggar.*)

¶ " I wold, [that] euery knyght dide now þe same,
　And were of good no morë coueytous
Than he was: what! to gete a noble fame,
　To knyghthode is tresór most precïous;
　But I was neuere so auenterous,
　　Renou*n* to wynnë by swerdës conquest,
　　ffor I was bred in á pesible nest.

[leaf 22 *a*]

1181　The Beggar has never fought;

1183

(170. *Beggar.*)

¶ " Vpon my bak come neuere haburgeou*n*,
　Ne my knyf drew I neuere in violence;
I may nat contrefetë Scipion
　In armës, ne his worthi excellence
　Of wilful pouert; but of indigence
　　I am as riche as was euere any man,
　　Suffre it in pacience if þat I can.

1184

1188　but he's as poor as any one.

1190

---

¹ there R, ther H.　　² riche R, rich H.
³ hert myght H R.　　⁴ sette R, set H.

(171. *Beggar.*)

¶ " No richer[1] am I þan þou maïst se ;   1191
    Of myne haue I[2] no thyng to takë to ;
I lyue of almesse. if it stood with þe
    So streyte, and lyuedest[3] as þat I do,
      I se þou woldest sorowe swychë two   1195
        As I ; but þou haast for to lyuen on
      A poore lyf ; and swych ne haue I non.   1197

(172. *Beggar.*)

¶ " Salamon yaf conseil, men shulden preye   1198
    Two thyngës vn-to god, in soothfastenesse :
Now herkne, sone, he bad men þus to seye :
    ' Enhancë þou me, lord, to no richesse,
    Ne by misérie me so sore oppresse,   1202
      That needë for to beggë me compelle :'
      In his *prouerbës* þus, lo ! can he telle.   1204

(173. *Beggar.*)

¶ " But þis pouert menë[5] conseiled he   1205
    Men to desyr, þat was necéssarye
To foode and clooth, dredyng lest plentee
    Of good hem myghtë makë to miscarie,
    And fro the knowlegyng of god to varie ;   1209
      And lest smert needë made hem god reneye :
      Now be war, sonë, lest þat þou folye.   1211

(174. *Beggar.*)

¶ " Sone, in þis menë pouert holde I þe,   1212
    Sauf þat þou canst nat taken it ful weel.

What thogh þou lesë þin annuytee,
    Yit mayst þou leuen on þat othir del,
    Thogh nat ful delecate schal be þi meel.   1216

      Of vj marc yeerly, mete & drinke & clooth
      Thow getë mayst, my child, with-outen oth." 1218

---

      [1] No richer R, Now riche H.   [2] I R, *om.* H.
[3] livedest R, lyuest H.   [4] tribue necessaria R.   [5] men R.

(175. *Hoccleve.*)

¶ " Ya, fadir myn, I am nat so per*fite*   1219   Hoccleve
    To take it so ; I haue had hábundance   pleads that
                                                           he's had
Of welfare ay ; and now stond in þe plite   plenty,
    Of scarsetee, it were a gret penance
ffor me : god scheldë me fro þat strait chance ! 1223
        Vj marc yeerly, to scars is to sustene   and cannot
                                                           get on with
        The charges þat I haue, as þat I wene.   1225   only £4 a
                                                           year.

(176. *Hoccleve.*)

¶ " Tow on my distaf haue I for to spynne,   1226   Moreover, he
                                                           has a Wife.
    Morë, my fadir, þan ye wot of yit,
Which ye schal know, or þat I fro yow twynne,
    Yf your good lust be for to heren it ;
But, for as moche as it nat to me sit,   1230
        Your talë for to[1] interrupte or breke,
        Here-after to yow wil I þer-of speke.   1232

(177. *Hoccleve.*)

¶ " Yit o worde, fader[2] ; I haue herd men seyn, 1233   [leaf 23 *a*]
    Who-so no good hath, þat he can no good ;
And þat fynde I, a plat sooth and a pleyn ;
    ffor al-thogh that myn heed, vndir myn hood,   Hoccleve
                                                           never was
    Was neuere wys, yit while[3] it with me stood, 1237   clever, but
                                                           had fair wits
        So þat I had siluer resonable,   while he had
                                                           cash.
        My litil wytte was sumwhat couenable.   1239

(178. *Hoccleve.*)

¶ " But now, for that I haue but a[4] lyte,   1240   But now he's
                                                           to get less
    And lykly am heer-aftir to han lesse,   income, his
My dul wit can to me no-thyng pro*fite* ;   wits grow
                                                           dull.
    I am so drad of monyës scantnesse,
    That myn hert is al nakid of lightnesse.   1244
        Wisseth me how to gete a golden salue ;   The Beggar
                                                           shall have
        And what I haue, I wele it wi*th* yow halue." 1246 half what he
                                                           gets Hoc-
                                                           cleve.

[1] to R, *om.* H.   [2] fader R, *om.* H.   [3] while R, wil H.
               [4] but a R, a large H.

(179. *Beggar.*)

¶ " Sone, as for me, nouthir avaunte ne rere ;   1247
　　　But if disese algatës schal bityde,
　ffor to be pacïent, rede I thow leere ;
　ffor any thyng, with-holde hir on þi side ;
　　　My reed wole it nat, sonë, fro the hide ;   1251

　　　Make of necessite, reed I, vertu ;
　　　ffor better rede can I non, by Ihesu.   1253

(180. *Beggar.*)

¶ " My sonë, they þat swymmen in richesse   1254
　　　Continuelly, and han prosperitee,
　And neuere han felt but welëful swetnesse,
　　　Vnscourgid ay of any aduersitee,

　Leest god forgete hem, oughten ferdful be ;   1258
　　　Syn god in holy writ seith in þis wyse,
　　　' Whom so I loue, hym wole I chastyse.' [1]   1260

(181. *Beggar.*)

¶ " Seint Ambroses legendë seith, how he   1261
　　　Ones to Romë-ward took his viage,
　And in Tuscië, tóward þat contree,

　　　With a riche ost he took his herbergage ;
　　　Of whom, as blyuë fair in his langage,   1265
　　　Of his estate enqueren he be-gan ;
　　　And vnto þat, answerde anon this man :   1267

(182. *Beggar.*)

¶ " ' Right at my lust haue I al worldely welth ;   1268

　　　Myn estat hath ben ay good, and yit is ;
　Richesse haue I, frendschipe, and bodyes helth ;
　　　Was neuere thynge me happid yit amys.'
　　　And seint Ambrose,[2] astonëd sore of this,   1272
　　　Anon right rowned to his compaignye,
　　　' Sires, it is tyme þat we hennës hye ;   1274

---

[1] Quem diligo, castigo R, *in margin.*
[2] Ambrose R, Ambroses H.

(183. *Beggar.*)

¶ " ' I am adrad, god is nat in þis place ;   1275 St. Ambrose
 Go we fast hennës, lest þat hys vengeance   feard God's
ffal on vs ! ' and with-in a litel space   vengeance,
 After they were agone, schop this myschance ; went away,
 The groundë[1] claue and made disseuerance, 1279 and soon the
  And in sank man, womman, childe, hous, & al Rich man
  That to hym appertened, gret and smal. 1281 sank into the
                 earth.

(184. *Beggar.*)

¶ " Whan þis come to Ambroses[2] audience, 1282 St. Ambrose
 He seidë[3] to his felacheepë þus :—   said,
' Lo, bretheren ! seeth heer in éxperience,   See how
 How merciáblely our lord Ihesus   Christ has
 Of his benyngë[4] grace hath sparid vs ! 1286 poor, and
  He sparith hem that vnwelthy heer ben, killd the rich!
  And to þe velthy[5] dooth as þat ye seen.' 1288

(185. *Beggar.*)

¶ " This lyf, my sone, is but a chirie faire ; 1289 [leaf 24 a]
 Worldly riches, haue ay in þi memórye,   This life
Schal passe, al look it neuer on men so feire ; is only a
 Whil þou art heer in þis world transitórie, Cherry-fair.
 Enable þe to wynne eternel glorie   1293
  Wher no pouert is, but perfite richesse
  Of ioye and blysse, and vertuous gladnesse. 1295

(186. *Beggar.*)

¶ " O thyng tel I þe, sonë, þat is soth :   1296
 Thogh a man hadde als moch as men han al, Unless Virtue
But vertu, þat good gye, al he mys dooth,   guides
 Al þat swetnessë tournë schal to gal.   Riches,
 Whan þat richesse is on a man yfal,[6] 1300
  If it be wrong dispendid or mys-kept, they'll bring
  Another day ful sore it schal be wept. 1302 Sorrow.

---

[1] groundë R, ground H. [2] Ambroses R, Ambrose H.
[3] seide R, seid H. [4] benigne R, benyng H. [5] welthy R.
      [6] falle R, fal H.

(187. *Beggar.*)

¶ " Sum riche is large, and his good mys despendith

  In mayntenance of syn and harlotrie ;

To swich despenses his lust hym accendith ;

  And on þat othir parte, his nygardie

Suffrith hys neghtburgh[1] by hym sterue & dye, 1307

  Rathir þan with a ferthyng hym releeue :[2]

  Tho two condicïons ben to repreue.   1309

(188. *Beggar.*)

¶ " Whoso moost hath, he moost of schal answere ;

  On day schal comë, sum men schal par chaunce

Desire he neuere haddë ben rychere

  Than heer han hadde his barë sustinaunce.

Whan þe day comth of ire and of vengeaunce,   1314

  Than schal men see,[3] how in þis world, I gesse,

  Richesse is pouert, and pouért richesse.   1316

(189. *Beggar.*)

¶ " Whyl er, my sonë, tolde I naght to þe   1317

  What hábundance in youth I hadde of good,

And how me blentë[4] so prosperitee,

  þat what god was, y nothing vnderstood ?

But ay whil þat I in my welthë[5] stood,   1321

  After my flesshly lust my lif I ledde,

  And of his wrechë no þing I me dredde.   1323

(190. *Beggar.*)

¶ " And as I seid, he smot me with þe strook   1324

  Of pouert, in which I contynue yit,

Whos smert my good blood first so sorë sook,

  Or þat I was acqueyntid wel with it,

þat nye it haddë refte[6] fro me my wit ;   1328

  But sithen, thanke I god, in pacïence

  I haue it take, and schal, for myn offence.   1330

---

[1] neighbore R.   [2] releueeue H, releeue R.   [3] see R, seeme H.
[4] blent H R.   [5] welthe R, welth H.   [6] refte R, reste H.

(191. *Beggar.*)

¶ " If þe list fle, þat may pouert engendre,   1331 Hoccleve is
to avoid Sin,
spend spar-
ingly,
  ffirst synne eschue, and god honoure & drede ;
Also, for þi lyflode is scars and sclendre,
  Despendë nat to largëly, I rede.
    Mesure is good ; let hir þe gye and lede ;   1335
    Be war of outrage, and be sobre & wys ;
    þus þou excludë hym, by myn avys.   1337

(192. *Beggar.*)

¶ " Nathëlees þou maist ágeyn me replie,   1338
  ' To sum folk, thogh þei doon al as I seye,
Agayn pouert it is no remedye ;
  þei mow it nat eschuë by no waye.'
    I grauntë wel, but þan take heede, I preye,   1342 take calmly
whatever
happens,
    The iugëmentȝ of god ben to vs hid ;
    Take al in gree, so is þi vertu kyd.   1344

(193. *Beggar.*)

¶ " To þe plesaunce of god þou þe conforme,   1345 [leaf 25 *a*]
and conform
to God's will.
  Aboutë þat be bisy and éntentif ;
þat þou mis-done hast, þou blyue it reforme ;
  Swych laborer[1] þe kythe heere in þis lyf,
    þat god þi soulë, which þat is his wyf,   1349
    Reioisë may, for it is to him due,
    And his schal be, but þou þe deuors sue.   1351

(194. *Beggar.*)

¶ " O þou, fortunë, fals and deceyuáble !   1352 Fortune is
false.
  fful soþ it is, if þou do a good deede,
þu nat purpósist it schal be duráble ;
  Of good ententë schal it nat procede.
    Wel oghte vs þi promesses blyndë drede ;   1356
    He sliperly stant who þat þou enhauncest,
    ffor sodeynlichë þou hym disauauncest.   1358

[1] a labour R.

(195. *Beggar.*)

Had the
Beggar
known

¶ " Hadde I donë, sonë, as I þe consayle,   1359
     Whan þat fortunës déceyuáble cheere
Lawhid on me, þan hadde I nat, sanȝ fayle,
     Ben in þis wrecched plyt as þu seest heere.

Fortune's
changeable-
ness, he'd
not have
trusted her.

     Not knew my ȝouthe[1] hir chaungeable maneere ;
     ffor whan I satte on hy vp-on hir wheel,
     Hir gladsum look me madë truste hire wel.   1365

(196. *Beggar.*)

¶ " I cowdë for no þing han wend or deemed   1366
     þat sche a-boutë baar dowble visage ;
I wende sche haddë ben swiche as sche semed.
     But nathëles, ȝit is it auantage
     To him þat woful is, þat hir vsage   1370

But it's of
use to some
folk.

     Is for to flyttë fro[2] placë to place ;
     Hire variance is vn-to sum folke grace.   1372

(197. *Beggar.*)

[leaf 25 b]

¶ " Whom so þat nedë greueþ & trauaylliþ,   1373
     Hire change is vn-to hym no grief or wo ;
But þe contrárie of þat no þing auaylliþ,
     As whan a man is wel, put hym þerfro.

Is she man's
Friend or
Foe ?

     What schal men calle hir ? frende, or ellys fo ? 1377
     I not ; but caH hire frend, whan þat sche esiþ,
     And calle hir fo, whan þat sche man displesiþ.

(198. *Beggar.*)

Tho' she's
changeable,

¶ " But who so calle hir schal a sikir name ?   1380
     Men mote hir clepe ' my lady chaungeabil,'
ffor hardily sche is þat seluë same ;
     A ! nay ! I gabbe, I am vn-resonabil ;

she's stedfast
in making
the Beggar
poor.

     Sche is ' my lady stidëfast and stabil,'   1384
     ffor I endure in pouertës distresse,
     And sche nat liste remuë[3] my duresse.   1386

---

[1] thought R.   [2] fro R, for H.
[3] releeue R.

(199. *Beggar.*)

¶ " I ymagynë whi þat nat hir list   1387   The Beggar
    With me now dele ; age is colde & drye ;   is old and worn-out.
And whan þo two ben to a lady wist,
    And þat I poore am eek for þe maystrie,
Swiche a man is vnlusty to hire ye,   1391   Lady Fortune
    And wers to gropë : straw for impotence !   likes the young and rich.
Sche loueþ yong folk, & large of dyspence.   1393

(200. *Beggar.*)

¶ " Al þis þat I haue of fortunë seyde,   1394
    Is but a iapë, who[1] seith, or a knak :
Now I a whilë bourdyd haue & pleyde,
    Resorte I wol to that þat[2] I first spake.
By-holde, & cast þou þine yë a-bak,   1398   Let Hoccleve
    What þou god hast a-gilt in tymë past,   correct his old faults.
Correct it, and to do so eft be a-gast.   1400

(201. *Beggar.*)

¶ " Of holy chirche, my sonë, I conceyue   1401   [leaf 26 a]
    As ȝit ne hast þou non a-vancëment :   He has had no promotion
Ye courteours, ful often ye deceyue   from the Church.
    Youre soulës, for þe désirous talént
Ye han to good ; & for þat þou art brent   1405
    With couetysë now, par auenture
Only for muk, þou ȝernest soulës cure.   1407

(202. *Beggar.*)

¶ " fful many men knowe I, þat gane and gape   1408   Many folk
    After som fat & richë benefice ;   gape after a fat benefice.
Chirche or prouendre[3] vnneþe hem may eschape,
    But þei as blyue it henten vp and trice :
God graunté þei accepte hem for þe office,   1412
    And noght for þe profet þat by hem hongeþ,[4]
ffor þat conceytë nat to prestehode longeþ.   1414

---

[1] as who R.   [2] þat, *om.* H R.   [3] prebende R.
[4] hongeth R, longeþ H.

(203.   *Beggar.*)

Now, one church doesn't suffice a man: he wants two or more.

¶ " A-dayës now, my sone, as men may se,   1415
　　O chirche vn-to a¹ man may not suffise ;
But algate he mote han pluralite,
　　Elles he can not lyuen in no wyse.

Then he stops at Court, and neglects his cures.

Ententifly he kepiþ his seruise   1419
　　In courte ; his labour þerë schal not moule ;
　　But to his curë lokiþ he ful foule.   1421

(204.   *Beggar.*)

He lets his church go to ruin,

¶ " Thogh þat his chauncel roof be al to-torn,   1422
　　And on þe hye² auter it reyne or snewe,
He rekkiþ noght, þe cost may be for-born
　　Cristes hous tó repare or makë newe ;
And þogh þer be ful many a vicious hewe   1426

and his people to rust.

　　Vnder his cure, he takiþ of it no kepe,
　　He rekkeþ neuer how rusty ben his schepe.³   1428

(205.   *Beggar.*)

[leaf 26 b]
He doesn't preach,

¶ " The oynëment of holy sermonynge   1429
　　Hym loþ is vp-on hem⁴ for to despende ;
Som person is so threde-bare of konnynge
　　þat he can noght, þogh he hym wys pretende,
And he þat can, may not his hertë bende   1433

is an absentee, but grabs his profits.

　　þer-to, but from his cure he hym absentiþ,
　　And what þer-of comeþ,⁵ gredyliche he hentith.

(206.   *Beggar.*)

¶ " How he despendiþ it, be as be may,   1436
　　ffor vn-to þat am I no-þing pryuee ;

He wears fine clothes,

But wel I wot, as nycë, fressh, and gay
　　Som of hem ben, as borel folkës be,
And þat vnsittynge is to hire degree ;   1440

and is gay and wanton.

　　Hem hoghtë⁶ to be mirours of sadnesse,
　　And wayuë iolitee and wantonnesse.   1442

---

¹ o R.　　² hye R, *om.* H.　　³ shepe R, chepe H.
⁴ hem R, hym H.　　⁵ comeþ = comþ.
⁶ ought R, hoght H.

(207.　*Beggar and Hoccleve.*)

¶ " But neuer þeles I wote wel þere-agayn,　　　　1443 Still, many Parsons are good.
　þat many of hem gye hem as hem ogħte,
And ellës were it grete pitee certayn :
　But what man wolt þou be for hym þe bogħte ? "
　(*Hoccl.*)　"ffadir, I may not chese ; I whilom þogħte
　Han ben a prest ; now past am I þe raas."
　(*Beg.*) " þan art þou, sone, a weddid man *per* caas ? "

(208.　*Hoccleve.*)

¶ " Ya, soþly, fadir myn, rygħt so I am.　　　　1450 Hoccleve waited long for a Benefice.
　I gasyd longë firste, & waytid faste
After some benefice ; and whan non cam,　　　　　None came, and so he married a Wife.
　By *proc*es I me weddid attë laste ;
　And god it wot, it sorë me agaste　　　　　　1454
　　To byndë me, where I was at my large ;
　　But do*n*e it was ; I toke on me þat charge." 1456

(209.　*Beggar and Hoccleve.*)

¶ " A, sone ! I haue espied, and now se　　　　1457 [leaf 27 a]
　þis is þe tow þat þou speke[1] of rygħt now." (l. 1226) She was the Tow on his Distaff, p. 45.
" Now, by þe rodë, fadir, soþ seyn ye."
　" Ya, sonë myn, þou schalt do wel y-now ;
　　Whan endyd is my talë, þan schalt þou　　　1461
　　Be put in swiche a way at[2] schal þe plese,
　　And to þin hertë do comforte and ese.　　　1463

(210.　*Beggar.*)

¶ " So longe as þ*o*u, sone, in þe priuë sel　　　1464
　Dwelt hast, & woldest fayn han ben auau*n*ced
Vn-to som chirche or þis, I demë wel　　　　　It wasn't God's will that he should be in Orders.
　þat god not woldë hauë þe enhanced
　In no swich plyt ; I holdë þe wel chaunced ;　1468
　God wot and know*ith* eu*er*y hyd[3] entente ;　God sent him his Wife.
　He, for þi best, a wyf vn-to þe sente.　　　1470

---

[1] spakest R.　　　[2] as (at = þat).　　　[3] mannes R.

(211.　*Beggar.*)

Had Hoccleve been a Priest, he might have been a bad 'un.

¶ "If þat þou haddest *per* cas ben a prest,　　1471
　　þou woldest han as wantonly þe gyëd
　As doþ þe nycest of hem þat þou seest ;
　And god for-beedë þou þe haddist tyëd
　　þer-to, but if þin hertë myght han plyëd　　1475

He's better as he is,

　　ffor to obserue it wel ! be glade and merye,
　　þat þou art as thou art,[1] god þanke and herie !

(212.　*Beggar.*)

¶ "þe ordres of prestehode and of wedlok　　1478
　Ben boþë *v*ertuous, *with*-outen fabil ;

tho' Priest-hood is more praiseworthy than Mar-riage.

But vnderstondë wel, þe holy ȝok
　Of prestehode is, as it is resonabil
　　þat it so be, þe morë *com*mendabil ;　　1482
　　þe lesse of hem, of mede haþ hábu*n*dance ;
　Men han meryt, after here goue*r*naunce.　　1484

(213.　*Beggar and Hoccleve.*)

[leaf 27 b] But who looks after Hoccleve's fellow-Clerks? Only, No-body; he's almost their only friend.

¶ " But how ben þi felawës lokyd to　　1485
　　At hoom ? ben þey not wel benéficëd ? "
" Ȝis, fadir, ȝis ! þer is on clept ' nemo ' ;
　He helpeþ hem ; by hym ben[2] þei chericëd :
　Nere he, þey weren porëly cheuycëd ;　　1489
　　He hem auanceth ; he ful hir frende is ;
　Sauf only hym, þey han but fewë frendes.　　1491

(214.　*Hoccleve.*)

Of all the men they've written for,

¶ " So many a man as þei þis many a yeer　　1492
　　Han writen for, ȝit[3] fyndë can þei[4] non
So gentel, or of hir estat so cheer,[5]
　þat onys liste for hem to ryde or gon,

not one'll speak a word for em.

　Ne for hem speke a worde ; but dombe as ston 1496
　　þei standen, where hir speche hem myght awayle ;
　ffor swiche folk is vnlusty to trauaile.　　1498

---

[1] as thou art R, *om.* H.　　　[2] ben R, *om.* H.
[3] ȝit, *om.* H R.　　[4] I R.　　[5] dere R.

(215. *Hoccleve.*)

¶ "But if a wyght hauë any[1] cause to sue   1499
  To vs, som lordës man schal vndertake
To sue it out; & þat þat is vs due
  ffor oure labour, hym deyneþ vs nat take;
    He seiþ,. his lord to þanke vs wole he make;   1503
      It touchiþ hym, it is a man of his;
    Where þe reuers of þat, god wot, sooþ is.   1505

(216. *Hoccleve.*)

¶ "His letter he takiþ, and forþ goþ his way,   1506
  And byddeþ vs to dowten vs no-thyng
His lord schal þanken vs an oþer day;
  And if we han to suë to þe kyng,
    His lord may þerë haue al his askyng;   1510
      We schal be sped, as fer as þat oure bille
    Wole specifie þe éffecte[2] of our wylle.   1512

(217. *Hoccleve.*)

¶ "What schol we do? we dar non argument   1513
  Make a-geyn him, but fayre & wel him trete,
Leste he roporte amys, & make vs schent;
  To haue his wil, we suffren him, & lete;
    Hard is, be holden suspect with þe grete: 1517
      His talë schal he leeuëd, but[3] nat ourys,
    And þat conclusïoun to vs ful soure is.   1519

(218. *Hoccleve.*)

¶ "And whan þe mater is to ende I-broght,   1520
  Of þe straunger, for whom þe suyte haþ be,
þan is he to þe lord knowén right noght;
  He is to him as vn-knowén as we;
    þe lord not wot[4] of al þis sotilte;   1524
      Ne we nat dar lete him of it to[5] knowe,
    Lest oure compleynte oure seluen ouerthrowe.

---

[1] a H R.   [2] effect R, fecte H.   [3] bileeued and R.
[4] ne wote not R.   [5] Ne we ne dar not lete hym of it R.

(219.　*Hoccleve.*)

Then this
Cheater of
the Privy-
Seal Clerks
declares he
has paid em:

¶ " And where þis bribour haþ no peny[1] payed　　1527
　　In oure office, he seiþ be-hynde our bak,
' He payde, I not what ' : þus ben we bytrayed,
　　And disclaundrid, and put in wyte and lak,

and thus
swindles the
suitor and
the Clerks
too.

fful giltëles ; & eeke by swiche a knak　　1531
　　þe man for whom þe suyte is, is deceyuëd,
　　He weneþ we han of his gold receyuëd.　　1533

(220.　*Hoccleve.*)

There are a
lot of these
Thieves, who
stop one
thriving.

¶ " fful many swychë púrsuours þere ben,　　1534
　　þat for vs take, & ȝeue vs nat a myte :
þis makiþ vs þat we may neuer þeen.
　　Eek where as lordës bydde hir men vs quyte,
　　Whan þat we for hemself laboure and write,　　1538
　　　And ben a-lowëd for oure payëment,
　　　Oure handes þer-of ben ful Innocent.　　1540

(221.　*Hoccleve.*)

[leaf 28 b]

¶ " I seyë nat, al[2] lordes men þus do　　1541
　　þat sue vnto oure court ; but many, I seye,
Han þus don oftë.　　lo ! my fadir, lo !

We lose both
our thanks
and our fees.

þus bothe oure þanke & lucre gon a-weye :
　　God ȝeue hem sorowe þat so *with* vs pleye !　　1545
　　ffor we it fynden ernest at þe fulle ;
　　þis makyth vs of oure labóur to dulle.　　1547

(222.　*Hoccleve and Beggar.*)

¶ " Now, fadir myn, how þinkiþ yow here-by ?　　1548

And it's very
hard lines.

Suppose ye not þat þis sittiþ vs[3] sore ? "
" Yis, certes, sonë, þat ful wel wote I ;
　Hast þou seyde, sonë ? wolt þou aght sey more ? "
　　" Nay, sir, as now ; but ay vp-on your lore　　1552
　　I herkne as bisily as I[4] best can."
　　　" Sonë, þan lat vs spek as we by-gan :　　1554

---

[1] peny R, *om.* H.　　　[2] I sey not all*e* R.
[3] ye that this sitteth vs not R, sit H.　　　[4] I R, *om.* H.

(223. *Beggar and Hoccleve.*)

¶ " Seye on þe soþe, I preye þe hertily, 1555 Hoccleve took
  What was þi causë why þou toke a wyf? his Wife,
Was it to getë children lawfully,
  And in clennessë to ledë þy lyf;
Or, for luste, or muk[1]? what was þi motyf?" 1559 not for lust
  ¶ " ffadir, no thyng wole I it queyntë make : or money,
  Only for loue, I chees hire to my make." 1561 but for Love.

(224. *Beggar.*)

¶ " Sonë, qwat[2] holdest þóu loue, I þe preye? 1562
  þow demest lust and loue conuertible,
Per cas; as whan þe list with þi wyf pleye, Does he know
  þi conceyt holdeþ it good and lisible when he may
  enjoy his
To doon; art þou oght, sonë myn, sensible 1566 Wife?
  In whiche cas þat þou oghtest the for-bere,
  And in whiche nat? canst þou to þis answere?"

(225. *Hoccleve and Beggar.*)

¶ " ffadir, me þinkeþ al is good y-nowe; 1569 [leaf 29 *a*]
  She is my wyf; who may þer-of me lette?"
" Nay, sone, a-byde; & I shal tellen how,
  If þat þou aght by goddës dredë sette, He may only
  do it for
Thre causes ben, whiche I þe wole vnschette 1573
  And open a-non, whi þou schalt with hire dele;
  Now herkne, sonë, for þi soulës hele. 1575

(226. *Beggar.*)

¶ þe firstë[3] causë, procreacïoun 1576 1. Procrea-
  Of children is, vn-to goddës honour; tion of
  Children,
To kepe eke thè fro fornicacïoun; 2. to prevent
  þe next is, & þe thridde, of þat labour Fornication,
Yildë þi dette in whiche þou art dettour 1580 3. to pay his
  Vnto þi wyf; & othire ententes al, Debt to his
  Wife.
  Ley hem apart, for aght þat may be-fal.[4] 1582

[1] Or first for mukke R. [2] what R. [3] first H R.
  [4] alle . . befalle R.

(227.   *Beggar and Hoccleve.*)

For no other cause is copulation lawful.

¶ " ffor þisë causes thow hire vsë muste ;   1583
  And for non othir, on peyne of dedly synne."
" ffadir, right now me thoghte, how a-geyn luste
  Ye helden, & children be goten therinne[1]
  Where is no luste ! "   " o sone, or þat me a-twynne,[2]
  þou shalt wel vnderstondë how þat I
  Not holde agaynës luste al vttirly.   1589

(228.   *Beggar.*)

¶ " I wote wel, leefful luste is necessarie ;   1590
  With-outen þat, may be non engendrure ;

Lust for lust only, is against God's hests.

But vsë luste for luste only, contrarie
  To goddës hestës is ; for I thensure,
  þogh þou take of it litel heede or cure,   1594
  A man may wyth his wyf do lecherie :
  The entente is al ; be war ay of folye.[3]   1596

(229.   *Beggar.*)

[leaf 29 b]
Many wedded folk live a holy life, and don't give way to their flesh.

¶ " Weddë[4] folk many leden holy lyf ;   1597
  flor þogh hire flesschly lustës hem assaile,
  And stire hem often, þe man to þe wif,
  And she to him ; þei maken swiche batail
  And strif a-gayn hir flesche, þat he shal fail.   1601

Others are like beasts.

  Of his purpos ; but somë[5] folke, as beestes
  Hire luste ay folwen ; in hem non areeste is.   1603

(230.   *Beggar.*)

Men who have paramours and wives use Provocatives to Lust.

¶ " A-dayës now þer is swyche gouernaunce   1604
  Among hem þat han paramours & wyues
  þat, for luste of hire wommen & plesaunce,
  Nat suffice hem metës restauratyues,
  But þei receyuen eeke prouocatyues   1608
  Tengendre hem luste, feyntyng[6] hire nature,
  And suche þing causiþ hastyf sepulture.   1610

---

[1] Therynne R, thinne H.   [2] twynne R.
[3] foly H, folye R.   [4] Wedded R.   [5] som H R.
[6] feyntyng R, feytyng H.

(231. *Beggar.*)

¶ " þis knowe I soþ is, & knew it[1] fern a-gon,   1611
 And *thei* þat so don, hyli god offende :
Swich folk holde I homicidës echon ;
 þei slen hemself, or god deþ to[2] hem sende.
 Mi sone, on goddës half I þe defende   1615
  Swiche medycynës þat þou noght receyue,
  Syn þei god wraþ,[3] & soule of man deceyue. 1617

Such men are Homicides: they slay themselves.

(232. *Beggar.*)

¶ " Pas ouer þis : þou seydest þenchesoun   1618
 Why þat þou took vp-on þè maryage,
Was vn-to non oþer entencïoun,
 But loue only þe sentë þat corage :
 Now, sonë myn, I am a man of age,   1622
  And many wedded couples haue I knowe,—
  Non of myn agë, many mo, I trowe,—   1624

Tho' the Beggar is old,

(233. *Beggar.*)

¶ " But I ne sawe, ne I ne spydë neu*er*,   1625
 As longe as þat I hauë lyued ȝit,
þe loue of hem dep*ar*ten or disseuere
 þat for goode louë bou*n*den were & knyt ;
 God loueþ loue, & he wole forþere it.   1629
  At longë[4] rennyng, louë beste schal preue ;
  þus haþ it ben, & ay schal, I bileue.   1631

[leaf 30 a] he has never known a couple separate, who married for Love.

(234. *Beggar.*)

¶ " But þey þat marien hem for muk & good   1632
 Only, & noght for[5] loue of þe p*er*sóne,
Not haue I wist þey any whylë stood
 In restë ; but of stryf is þere swiche wone,
 As for þe morë part, twixt hem echone,   1636
  þat al hir lyf þei lede in heuynesse :
  Swich is þe fruyte to weddë for rychesse.   1638

But those who marry for money,

live in strife and heaviness.

---

[1] it R, *om.* H.   [2] do for R.   [3] wraþþen R.
[4] longe R, long H.   [5] for R, for þe H.

(235. *Beggar.*)

Rich folk too
marry their
children be-
fore puberty.
[See my
*Child-Mar-
riages*, E. E.
T. Soc., 1897.]

¶ " Among þe ryche also is an vsage,   1639

Eche of hem his childe vn-to oþres wedde,

þogh þei be al to yong & tendre of age,

No-wher my ripe ynow to go to bedde ;

And hire conceyt in loue is leyde to wedde,   1643

Men wit it wel, it is no questïoun,

Tyl yeerës come of hire discrecioun.   1645

(236. *Beggar.*)

And when
they grow up,
they can't
love one
another.

¶ " And whan þei han þe knoweleche of resoun,   1646

þan may þei noþer fynden in hire herte

To louë oþer ; al out of sesoun

þei knyt ben, þat in-tó wedlók so sterte :

þis makeþ many a couple for to smerte.   1650

This is done
for Covetous-
ness.

O couetyse ! þin is al þe gilt

Of þis ; & mo deceyuë ȝit þow wilt.   1652

(237. *Beggar.*)

[leaf 30 b]
Those who
marry for
Lust only,

¶ " Also þey þat for luste chesen hir make   1653

Only, as oþer while it is vsage,

Wayte wel, þat[1] whan hir luste is ouerschake,

And þere-with wole hir louës hete asswage,

find marriage
a Hell.

þanne is to hem[2] an helle, hire mariage   1657

þanne þei desyren for to be vnknyt,

And to þat ende studie in al hir wyt.   1659

(238. *Beggar.*)

¶ " Styntynge þe cause, þe éffect[3] styntiþ eek ;   1660   ¶ Cessante
causa.

No lenger forster, no lenger lemman ;

Love ground-
ed on Lust
isn't worth
a leek.

Loue on lust groundid, is not worþ a lek.

But who for vertu weddeþ a womman,

And noþer for muk ne for lust, þat man   1664

þe formë due of matrimoignë sueþ,

And soulës hurt & bodyes grief eschueþ.   1666

---

[1] that R, *om.* H.   [2] hem R, hym H.

[3] þe cause theffect R, cause þe feffect H.

(239. *Beggar.*)

¶ "I dar not medle of lordes mariágis,   1667
  How þey hem knytten, hir makës vnseen ;
But as to me it semeþ¹ swiche vságe is
  Not worþ a strawe ; for, also mot I theen,
    Reportës not so sikyr iuges ben,   1671
      As man to se þe womannës persóne ;
      In whiche a choys, lat man hymself allone.   1673

Some Lords never see their Brides before Marriage.

(240. *Beggar.*)

¶ "Weddyng at hoom in þis land, holsom were,   1674
  So þat a man hym weddë duëly ;
To se þe flesche firste, it may no þing dere,
  And hym avisë how hym lykiþ² þer-by
Or he be knyt ; lo ! þis conceyt haue I ;   1678
    In þis materë³ depper cowde I go,
    But passe I wole, & slippe away þer-fro.   1680

Let English men wed English women.

(241. *Beggar.*)

¶ "Now sythen þou hast, to my Iugëment,   1681
  þe maryëd vn-to goddës plesaunce,
Be a trewe housbounde, as by myn assent ;
  kepë þi bond ; be war of þencombraunce
Of þe feend, which, with many a circumstaunce 1685
    fful sly, him castiþ þë wrappe in & wrye,
    To stirë þe for to done aduoutre.   1687

[leaf 31 *a*]

Be a faithful Husband.

(242. *Beggar.*)

¶ "Aduoutrie and periurie, and wylful slaghtre,   1688
  þe book seiþ, lik ben, & o peys þei weye.
War aduoutre ! it is no pleye or laghtre
  To don it ; fle also þise oþer tweye !
ffor þus wot I wel, seint Ierom can seye :   1692
    'In peyne, aduoutre haþ þe secounde place.'
    þo þre to eschue, god þe grauntë grace !   1694

Adultery and Perjury are as bad as Murder.

¶ In canoni-
bus. Adul-
terare sponte
periurare,
& hominem
sponte occi-
dere, equipa-
rantur. Iero-
nimus dicit,
Adulterium
secundum
locum habet
in penis.

---

¹ seemeth R, seme H.   ² lykiþ = lykþ.
³ matere R, mater H.

(243. *Beggar.*)

When Abram
went to
Egypt

he told Sarai

¶ " I, in þe bible, rede how þat abram   1695

    To Egipt wentë, wíth his wyf saray,

And whan þat þei ny vn-to Egipt cam,

þus seyde he vnto his wyf by þe way :

' I wote wel þou art fair ; it is no nay ;   1699

Whan þei of Egipt se þe, þei wol seye,

" þou art his wyf," & for þe, do me deye.   1701

(244. *Beggar.*)

to say she
was his
Sister,

so as to save
his life.

¶ " ' Thei welen kyllë me and þe reserue ;   1702

ffor-þi, vnto hem seye, I þe be-seche,

þou art my sustre, leste I for þe sterue ;

þus may I wel ben esyd by þi speche ;

And þus þou mayste lengþe my lyf & eche.'   1706

And whan þei into Egipt entred were,

þe gipcïans¹ fastë behelden here,   1708

(245. *Beggar.*)

[leaf 31 b]

She was
taken by
Pharaoh,

whom God
then punisht.

¶ " And of hire beaute maden þei report   1709

    To pharäo ; & sche as blyue is take

In-to his hous ; & done is gret comfort

Vnto Abram, for þis wommanës sake ;

And grete desport and cherë men hem make.   1713

But for saray, greuously pharäo

Punysshyd was, & eke his hous þerto.   1715

(246. *Beggar.*)

Pharaoh
reproacht
Abram,

and sent off
him and
Sarai.

¶ " Pharäo clepte abram, & hym abreyde :   1716

' What is it þat þou hast don vn-to me ?

' Why naddest þou tolde vn-to me,' he seyde,

' How þat þis womman, wyf was vnto the ?

ffor what enchesoun seydestow,' quod² he,   1720

' Sche was þy suster ? takë þi wyf here,'

Quod he, ' and boþë go youre wey in fere ! '   1722

¹ Egipciens R.   ² koth (always).

¶ *Genesis* xijᵒ. Cumque prope esset ut ingrediretur Egiptum, dixit Saray vxori sue, " Noui quod pulcra sis mulier, & quod cum te viderunt Egipcii, dicturi sunt, ' vxor illius es,' & interficient me, & te reseruabunt ; dic ergo, obsecro, quod soror mea sis, vt bene sit mihi propter te, & viuat anima mea ob graciam tui," &c.

¶ Item, eodem capitulo: fflagellauit autem dominus pharaonem flagellis maximis, & domum eius, propter Saray vxorem Abraham ; vocauit quoque pharao Abraham, eciam dixit ea : ' Quidnam est hoc quod fecisti michi ? ' &c.

(247. *Beggar.*)

¶ "The bible makiþ no man*ér* of mynde   1723

  Wheþer þat pharäo lay by hire ogħt ;

But looke in lyre,[1] & þerë schalt þou fynde,   *N. de Lyra*

  ffor to han don*e* it, was he in ful þogħt ;   *says God kept Sarai from Pha-*

But god p*r*eserued hire ; he myghtë[2] nogħt ;   1727   *raoh's bed.*

  And sethyn, for wil, god hym punissched[3] so,

  How schal þe dedë vnpun*ý*sshed go ?   1729

(248. *Beggar.*)

¶ "Also not knewe he þat a wif sche was.   1730

Non solum eternaliter, verum eciam temporaliter in ista vita, adulter mani- festus est pu- nitus, iuxta illud versus : 'Ex istis quidem,' &c.

  Now þannë, þey þat wyuës wetyngly   *Adulterers are in hard plight.*

Takyn and holde, and w*i*th hem don trespas,[4]

  Stonde in harde plyt ; son*ë*, be ware, rede I ;

If þou þere-inne agylte, eternelly[5]   1734

  þou smert*ë* schalt, & in þis lif prés*é*nt

  Han scharp adu*er*sitee & gret turment.   1736

(249. *Beggar.*)

¶ Genesis xx°. Redde vxorem viro suo ; si au- tem nolueris, scito quod morte morie- ris tu & omnia que tua sunt.

¶ "And to abymalech, god bade he shulde   1737   *[leaf 32 a]*

  Ʒildë sara also to hir housbonde ;   *Abimelech also had to give up Sarah. (Genesis xx.)*

ffor he and his, echon, if he ne wolde,

  Shulden ben dede, he did hem vndirstonde.

Take heede, o son*ë*, þat þou clere ay stonde,   1741

¶ Item in eodem. Con- cluserat au- tem dominus omnem vu- luam domus Abymalech, propter Sa- ram vxorem Abrahe.

  ffor god stoppid eke the concepciou*n*

  Of eu*er*y woman of his manciou*n*.   1743

(250. *Beggar.*)

¶ "Ne þat she was a wif, wist he no þing ;   1744

  Ne nogh[6] hir knew in no flesshly folye.   *David ravisht Bathsheba and had Uriah slain.*

My godë son*ë*, rede of dauid kyng,

  How he bersabe toke, wyf of vrie,

¶ Regum ij° capitulis x° & xj^mo

Into his house, and did aduout[e]rie ;   1748

  And how he made vrië slayne to be,

  And how þer-forë[7] punysshed was he.   1750   *He was punisht.*

---

[1] Nicolaus de Lyra, the celebrated medieval commentator on the Scriptures.—T. Wright.   [2] mygħt H R.

[3] for that will . . . punysshed R, punissche H.

[4] Compare Robert of Brunne's (*Handlyng Synne*, l. 7420-7, A.D. 1303) reproach to the nobles for ravishing maidens and wives, and then boasting of it. See also *H. S.*, lines 2928-83.

[5] eternelly R, enternelly H.

[6] nought R, nogh H.   [7] fore R, for H.

(251. *Beggar.*)

The tribe of
Benjamin
was destroyd
for Adultery.

¶ " How was þe tribe also of beniamyn 1751
 Punysshid, & put to destruccioun,
ffor aduoutr[i]ë which þei lyued inne,
 In þe abhomynable opp*ress*ioun
 Of þe leuytës wyfe : lo ! mencioun 1755
  þer-of is made, if þou loke holy writte,
  In iudicium, ful redily[1] it syt. 1757

¶ Iudicum
xx° Egressi
sunt &c.

(252. *Beggar.*)

¶ " Who-so lith wi*th* his neyghëburës[2] wyfe 1758
 Is cursyd ; & who is any aduoutoure,
þe kyngdome faillë shal of endles lyfe ;
 Of þat ne shal he be no póssessoure.

Englishmen
are the worst
Adulterers
living.

 Alasse ! this likerous dampnáble errour, 1762
  In this londe hath so large a þrede I-sponne,
  þat wers peple is non vndir the[3] sonne. 1764

¶ Deutro-
nomi xxvij°.
Male*dictus*
qui dormierit
cum vxore
proximi sui.
Ad *corinthos*
vj^to. Ne*que*
fornicarii,
ne*que* idolis
seruientes,
neque adul-
teri, regnum
dei posside-
bunt.

(253. *Beggar.*)

[leaf 32 *b*]

¶ " Of swichë stories cowde I telle an[4] heepe, 1765

But enough
of this.

 But I supposë þisë schol suffise ;
And for-þi, sonë,[5] wole I make a leepe
 ffrom hem, and go wole I to þe empryse
 þat I first took ; if þu þe wel auyse, 1769
  Whanne I þe mette, & sy þin heuynesse,
  Of comfort, sonë, made I þe p*romesse* : 1771

(254. *Beggar and Hoccleve.*)

¶ " And of a trewë man, be-heste is dette." 1772
 "ffader, god ȝilde it ȝow, and so ȝe diden ;
Ye hyghten me in esë me to sette."
 " Now, sone, & þogħ I longë haue abiden,

Let's go back
to the trouble
of you, Hoc-
cleve.

 Thi gryfe is noght out of my myndë slyden ; 1776
  To þi greuancë wole I now resorte,
  And schewë þe how þou þe schalt comforte. 1778

---

[1] Iudicum fuħ redily R, redy H.
[2] neighbores R, neyghburs H. [3] the R, *om.* H.
[4] an R, and H. [5] sone R, p*er*sone H.

(255. *Beggar.*)

¶ " In schort, þis is of þi grief énchesou*n* :   1779

  Of þin annuitee, þe paiëment,

Whiche for þi long se*r*uyse is þi guerdou*n*,

  þou dredest, whan þou art from court absent,

  Schal be restreynëd, syn þou now p*re*sent   1783

   Vnneþës mayst it gete, it is so streit ;

   þus vnder-stode I, sonë, þi conceit ;   1785

(256. *Beggar and Hoccleve.*)

¶ " ffor of þi liflode is it þe substaunce ;   1786

  Is it nat þus ? "   " 3is, sooþly, fader, it."

" Now, sone, to remedïe þis greuánce,

  Canstow no weyës fynden in þi wyt ? "

  " No, certes, fader, neuere koude I 3it.'   1790

   " May no lordschepë, sonë, þe auayle,

   ffor al þi long seruice & þi trauaile ? "   1792

(257. *Hoccleve.*)

¶ " What, fadir ? what ? lordës han for to done   1793

  So mych for hem-self, þat my mateere

Out of hir myndë slippith away soone.

  The world is naght swich now, my fadir deere,

  As ye han seen*e* ; farwel, frendely maneere !   1797

   So go[d] me amende, I am al destitut

   Of my lyflodë ; god be my refut !   1799

(258. *Hoccleve.*)

¶ " I am vn-to so streyt a poynt ydryue,   1800

  Of thre conclusïons moot I cheese one :

Or begge, or stele, or sterue ; I am yschryue

  So ny, þat oþ*er* way ne se I noon.

  Myn hert is also deed as is a stoon ;   1804

   Nay, ther I faile, a stoon no thyng ne felith ;

   But thoght me brenneth, and freesyngly keeliþ

REGEMENT.   F

(259. *Hoccleve.*)

<table>
<tr><td>Hoccleve is asham'd to beg:</td><td>¶ "To beggë, schame is myn impediment;
I wot wel, rather schulde I die and sterue;
And steltlës guerdon is swich paiëment,
þat neuer thynke I his wages disserue.[1]</td><td>1807</td></tr>
<tr><td>he longs for Death.</td><td>Wolde honest deth come, and me ouerterue,
And of my grauë me put in seisyne,
To al my greef þat were a medecyne."</td><td>1811

1813</td></tr>
</table>

(260. *Beggar.*)

<table>
<tr><td>The Beggar reproves him.</td><td>¶ "What, sone ! how now ? I se, wel smal effecte,
Or ellës non, my wordës in thè take ;
Outhir ful symple is þin intellect,
Or hokirly thow hast hem ouershake,
Or þi goost slept hath ; what, my sone ! a-wake !
Whyl er þou seydist þou were of me glad,
And now it semeth þou art of me sad.</td><td>

1820</td></tr>
</table>

(261. *Beggar and Hoccleve.*)

<table>
<tr><td>[leaf 33 b]</td><td>¶ "I demë so, syn þat my longe sermoun
Profitith naght, it sorë me repentith."</td><td>1821</td></tr>
<tr><td>Hoccleve promises to do as he's told.</td><td>" ffadir, beth nat of þat opynyoun ;
ffor as ye wele I do, myn hert assentith ;
But ay among, fadir, thoght me tormentith
So sharply, ánd so trowblith and dispeireth,
That it my wit foule hyndryth and appeireth."</td><td>

1825</td></tr>
</table>

(262. *Beggar.*)

<table>
<tr><td></td><td>¶ "O my good sonë, wolt þou yit algate
Despeirëd be ? nay, sonë, lat be þat !
þou schalt as blyue entre in-to þe yate
Of þi comfort. now telle on pleyn and plat :</td><td>1828</td><td>Parascenes ad opus De regimine principis.</td></tr>
<tr><td>Doesn't he know Prince Henry ?</td><td>My lord þe princë, knowyth he þe nat ?
If þat þou stonde in his beneuolence,
He may be salue vn-to þin indigence.</td><td>1832

1834</td><td>(*In the* 1700 *hand.*)</td></tr>
</table>

[1] deserue R.

(263. *Beggar and Hoccleve.*)

¶ "No man bet, next his fadir, our lord lige." 1835

"Yis, fadir, he is my good gracious lord."

"Wel, sonë, þan wole I me oblige,—

And god of heuen vouch I to record,—

þat if þou wolt be ful of myn accord, 1839

Thow schalt no cause haue morë þus to muse,

But heuynessë[1] voide, and it refuse. 1841

Yes. Hoccleve knows Prince Henry very well.

(264. *Beggar.*)

¶ "Syn he þi good lord is, I am ful seur 1842

His gracë to þe schal nat be denyed;

þou wost wele, he benyng is and demeur

To sue vnto; naght is his goost maistried

With daunger, but his hert is ful applied 1846

To graunte, and nat þe needy werne his grace;

To hym pursue, and þi releef purchace. 1848

The Prince is kind-hearted.

(265. *Beggar.*)

¶ "Compleyne vnto his excellent noblesse, 1849

As I haue herd þe vn-to me compleyne;

And but he qwenche þi gretë[2] heuynesse,

My tongë[3] take, and slitte in peeces tweyne.

What, sonë myn! for goddës derë peyne, 1853

Endite in frenscħ or latyn þi greef clere,

And, for to write it wel, do thi poweer. 1855

[leaf 34 a] Let Hoccleve apply to him, and write him a French or Latin Appeal.

(266. *Beggar and Hoccleve.*)

¶ "Of allë[4] thre þou oghtist be wele leerid, 1856

Syn þou so long in hem labóurëd haast,

þou of þe pryue seel art old I-yeerid."

"Yit, fadir, of hem[5] ful smal is my taast."

"Now, sonë, þan, foulë hast þou[6] in waast 1860

Despent þi tyme; and nathelees, I trowe

þou canst do bet þan þou wilt do me knowe. 1862

He must know both, and English too, as he's been so long at the Privy-Seal.

Vide supra, folio 15 [*in* 1700 *hand*].

---

[1] heuynesse R, heuynes H.   [2] grete R, gret H.
[3] tunge R, tong H.   [4] alle R, al H.   [5] hem R, hym H.
[6] thou foule hast R.

(267.   *Beggar and Hoccleve.*)

¶ " What schal I callë þe? what is þi name?"   1863
    " Hoccleuë,[1] fadir myn, men clepen me."

    " Hoccleuë,[1] sone?"   " I-wis, fadir, þat same."
    " Sone, I haue herd, or this, men speke of þe ;

    þou were aqueynted with Caucher,[2] pardee—   1867
    God haue his soulë best of any wyght !—
    Sone, I wole holdë þe þat I haue hyght.[3]   1869

(268.   *Beggar.*)

¶ " Al-thogh þou seyë þat þou in latyn,[4]   1870
    Ne in frenssh nowther, canst but smal endite,
In englyssh tongë canst þou wel afyn,[4]
    ffor ther-of can I eekë[5] but a lite ;
    Ye[6] straw ! let be ! þi pennë take, and write   1874
    As þou canst, and þi sorowe tourne schal
    Into gladnesse ; I doute it naght at al.   1876

(269.   *Beggar and Hoccleve.*)

¶ " Syn þou maist nat be paied in thescheqer,   1877
    Vnto my lord þe princë make instance
    þat þi patent in-to þe hanaper
    May chaunged be."   " fadir, by your suffrance,
    It may not so, bi-cause of þe ordenance ;   1881
    ' Longe aftir þis schal no grant chargeable
    Out passe ;' fadir myn, this is no fable."   1883

(270.   *Beggar.*)

¶ " An egal change, my sonë, is in soothe   1884
    No charge, I wot it wel ynow in dede.
What, sonë myn ! good hert take vnto þe !
    Men seyn, who-so of euery grace hath drede,

    Let hym beware to walk in any mede.   1888
    Assay ! assay ! þou simple-hertid goost !
    What grace is shapen þe, þou naght ne woost."

[1] Occleve R.   [2] Chaucers R.   [3] the hight R.
[4] latyne, afyne R.   [5] Truly therof kan I R.   [6] Ye R.

(271. *Hoccleve.*)

¶ " ffadir, as siker as I standë here, 1891
  Whethir þat I be simple, or argh or bolde,
Swych an eschangë get I non to yeere ;
  Do as I can, with þat I haue in holde ;
ffor, as for þat, my comfort is but cold ; 1895
  But wel I fyndë your good wyl alway
  Redy to me, in what ye can and[1] may." 1897

Hoccleve 'll get nothing this year:

(272. *Beggar.*)

¶ "That is sooth, sonë ; now, syn þou me toldist 1898
  My lord þe princë is good lord þe to,
No maistri[2] is it for þe, if þou woldist
  To be releeuëd ; wost þou what to do?
Writtë to hym a goodly tale or two, 1902
  On which he may desporten hym by nyghte,
  And his fre gracë schal vp-on þe lighte. 1904

but he's to write Prince Henry a Tale or two, to amuse him at night,

(273. *Beggar.*)

¶ "Sharpë thi penne, and write on lustily ; 1905
  Lat se, my sonë, make it fresh and gay,
Outë thyn art if[3] þou canst craftily ;
  His hyë[4] prudence hath insighte verray
To iuge if it be wel y-made or nay ; 1909
  Wher-forë,[5] sone, it is vn-to the neede,
  Vn-to þi werk, takë[6] þe gretter heede. 1911

[leaf 35 a]

something fresh and gay,

(274. *Beggar.*)

¶ "But of a thyng be wel waar in al wise, 1912
  On flaterië þat þou þe nat founde ;
ffor þer-of, sonë, Salamon þe wise,—
  As þat I haue in his *prouer*bës found,—
Seith thus : 'thei þat in feynëd speche haboundë,
  And glosyngly vnto hir freendës talke, 1917
  Spreden a net bi-forne hem wher they walke.'

but with no Flattery in it.

¶ Pr*o*uerbi-
arum xxix°.
Qui blandis
fictis que ser-
monib*us* lo-
quitur amico
suo, expandit
rethe gressi-
b*us* suis.

---

[1] or R.   [2] maistrie R.   [3] Uttre . . as R, Out . . if H.
[4] hye R, hy H.   [5] Wherfore R, Wher for H.   [6] to take R.

(275. *Beggar.*)

¶ " If a deceyuo*ur* yeue a man to sowke   1919
    Word̈es plesant, in hony al by-wrappid,
Good is a man eschewë[1] swich a powke ;
    Thurgh fauel haþ ful many a man mys-happid ;
    ffor when þat he hath ianglid al and clappid   1923
        With his freend, tretyng of pees openly,
        He in a-wayt lith of hym couertly.   1925

(276. *Beggar.*)

¶ " Þe mostë lak þat han þe lord̈es grete,   1926
    Is of hem that hir soothës shuld hem telle ;
Al in þe glosë folk labour and swete ;
    Thei stryuen who best ryngë[2] shal þe belle
    Of fals plesance, in þat hir herẗes swelle   1930
        If þat oon can bet than othér deceyue ;
        And swich deceyt, lord̈es blyndly receyue.   1932

(277. *Beggar.*)

¶ " The worldly richë men, han no knowleche   1933
    What þat thei bene of hir condicio*un* ;
Thei ben so blent with fauell̈es gay speche,
    Wich réportith to hem, þat hir reno*un*
    Is eue*ry*wherë halwid in the toun,   1937
        That in hem-self they demen gret vertu,

        Where as þe*r* is but smal or naght a gru,   1939

(278. *Beggar.*)

¶ " ffor vnneth á good word men speke of hem :   1940
    This falsë[3] treso*un* comon is and rif ;

Bet were it the ben[4] at ierusalem,
    Sonë, þan þou were in it defectif.
    Syn my lord þe prynce is, god help his lyf,   1944
        To thè good lord, good *ser*uant þou þe quyte
        To him, and trewe, and it shal the profyte. 1946

¹ to eschewe R, eschew H.   ² rynge R, ryng H.
³ fals H R.   ⁴ thou were R.

(279. *Beggar and Hoccleve.*)

¶ " Write him no thyng þat sowneth in-to vice ;   1947
     Kythë thi loue in matere of sadnesse ;
looke if þou fyndë canst any tretice
     Groundid on his estatës holsumnesse ;
     Swych thing *tra*nslate, and vnto his hynesse,   1951
          As humblely as þat þou canst, p*r*esent ;
          Do thus my sone."   " fadir, I assent.   1953

Hoccleve is to english some Treatise on the Prince's duties.

(280. *Hoccleve.*)

¶ " With hert as tremblyng as þe leef of asp*e*,   1954
     ffadir, syn ye me redë to do so,
Of my symple conceyt wole I the clasp*e*
     Vndo, and lat it at his largë go.
     But weylaway ! so is myn hertë[1] wo,   1958
          That þe honour of englyssh tonge is deed,
          Of which I wont was han consail and reed.   1960

He agrees,

but laments that the Honour of English,

(281. *Hoccleve.*)

G. Chaucer [*in* 1700 *hand.*] .

¶ " O, maist*e*r deere, and fadir reue*r*ent !   1961
     Mi maist*e*r Chaucer,[2] flour of eloquence,
Miro*u*r of fructuous entendëment,
     O, vniue*r*sel fadir in science !
     Allas ! þat þou thyn excellent p*r*udence,   1965
          In þi bed mortel mightist naght by-qwethe ;
          What eiled deth ? allas ! whi wolde he sle the ?

[leaf 36 *a*]
CHAUCER, the Flower of Eloquence, is dead.
[Did Hoccleve see him on his deathbed ?]

(282. *Hoccleve.*)

¶ " O deth ! þou didest naght harme singuleer,   1968
     In slaghtere of him ; but al þis land it sm*e*rtith ;
But nathëlees, yit hast þou no power
     His namë sle ; his hy v*e*rtu astertith
     Vnslayn fro þe, which ay vs lyfly hertyth,   1972
          With bookës of his ornat éndytyng,
          That is to al þis land enlumynyng.   1974

But tho Death could slay the Man his Fame still lives. ,

----

[1] hert R H.   [2] Chaucers R.

(283. *Hoccleve.*)

Gower, too,
is dead.
¶ " Hast þou nat eeke my maister Gower slayn,   1975 J. Gower [in
1700 *hand*].
  Whos vertu I am insufficïent
ffor to descreyue[1] ? I wote wel in certayn,
  ffor to sleen al þis world þou haast yment[2] ;
    But syn our lorde Crist was obedient   1979
      To þe, in feith I can no ferther seye ;
All must die.   His creäturës mosten þe obeye.   1981

(284. *Hoccleve and Beggar.*)

Tho Hoccleve
speaks and
writes poorly,
¶ " ffadir, ye may lawhe at my lewdë[3] speche.   1982
  If þat þow list ; I am no thyng fourmeel[4] ;
My yongë[5] konyng may no hyer reche,
  Mi wit is[6] also slipir as an eel ;
he means
well.   But how I speke, algate I menë weel."   1986
      " Sone, þou seist wel I-nogh, as me seometh,[7]
        Non oothir feele I, so my cónceyt demeth.   1988

(285. *Beggar.*)

[leaf 36 *b*]
Hoccleve and
the Beggar
are to go to
their meals.
¶ " Now, farwel, sone ! go homë to þi mete,   1989
  It is hy tyme ; and go wil I to myn ;
And what I haue y-seid þe, naght forgete ;
  And swych as þat I am, sone, I am thyn.
    Thow seest wel, age hath put me to declyne,   1993
      And pouert hath me maad of good al bare ;
        ¶ I may naght but preyë[8] for þi welfare."   1995

(286. *Hoccleve and Beggar.*)

" What, fadir ? wolden ye thus sodeynly   1996
  Depart fro me ? Petir ! crist, for-beede !
Ye shal go dynë *with* me, trewëly."[9]
The Beggar
won't dine
with Hoc-
cleve.   " Sone, at a word, I moot go fro þe neede."
      ¶ " Nay, fadir, nay !" " Yis, sone, as god me speede !"
        " Now, fadir, syn it may non othir tyde,
          Almyghty god yow saue, and he your gyde ! 2002

---

[1] discrive R.   [2] yment R, ment H.   [3] nyce H.
[4] formeel R.   [5] yonge R, yong H.   [6] is R, *om.* H.
[7] seemeth R.   [8] prey H, pray R.   [9] trewly H, truly R.

(287. *Hoccleve and Beggar.*)

¶ " And grautë gracë me þat day to se,   2003.
    That I sumwhat may quytë your goodnesse.
But, goodë¹ fadir, whan and wher schul ye
    And I efte metë?"   "Sone, in soothfastnesse,   *Hoccleve and the Beggar*
I euery day heere at þe Carmes messe,²   2007   *can meet any day in White-friars at 7 a.m.*
    It faileth naght o-boute þe hour of seuene."
    " Wel, fadir, god bytake I yow, of heuene ! " 2009

(288. *Hoccleve.*)

¶ Recordyng in my myndë þe lessoun   2010
    That he me yaf, I hoom to metë wente ;
And on þe morowe sette I me adoun,   *Next day Hoccleve sets to work at this Poem.*
    And penne and ynke and parchemyn I hente,
    And to performe his wil and his entente   2014
    I took corage, and whiles it was hoot,
    Vn-to my lord the princë thus I wroot³ :— 2016

[*HOCCLEVE'S "REGEMENT" FOR HENRY V.*
      WHEN PRINCE OF WALES.]

[*Proem.*]   (289,⁴ *MS. Reg.* 17, D vi, to st. 293.)

Hyë and noblë princë excellent,   2017   [leaf 40 *a*
    My lord the prince, o my lord gracïous,   *His Proem to Henry, Prince of Wales.*
    I, humble seruaunt and obedient
Vnto your éstate hye & glorious,
Of whiche I am full tendir & full ielous,   2021
    Me recomaunde vnto your worthynesse,
    With hert entier, and spirite of mekenesse. 2023

---

¹ goode R, good H.
² The house and church of the Carmelites, or White Friars, stood on the South side of Fleet Street, between the Temple and Salisbury Court.—T. Wright. Not far, therefore, from Hoccleve's "cote" in Chester's Inn, Somerset House.
³ The original leaf 37—a Picture and 5 stanzas—has been torn from the Harl. MS. by some "furious Foole." The 5 stanzas are inserted here from MS. Reg. 17 D vi, leaf 40.
⁴ This stanza is under an illumination of a little poet on his knees presenting his book bound in pink to a tall crownd man standing, clad in a blue cloak, collard and lined with ermine. His under robe is colourd lake, with a black belt, studded with gold. The robe has a white-borderd pocket-slit near the top of the left thigh. The poet is in a dull brick red gown, borderd with yellow, and has lake hose. At foot is a coat of arms hung on the ornament, a fret, or, on sable, quartering a lion rampant or, gules. The arms of ? Rich. Durrundill.

(290)

Right humbly axyng of you [the] licence,   2024

That witħ my penne I may to you declare

(So as that kan my wittës innocence,)

Myne inward willl that thursteth the welefare

Of your persone; and ellës be I bare   2028

Of blisse, whan þat the coldë stroke of detħ

My lyfe hatħ quenched, & me byraft my bretħ.

(291)

Thougħ that my livelode and possession   2031

Be skant, I riche am of beneuolence;

To you therof kan I be no nygon:

Goode haue I none, by whiche your excellence

May plesëd be; &, for myne impotence   2035

Stoppetħ the way to do as I were holde,

I write as he þat your goode lyfë faynë wolde.

(292)

Aréstotle, most famous Philosofre,   2038

His Epistles to Alisaundre sent,

Whos sentence is wel bette than[1] gold in cofre,

And more holsomer grounded to trewe entent:

For aH þat euer tho Epistles ment,   2042

To settë was þis worthy Conquerour,

In reulë, how to sústene his honour.   2044

(293)

The tendir loue, and the feruént chiertee   2045

That this worthy clerk ay to this kyng bere,

Trustyng his welthë durable to be,

Vnto his hert[è] stak and satte so nere,

That by writýng his counseiH yave he clere   2049

Vnto his lord, to kepe hym fro myschaunce,

As witnessetħ his booke of gouernaunce.   2051

---

[1] that R.

(294) (*Harl.* 4866 *again.*)

¶ Of which, and [eek] of Gyles of regyment   2052   [leaf 37 *a*]
   Of princes, plotmel thynke I to translate.
And thogh that[1] senple be my sentément,
   O worthi prince, I yow biseeche al-gate
     Considerith, how endityng hath in hate   2056
      Mi dul conceyt, and nat accordë may
      With my childhode ; I am so childissh ay.   2058

From this, and Guido's *De Regimine,* Hoccleve will english a Poem for the Prince,

(295)

¶ Also byseeche I that þe altitude   2059
   Of your estate—þogh þat þis pamfilet
Non ordre holdë, ne in him include—
   Nat greuëd be, for I can do no bet.
     Anothir day, whan wit & I be met,[2]   2063
      Which longe is to, and han vs freenly[3] kist,
      Descouere I wole, thát now is nat wist.   2065

praying his Highness not to be annoyd,

(296)

¶ Nathëles, swich as is my smal konyng,   2066
   Withal so treewe an[4] herte, I wole it oute,
As þo two dide, or euere Clerc lyfynge ;
   But tremblyng is my spirit out of doute,
     That to performë þat I am a-boute ;   2070
      Allas ! þe stuf of sad intelligence
      Me faillith, to speke in so hy presence.   2072

as Hoccleve knows little,

and is fearful,

(297)

¶ Simple is my goost, and scars my letterure,[5]   2073
   Vnto your excellencë for to write
Myn inward loue, and yit in áuenture
   Wyle I me puttë, thogh I can but lyte.
     Mi derë maistir—god his soulë quyte !—   2077
      And fadir, Chaucer, fayn wolde han me taght ;
      But I was dul, and lernèd lite[6] or naght.   2079

and simple.

Chaucer [*in* 1700 *hand*].

Chaucer tried to teach him, but he was too stupid.

---

[1] that R, *om.* H.   [2] bette . . mette R.   [3] frendely.
     [4] and H, an R.   [5] scarce my lettrure R.
       [6] lerned? right? R.

(298)

¶ Allas! my worthi maist*er* honorable,   2080
    This landës verray tresor and richesse,
Deth, by thi deth, hath harme irreparable
    Vnto vs doon; hir vengeable duresse
        Despoilèd hath þis land of þe swetnesse   2084
            Of rethorik; for vn-to[1] Tullius
            Was neu*er* man so lyk a-mongës vs.   2086

(299)

¶ Also, who was hiër in philosophie   2087
    To Aristotle, in our tonge, but thow?
The steppës of virgile in poesie
    Thow filwedist eeke, men wot wel y-now.
        That combre-world, þat þe, my maistir, slow, 2091
            Wold I slayn were! deth was to hastyf
            To renne on þe, and reuë the thi lyf.   2093

(300)

¶ Deth hath but smal consideracïoun   2094
    Vnto þe v*er*tuous, I haue espied,
No more, as shewith þe *pro*bacïoun,
    Than to a vicious maistir losel tried;
        A-mong an heep, eu*er*y man is maistried;   2098
            With hire, as wel þe porre as is þe riche;
            lered[2] and lewde eeke standen al y-liche. 2100

(301)

¶ She myghte han taried hir vengeance awhile,   2101
    Til that sum man had egal to thè be.
Nay, lat be þat! sche knew wel þat þis yle
    May neu*er* man forth bryngë lyk to the,
        And hir officë needës do mot she;   2105
God bad hir so, I truste as for thi[3] beste;
            O maister, maist*er*, god þi soule reste! 2107

---

¹ fro vs to R.   ² Lered' R, lerd H.   ³ the R.

¹(302. *The Regement. From MS, Reg.* 17 D *vi,*
        to line 2160.)

Now to my matere, as that I began :   2108   [leaf 42]
  There is a booke, Iacob de Cessoles,   Hoccleve will
Of þe ordre of Prechours, made, a worthy man,   also translate
                                                              from the
That "the Chesse moralisèd" clepeð is,   *Libellus de*
  In whicħ I purpose eke to laboure y-wis,   2112   *Ludo Scacho-*
                                                              rum by Jaco-
    And here & there, as that my liteħ witte   bus de Cesso-
    Afforthë may, I thynkë tránslate it.   2114   lis.

(303)

And al be it that in that placë square   2115
  Of the lystës, I mane þe eschekere,
A man may lernë to be wise & ware,
  I, that haue auentureð many a yere,
  My witte there-in is but litiħ the nere,   2119
    Save that somwhat I knowe a kyngës draught ;   He knows
                                                              only a king's
    Of other draughtës, lerneð haue I naught.   2121   draught.

(304)

And, for that amongˈ the draughtës euerychone   2122
  That vnto þe chessë appertenë may,
Is none so nedëfuħ vnto your persone
  To knowe, as that of the cheertë verray
  That I haue hade vnto your noblesse ay,   2126
    And shaħ, yf your plesaunce it be to here,   This he will
                                                              now report.
    A kyngës draught, reporte I shaħ now here. 2128

(305)

I am sure that thɔ bookës allë thre,   2129   Prince Henry
                                                              must know
  Redde hatħ & seen your Innat sapience ;   Hoccleve's
And, as I hope, her vertues folwen ye ;   three Author-
                                                              ities.
  But vnto you compile I this sentence,
  That, at the goode luste of your excellence,   2133
    In short ye may beholð and rede   Hoccleve puts
                                                              their scatterd
    That in hem thre is skatereð ferre in brede. 2135   maxims to-
                                                              gether.

¹ The original leaf 39 of the Harl. MS. 4866 is out. It con-
taind lines 2108—2160. They are inserted here from MS. Reg.
17 D vi.

(306)

And álthougħ it be no manér of nede [leaf 42, back] 2136
  Yow to counseilë what to done or leve,
Yf þat you liste of stories to take hede,

This Rege-
ment will,
at worst,
do to while
away the
night.
  Somwhat it may profitë, by your leve :   2139
At hardest, when[1] þat ye ben in Chambre at eve,
  They ben goodë to drivë fortħ the nyght ;
  They shuħ not harme, yf þey be herdˡ a-right.

(307)

The Prince
mustn't think
it too long.
To your hyenessë, thynke it not to longe,   2143
  Thougħ in that draught I somwhat wadë deepe ;
The thewës vertuous that to it longe
  Wacchen my gost, & letten him to slepe.
Now God in vertu mayntene you and kepe !   2147
  And I besechë your magnificence,
  Yeve vnto me benignë audience.   2149

(308)

Hoccleve is
not as good
as his three
Authorities.
For thougħ I to the steppes clergyaħ   2150
  Of thisë clerkës thre [may] not atteyne,
Yit, for to putte in prees my cónceyte smaħ
  Goode wille me arteħ take on me the peyne ;
But sorë in me quappeħ euery veyne,   2154
  So dredefuħ am I of myne ignoraunce ;
  The crosse of criste me spedë and auaunce !   2156

(309)

He prays for
success to
the Prince
when he
becomes
Henry V.
Now, gracious prince, agayn that the corone   2157
  Honoure you shaħ witħ roial dignitee,
  Beseche I hym that sitte on hye in trone,
That, when þat chargë réceyuedˡ han ye,[2]
[leaf 38 a]
Swych gouernancë men may feele and se   2161
  In yow, as may ben vn-to his plesance,
  Profet to vs, and your good loos avance.   2163

---

[1] whan that R.
[2] This line ends the extract from MS. Reg. 17 D vi. With
the next line, Harl. 4366 begins again, and runs on to the end.

[§ 1. *ON THE DIGNITY OF A KING.*]

(310)

¶ ffirst and foreward, the dignitee of kyng
   Impressid be in the botme of your mynde,
Consideryng how chargeable a thyng
   That ofice is; for so ye schul it fynde.
   Vn-to good reulë ye yow knytte and bynde;
     Of goddës¹ wrechë haue ay drede and awe;
     Do right to grete and smale, and keepë² lawe.

2164 Let kingly dignity be deeply imprest in your mind.

2168

(311)

¶ Onës þer was a kyng, as I haue rad,
   Whan his coronë was vn-to hym broght,
Or he it tok, in thoght he stood al sad,
   And þus he seidë, after he had thoght:
   " O þou corone, noble and faire y-wroght,
     What man that þe receyueth or admittith,
     More esë þan he weneth from hym flittith.

2171 A King once

2175 told his Crown that it cost him his ease.

2177

(312)

¶ Who-so þe peril know, and charge and fere
   That is in the, thogh þou at therthe³ lay,
He woldë noght the vp areyse or rere,
   But lat þe lyë stille, and go his way.
   ffor sooth is þis, and hath & schal ben ay,
     This worldës hook, enuye hath to his bayt,
     And ay hath hye degree sore in a-wayt."

2178 Whoever knew the Danger of it, would never be crownd.

2182

2184

(313)

¶ Now, noble princë, thogh I be nat wys,
   Wel-willed am I, as I first yow tolde;
In þe name of ihesu, wirke after þe auys
   That I compyle oute of this auctours olde.
   And if I nat the wey of reson holde,
     ffolwe me nat; and if þat I do, thenne
     Do as I schal reportë with my penne.

2185 Prince Henry,

work after my old authors' advice!

2189 [leaf 38 *b*]

2191

---

¹ goddes R, god H. ² yᵉ overline, later H, kepe your R.
³ thoght þou at hert H, though thou at the erthe R.

[§ 2. *ON A KING'S KEEPING HIS CORO-*
NATION OATHS; AND ON TRUTH AND
CAUTIOUS SPEECH.]

(314)

Keep your Coronation Oaths!

¶ Tho othës that at your creacïoun   2192
    Shul thurgh your tongë[1] passe, hem wel observe;
Lat no colóurëd excusacïoun
    Yow makë fro hem slippe aside or swerue;
    Holde vp hir lyf,[2] lat hem nat in yow sterue;   2196
      It is nat knyghtly[3] from an oth to varie;
      A kyng of trouth, oweth bene exemplarie.   2198

(315)

¶ Lo! thus this Aristotle in his book seith   2199
    To Alisandre, and to be war hym bit,
That he ne breke his bondës ne his feith,
    ffor vn-to folke vntrewë longith it;

He who breaks his Oath, ends badly.

He seith þat gracë nat in hym abit,   2203
    But wikked ende and cursid áuenture
    Hym folowith, that forswere[4] hym hath no cure.

(316)

Faith-keep-ing gives Kings power,

¶ By[5] feith, is maad the congregacïoun   2206
    Of peple, and of cités enhabitynge;
By feith, han kyngës dominacïoun;
    ffeith causith eek of men þe comunynge;
    Castelx, by feith, dreden non ássailynge,   2210

and subjects' obedience.

    By feith, þe Citees standen vnwerréyed,
    And kyngës of hir sogetȝ ben obeyed.   2212

(317)

No greater thing can a man lose, than Faith.

¶ Who leeseth feith, gretter thyng may non leese. 2213
    Or a man speke, or bynde hym by his sel,
And hath his ful libérte, and may cheese
    What he do schal, hym oghte auyse hym wel

[leaf 39 a]

    Or he promette; and[6] heetë naght a deel   2217
      By word ne bond, but if he wole it laste;
      ffor who so dooth, schal smerten at þe laste. 2219

---

[1] Shuly . . tong H, Shalt . . tonge R.   [2] hede R.
[3] knygly H, knyghtly R.   [4] to forswere R.
[5] By the H R.   [6] and R, *om.* H.

(318)

¶ Litel encheson haþ he for to speke,   2220
   To whos wordës is[1] ȝeuen no credence :
Perillous is,[2] a man his feith to breke.
   ffeith, by necessite ne indigence
Naght artid is : disceyt,[3] & apparence   2224
   Of trouthe outward, and inward fikilnesse,
   Bulteth[4] out schame, and causeþ gret smartnesse.

*It's danger-
ous for a man
to break
Faith.*

(319)

¶ What was þe cause of þe destruccïoun   2227
   Of þe peple of Scites & of Arabiee,
But for hir kyngës, in decepcioun
   Of men and Citees nyh to hir contre,
Hir othis vseden, by sotilte   2231
   Brekyngë bondës þat stablisshed were
   Mankynde to profitë, and not to dere ?   2233

*Their kings'
deceit ruind
Scythia and
Arabia.*

(320)

¶ And for þat synnë, goddës riȝtwisnesse,   2234
   That punnysshith falshood and trecherie,
Nat myghte hem suffre endure in þat woodnesse ;
   But þey destroyed were, it is no lye.
Vntrouthe, allas ! þe ordre of chyualrie   2238
   Dampneth it ; thogh þat þe persone it vse,
   Knyghthode itself mot algate it refuse.   2240

*For it, God
had them
destroyd.*

(321)

¶ To god truste I, no lord in al þis lond   2241
   Is gilty of þat inconuenience ;
ffy ! what ? a lord breke his byheste or bond ?
   Nay, god forbedë þat that[5] pestilence
In a lord dwelle, or holdë residence ;   2245
   ffor if þat he that wicked geste recette,
   By suche a lorde wole honour no thing sette. 2247

*I hope no
English lord
is faithless.*

[leaf 39 *b*]

---

[1] is R, *om.* H.   [2] is it R.   [3] disceyue H, disceyte R.
     [4] Bulteth R.   [5] such R.

(322)

¶ Whan Marcus Regulus was, as I rede,   2248
   Venqwisshèd in a bataile of þe see
By hem of Cartage, hoom wiþ hem þey lede
This prisoner ; and aftir, sent was he
   By hem to Romë, his ownë contre,   2252
      Sworn to retournë to Cartage ageyn,
      As tullius And eek seint Austyn seyn.   2254

(323)

   ¶ The causë whi þey hym to Romë sente,   2255
     Was for to do to Romayns hir message,
He was to try
to arrange an
exchange of
Prisoners. Wityng of hem, if þat þey wolde[1] Assente,
   That, syn[2] ther werë Romayns in cartage
     In prisoun, and Romayns hadde eek in cage   2259
      Cartagiens, suffre hem at largë goo,
      And þe Romayns go schulden[3] [fre] also.   2261

(324)

   ¶ Whan Marcus doon hadde as þat he was bode,   2262
     The senat axid hym what was his reed ;
And he answerde, and seidë[4] þus for gode :—
    " Al þis, rede I, lat slepen,[5] & ben deed ;
     It may by no way sinke in-to myn heed,   2266
      That to vs Romayns were it couenable,
      Swiche an eschaungë ; but[6] vnprofitable.   2268

(325)

¶ " We Romayns þat þey han in prison loke,   2269
     Ben but ȝonge froth, vnlernëd in batayle,
And othir feble folk with age I-broke,
     Of whiche I am on ; we may nat availe ;
    Of vs no losse is ; but with-outen faile,   2273
      Ȝoure prisoners[7] ben myghty men and wyse,
      And folk in armës preeuëd at deuyse."   2275

---

[1] wolde R, worde H.   [2] sithin R.
[3] shulde R, schuld H.   [4] seid H, seide R.   [5] slippen R.
[6] is but R.   [7] prisoners R, prioners H.

(326)

¶ His freendës wolde han holde hym stillë there, 2276
  But thei nat myghte; he wolde alwey retourne;
To breke his oth, his goost was ay in fere;
  He þoghte noght in his[1] contre soiourne.
  Do qwat hem list, whether *the*i glade or mo*ur*ne,
    Vnto his foos as bliuë he hym dressith,
    And knewe wel to be deed, the book witnéssith.

Regulus insisted on returning to Carthage,

to be kild.

(327)

¶ He held[2] it bette his oth for to obserue, 2283
  And dye in honur, as þat a knyght oghte,[3]
Than by periúrie his lif for to preserue;
  Of suche vnknyghtly trikkës he nat roghte.[3]
  I trowë now-a-dayës, thogh men soghte,[3] 2287
    His heir ful hard were in þis land to fynde;
    Men list not so ferforth to trouthe he*m* bynde.

He'd rather die than break his Oath.

Englishmen aren't like him.

(328)

¶ Ʒit nat only to preyse is this Marcus 2290
  ffor trouthë, but eek, as it semeth me,
His renoun oghtë doubled ben, as þus—
  Where as theschangë myghte han maad hy*m* fre,
  Qwit of his foos[4] prisou*n*, gretter cheerte 2294
    He hadde of the profet vniuersel
    Than of hym self: his deeth it preued wel. 2296

Regulus might have been freed, but died for the general good.

(329)

¶ Nota de Alexandri iuramento.

¶ Amongës allë[5] þingës in a knyght, 2297
  Trouthe is a þing that he ne lakkë may,
If his honur schal bere his heed vp right.
  Valerie tellith how, wiþ greet array,
  Kyng Alisandre and his oost, on a day, 2301
    Meeued of ire and maléncolye,
    Vn-to a citee dressid hym in hye, 2303

(R) De iuramento regis Alexandri observato.

Truth is the first requisite of a Knight.

[lf. 42 (40) b]

Alexander once besiegd

---

[1] his R, *om.* H.   [2] heled H, helde R.
[3] sholde . . wolde . . be olde R.   [4] fees (*altered to* foos) of R.
[5] alle R, al H.

(330)

Lampsacus.   ¶ Whichë þat clept and called was Lapsat,   2304
                 Purpósynge[1] bete it to þe erthe adoun ;
              And or þat this kyng fully cam ther-at,
His old   Ther was a Philosophere in þe toun,—
Master
                 A man of excellent discrecïoun,   2308
                 That to this kyng somtyme had maister be,—
                 fful sore abasshed of him & his meyne.   2310

(331)

came to pray ¶ Out of þe toun he spedde hym on his weie,   2311
him for
Mercy.   As hastely as þat he coude or myghte,
              Toward þe kyng, of grace hym for to preie ;
                 And ás swithe as þe kyng hadde of hym sighte,
                 He knewe him and his menynge ; and on highte[2]
Alexander   He seide him þus : "by þe goddës I swere,
swore he'd do
nothing that   Al þi labour schal nat be worth a pere ;   2317
he askt.

(332)

              ¶ At þi prayerë do wole I no þing."   2318
                 This Philosophre of his ooth took good hede,
So the Master And seide, "o worthy conquerour and kyng,
said, 'De-
stroy this   Than prey I þe, vnto the toun þè spede,
town at
once!'   And it destroyë bothe in lengthe & brede ;   2322
                 Haue on it no pitee, but al down caste ;
                 This pray I þe, þat may[3] be done as faste." 2324

(333)

Alexander   ¶ And whan þe kyng his prayere vnderstood,   2325
                 Al his angir and his irrous[4] talent
spard the   Refreynèd he ; he woldë for no good
town,
                 On þe toun vengë him, as he had ment ;
[leaf 41 a]   He rathir chees be disobedient   2329
rather than   To his vengeáble wil, and his oth kepe,
break his
Oath.   Than be forsworn of þat he swoor so depe.   2331

---

[1] H R insert "him."   [2] Harl. MS. "zighte," hight R.
     [3] þat it R.   [4] errenous R.

(334)

¶ Or a kyng swere, it is ful necessarie
A-vise hym[1] wel; for whan þat it is past,
He may his oth in no wise contrarie,
If he of sham or repreef be agast.
A kyng owéth of word be stidëfast;
No thing byhetë, but he it performe,
If he wole hym vnto his state conforme.

2332 A King must take heed before he swears an oath.

2336

2338

¶ Crisosto-*mus super Matthaeum* omelia 12. Nisi consue-tudo interdi-catur *non* possunt am-putari per-iuria. Ex iuramento enim periu-rium genera-tur; sicut enim qui *habet* in con-suetudi*ne* multu*m* loqui neccesse est vt aliqua*ndo* importune loqu*itur*, sic, qui *habet* consuetudi-ne*m* iurare in rebu*s* ydoneis freque*n*ter & in rebu*s* superfluis & nolens con-suetudine trahente periurat. In Canone xxij. q. ij ¶ Isti tres. Iuramentu*m* tres *habet* condiciones, videl*icet*, ve-ritatem, iudi-cium & iusti-ciam: verita-tem silicet, vt iurans sciat vel credat verum esse quod iurat; Iudici*um*, i*d est*, discre-cionem vt discrete iuret, non *precipi-*tanter.

(335)

¶ A greet clerk, whiche clept is Crisostomus,
Where he of the[2] matir of sweryng tretith,
Thyse arn the wordës that he writ to vs :—
"What man þe custume of othës nat letith,
In sweryng oftë, what he seith forgetith;
Vsage of othes, of periurie is cause."
And more he seith eke in þe samë clause.

2339 St. Chrysos-tom

says that often swear-ing leads to Perjury.

2343

2345

(336)

¶ He seith, "periurie engendrid is of othis;[3]
ffor right as he þat custumably
Clappith and ianglith, and to stint loth is,
Moot othir whilë speke vnsittyngly,
Right so, vsage of swering, enemy
To trouthe is, and makith men hem forswere;"
fful necessarie is, othis to for-bere.

2346

2350

2352

(337)

¶ Swering haþ thisë[4] thre condicïouns
ffolwynge, as trouthë, doom, and rightwisnesse.
Oth axiþ trouthe, and no decepcïouns,
But swere in his ententë sothfastnesse.
Doom moot discreetly, left[5] al hastynesse,
Swere, and nat needles; and iustice also,
Leeffuly swere, and iustly euermo.

2353 Oath-taking requires Truth, Judg-ment and Righteous-ness.

2357 [leaf 41 *b*]

2359

---

[1] hem H, hym R.   [2] the, *om.* H R.   [3] othis R, this H.
[4] thise R, this H.   [5] left R, lest H.

(338)

Kings should
swear only
in cases of
Necessity.
¶ Quintilian seith, þat vn-to hygh degre,   2360

   Vnsittynge is to swere in any wise,

Bút it be causid of necessite ;

   ffor, as he seiþ, and othir clerkis wise,

     A kyng or princes word oghtë suffise   2364

      Wel morë than, oghte a marchántes oth,

      And to go ther ageyn be morë loth.   2366

¶ Quintili-
anus dicit,
iurare nisi
vbi *neccesse*
est, graui
viro,—*id est*,
nobili & fa-
moso,—*pa-
rum* conuenit ;
verb*um* enim
satis simplex
in R*ege* vel
in *principe*
firmior sit
q*uam* iura-
ment*um* in
mercatore.

(339)

   ¶ And syn a princes oth, or his promesse,   2367

     Whan þei nat holden ben, him dishonure,[1]

They should
keep to what
they write
and seal.
His lettre and seel, whiche more open witnesse

     Beren than þei, good is take hede and cure[1]

      That þei be kept ; writingë wil endure ;   2371

       What a man is, it prest is for to preue ;

       Outhir, honure it shal him, or repreue.   2373

[R] Litera
scripta ma-
net.

(340)

   ¶ Now if it happe, as it haþ happed ofte,   2374

Kings should
pay what
they borrow
of Merchants.
     A kyng in nedë borwe of his marchántis,

Greet wisdom were it tretë faire & softe,

     And holde hem truëly her couenantis ;

      ffor trust it wel, whan hir couénant is   2378

       Nat to hem kept, as þat hir bonde requerith,

       The kyng haþ schame, and eke it hem mys-cherith.

(341)

Otherwise
they'll hardly
lend again.
¶ Loth wolde hem ben eft-sonës for to lene ;   2381

     He þat is brent, men seyn, dredith þe fire.

Be his day kept, he rekkeþ nat a bene,

     But elles, siker, "don is in þe myre."[2]

[leaf 42 *a*]
     Wiþ-outen dowte, a Marchantës desir   2385

      Is with good herte his kyng honour and plese,

      And, to his myght, refresche & doon him ese.

---

[1] An instance of Hoccleve's false ryme of *-oure -ure.* See
p. 21 above, and 'Minor Poems,' I, p. xxxix.
[2] Cp. 'Chaucer' and 'Towneley Plays,' &c.

(342)

¶ In hem is þe substaunce of euery lone : 2388
  What folk cheuyce, as mochil as doon they ?
Excellent Prince, I demë your persone, *My Prince,*
  To hem and to al othir, in good fay, *I'm sure you'll keep your*
  Wole holdë þat ye heeten hem alway, 2392 *Promise.*
    And so to do, god, þe auctour of trouthe,
    Yow graunte ! and elles certes were it routhe.

(343)

¶ If þat a poorë man breke his byheste, 2395 *If a poor man breaks his,*
  Or do ageyn his oth, or seel, or lettre,
Men hente him by þe heed, and him arreeste,
  And to prisón he gooth ; he gette no bettre, *he's sent to prison.*
  Til his mainpernour his arrest vnfettre ; 2399
    And yit he moot þe cours of lawe abyde,
    Or his mainpernour mot deffende his syde. 2401

(344)

¶ Among the poorë peple thus it goth, 2402
  Thei, for vntrouthe, han smert & open schame ;
And if a lorde his bond breke, or his oth, *If a lord does,*
  ffor soþe it is a foul spot in his name ;
  Thogh men dare not opynly him diffame, 2406
    Thei þinke, al be it þat þei no thing speke ; *folk think ill of him.*
    In swichë lordës is vntrouthe I-reke. 2408

(345)

¶ And syn a kyng, by wey of his office, 2409 *As a King is like God,*
  To god I-likned is, as in manere,
And god is trouthe itself, þan may the vice *he should not be untruthful.*
  Of vntrouthë, naght in a kyng appeere,
¶ Iacobus iij. If his officë schal to god referre. 2413 [leaf 42 b]
Si quis verbo
non offendit,   A besy tongë bringeth in swiche wit,
perfectus est
vir.   He þat by word naght gilteþ, is perfit. 2415

(346)

A King
should not
talk too
much.

¶ A ! lord, what it is fair and honurable,   2416
   A kyng from mochil spechë him refreyne ;
It sitte him ben of wordes mesuráble,
   ffor mochil clap wole his estate desteyne.
If he his tongë with mesurës reyne   2420
   Gouernë, than his honur it conserueth ;
   And by þe reuers, diëth[1] it and sterueth.   2422

(347)

Folk should
long for his
words, and
not be duld
by a lot of
em.

¶ Bet is, þe peples erës thriste and yerne   2423
   Hir kyng or princes wordës for to here,
Than þat his tongë goo so faste & yerne
That mennës erës dul of his mateere ;
   ffor dullynge hem, dulleþ þe herte in fere   2427
   Of hem þat yeuen to him audience ;
   In mochil spechë wantiþ not offence.   2429

(348)

¶ Who so þat hatiþ mochil clap or speche,   2430

He who holds
his Tongue,
preserves his
Soul.

   Qwenchiþ malice ; and he þat his[2] mouth kepiþ,
Keepith his soule, as þat þe bookës teeche.
Vnbridlid wordës oftë man by-weepiþ ;
   Prudencë wakiþ whan þe tongë sleepiþ,   2434
   And slepith oftë whan þe tongë wakiþ ;
   Moderat speche engendrith reste, and makith.

(349)

Wild animals
can be tamed,

¶ Allë[3] naturës of bestës and briddes   2437
   And of serpentës ben ymakid[4] tame,

but not man's
Tongue.

But tonge of man, as it wel knowe & kid is,
Nat may be tamed ; o, fy ! man, for schame !
   [5]Silence of tunge is wardein of good fame ;   2441
   And after repreef fissheth, clappeth, fouleth ;
   The tunge of man, all the body defouleth.   2443

¶ Aristoteles
(de regis con-
tinencia a
multiloquio
dicit R):
Melius est
quod aures
hominum
sint sitibundi
ad Regis elo-
quia, quam
suis affatibus
sacientur :
quia saturatis
auribus ani-
ma eciam
saturatur.
Prouerbia-
rum x.
In multilo-
quio non
deerit pecca-
tum.
¶ Ecclesias-
tici capitulo
xixº. Qui
odit loquaci-
tatem, extin-
git maliciam.
Prouerbia-
rum xiij.
¶ Qui custo-
dit os suum,
custodit ani-
mam, qui
autem &c.

¶ Iacobi iij.
Omnes nature
bestiarum,
volucrum &
serpentum
domantur.
[R] Item in
eodem : Lin-
gua maculat
totum corpus
nostrum, &c.

[1] deyeth R, dith H.
[2] his R, þis H, with 'his' in corrector's hand in margin.
[3] Alle R, Al H.   [4] ymaked R, makid H.
[5] Leaf 45 is out of the Harl. MS. 4866. It contained lines
2441—2492. They are supplied here from MS. Reg. 17 D, vi,
leaf 47 back, leaf 48.

(350)

And that [þat] oute of tunge of kyng procedeth, 2444   [*MS. Reg.*
    The peple specially beren awey.   17 D 6.]

Wherfore, vnto a kyng þe more it nedeth   A King
    Avise hym what he spekë shall alwey,   should be
    In mochell spechë som behestë[1] may   2448 specially
                                      cautious in
      Lightly astertë, that may not be holde;   what he says.

      And than [þe] trouthë begynneth to colde. 2450

(351)

O worthy princë, this, loo, meveth me   2451
    Of trouthë for to touchë thus sadly,

For that I woldë that the hye degree   I wish our
    Of Chiualrië vniuersally   Knights kept
    Bare vp his hede, & bentë[2] not awry; 2455 straight, and
                                   not awry.
      Of his honour, vntrouthe a knyght vnlaceth,

      And his renoun all vttirly defaceth. 2457

(352 *abb aa cc.*)

And failyng it, the chief flour of his stile   2458
    Fadeth & falleth, & begynneth dye.[3]

Honoure appropred is to chiualry[e].

    But now passe ouer; touche I wole a while I'll now treat
    Of rightwisnesse, which that out of this ile 2462 of Justice,
                                which is like
      Purpóseth fully for to fare & wende,   to leave us.

      So is our reule vnthrifty & vnthende. 2464

[§ 3. *OF JUSTICE.*]

(353)

[R] Ansel-
mus *libro* Cur
deus homo.
Justicia est
animi liber-
tas, tribuens
vnicuique
quod suum
est *secundum*
propriam
dignitatem,
&c.

Seint Ancelme seith, Iustice is liberte   2465 Justice is
    Of will, yeuyng vnto euery wight   giving every
    Thát longeth to his propre dignite;   one his due.
    To god, obedience, as it is right;

    And he þat poor is of degree & myght, 2469
      Vnto his better, honour & reuerence;

      The grete eke to the smale, lore & science. 2471

[1] MS. behest.   [2] MS. bent.   [3] MS. to dye.

(354)

[MS. Reg.
17 D 6]
Justice de-
fined by St.
Anselm.

To thyne egaⱦ, concorde ; vnto thy foo,　　2472
　Suffraunce ; & to thy self, holynesse ;
To the nedy, greved with wreccheⱦ wo,
　Mercy in dede, & rewë his distresse
After thy power', & releve in heuynesse ;　2476
　And rewe vpon) hym, yf that thy myght faile,
For þat wiⱦ shaⱦ þy dedë countervayle.　2478

¶ Scriptum
est : Sola be-
neuolencia
sufficit aman-
ti, si facultas
deest bene-
ficiendi, &c.

(355)

To follow
Justice, first
love God.

Who-so it be that Iusticë verray　　2479
　Desireth folowe, first mote he god drede,
And loue as hertly[1] as he kan & may.
　It not suffiseth to do no noyous dede,
But who annoyë hym wolⱦ it forbede ;　2483
　For none anoyë is no righwisnesse,
But it is abstinence of wickkednesse.　2485

Si quis es
qui iusticiam
veram sectari
desideras,
time prius
deum.

Scriptum est:
Non nocere,
non est ius-
ticia, sed mali
abstinencia,
&c.

(356)

We owe each
other, Advice
and Help.

Of counceiⱦ & of helpe we be dettoures[2]　2486
　Eche to other, by right of bretherhede ;
For whan a man y-falle in-to errour is,
　His brother ought hym counceille & rede
To correcte & amende his wikked dede ;　2490
　And yf he be vexeⱦ witⱦ maladie,
Mynystre hym helpe, his greef to remedie.　2492

Scriptum est:
Ipso iure fra-
ternitatis &
societatis
humane con-
silii & auxilii
debitores su-
mus. Hoc
enim volu-
mus vt & ipsi
nobis impen-
dant consili-
um, quo nos-
tra erudiatur
ignorancia,
& auxilium
quo iuretur
infirmitas
nostra.

(357)

[Harl. 4866,
leaf 43 a]
Each should
teach others
what to do,
and what to
refuse.

[3]¶ Euery man owiþ studien[4] and muse　2493
　To teche his brothir what þing is to do,
And what be-houëiy is[5] to refuse ;
　That þat is good, prouokyng him þerto ;
And þus he mote conseille his brothir, lo !　2497
　" Do þat right is, and good, to goddës pay,
In word nat only, but in werk al-way."　2499

[R]Vnusquis
que fratrem
suum docere
studeat, que
oporteat vel
non oporteat
facere, prouo-
cans eum ad
meliora, &
consulens que
recta sunt
coram Deo ;
et hoc non
verbo tan-
tum, sed
opere &c.

---

[1] MS. also hertily.　　[2] MS. doctoures.
[3] Harleian MS. 4866 begins again.　　[4] to studie R.
[5] byhoveth for.

(358)

¶ Lawëful iustice is, as in manere,
  Al vertu ; and who wole han þis iustice,
The lawe of crist, to kepë mot he leere.
  Now if þat lawë fórbeede euery vice,
  And cómande al good þing, and it cherice,
    ffulfillë lawë, is[1] vertu perfyt,
    And in-iustice is of al vertu qwyt.

2500 Justice contains the whole of Virtue.

2504

2506

(359)

¶ Iustice is of the kynde and the nature
  Of god ; and he haþ made it, and ordeyned
On remës and on euery crëature.
  By iustice, is schedyng of blood refreyned,
  And gilt punýsched, whan it is compleyned.
    Iusticë déffendeth possessions,
    And peple kepeþ from oppressions.[2]

2507 It is of the nature of God,

it stops bloodshed

2511

2513 and oppression.

(360)

¶ A kyng is made to kepen and maynteene
  Iustice, for she makith obéisant
The mysdoers þat proudë ben & keene ;
  And hem þat ben in vertu hábundant
  Cherisith ; a kyng is, by couenant
    Of ooth maad in his coronacioun,
    Boundë[3] to iustices sauuacioun.

2514 Kings are made to maintain Justice.

2518

2520

(361)

¶ And a kyng, in fulfillinge of þat, is
  To god.lik, whiche is verray rightwisnesse ;
And men of yndë seyn and holden þis—
  ' A kyngës iustice is a greet richesse
  Vnto his peple, as plentee or largesse
    Of erthly good, and bettre þan reyn
    ffallynge at eue from heuen,' þei seyn.

2521 [leaf 43 b] And, in doing it, are most like God.

2525

2527

---

[1] it is R.   [2] oppressions R, appressions H.
[3] And bounden R.

(362)

¶ fful often sithë[1] it is wist and seen, 2528
  That for þe wrong and þe vnryghtwisnesse
Of kyngës mynistres, þat kyngës bene
  Holden gilty, where-as in soothfastnesse
  Thei knowen no þing of þe wikkednesse; 2532
   Vniust mynístres ofte hir kyng accusen,
   And thei þat iust ben, óf wrong hem excusen.

(363)

¶ If þe ministres do naght but iustice 2535
  To poorë peple, in contre as þei go,
Thogh þe kyng be vniust, yit is his vice
  Hid to þe peple; thei wene eueremo
  The kyng be iust, for his men gye hem so. 2539
   But ministres to seelde hem wel gouerne;
   Oppressïoun regneth in euery herne. 2541

(364)

¶ A kyng, me thinkeþ, for þe seuerte 2542
  Of his good loos, by-houeþ it enquere
Of hem þat han his éstate in cheerte,
  What famë þat his poore peple him bere;
  He of iustice is bounden hem to were 2546
   And to diffende; and if þat þei be greued,
   By him thei mot be holpen and releued. 2548

(365)

¶ Excusë schal hym naght his ignorance; 2549
  He mot enquere of wrong, and it redresse;
ffor þat he peple haþ in gouernance,
  He clept is kyng: if his men peple oppresse,
  Witynge hym, and noght rekke of the duresse, 2553
   He may, be ryght, be clept no gouernour,
   But of his peple a wilful déstroyour. 2555

[1] sothe R.

(366)

¶ O worthi king! benyngne Edward þe laste!　2556　Good Edward III,
Thow haddist ofte in herte a drede impressid,
Whiche þat þyn humble goost ful sore a-gaste;
And to know if þou cursed were or blessid,
A-mong þe peple ofte hastow þe dressed　2560　you often went alone among your people!
In-to contre, in symple array allone,
To herë what men seide of þi persone.[1]　2562

(367)

¶ Sapientie. vo [i. e. cap. 6]. Quia non recte iudicas-tis [R. neque custodistis legem iusticie &c.].

¶ Al-thogh a kyng haue hábundance of myght　2563　A King should
In his land, at his lust knytte & vnknytte,
Good is þat he his power vse ariȝt,
That fro the wey of iustice he ne flitte,　　be just, or God'll punish him.
Leste oure lord god hym from his gracë schitte,　2567
Of whom al rightwis power is deryued;
ffor if he doo, of blisse he schal be pryued.[2]　2569

(368)

¶ Refert valerius maxi-mus qualiter Theodorus sirenus cruci-figebatur quia regem de lisemaco arguebat pro suis defecti-bus &c.

¶ I fynde how þat Theódorus sireene,[3]　2570　Theodorus Cyrenaicus was crucified for telling King Lysi-machus his faults.
ffor þat he to þe kyng of Lysëmak
Tolde his defautës, þe kyng leet for teene
Crucifie him; and as he heng & stak
Vppon þe croys, þus to þe kyng he spak:　2574
"This peyne, or othir like þer-to, moot falle
Vppon þi falsë counsaillourës[4] alle.　2576

(369)

¶ "Nought rekke I thogh I rote an hy or lowe,[5]　2577　[leaf 44 b]
As he þat of þe deth hath no gastnesse;
I dye an innocent, y do the knowe;　　He died in defence of Justice.
I dyë to defendë rightwisnesse.
Thy flatereres, en-haunced in richesse,　2581
Dreden to suffre for riȝt suche a peyne,
But I thereby nat settë resshës tweyne."　2583

---

[1] See, among others, "A Tale of King Edward and the Shepherd," in *Hartshorne's Metrical Tales* (from T. Wright).
[2] pryved? R, preyued H.
[3] Surcene R. (See Smith's *Dict. Greek and Roman Biography*. Theodorus 32. Cyrenaicus.)
[4] Counsaillours, H, counceilours R.　　[5] lowe R, lawe H.

(370)

¶ Ther was a duke Romayn, clept Cámilus, 2584
  Leyde onës seegë vn-to a citee,
ffalisk[1] namèd, as seiþ valerius,
Of whiche the men of moost auctorite,
  And grettest of power and of degre, 2588
    To a Maister in þe citee dwellinge,
    Bytook hir children, by wey of lernynge. 2590

(371)

¶ What doth me this maister, but on a day 2591
  Somme of tho children out of þe tounë[2] ledde,
The most expert in science, and þe way
  Streight to þe Romayn tentës he hym spedde;
  And þe duke þus counsailled he, and redde: 2595
    " Haueth this children in possessïoun,
    And kepith hem in holde and in prisoun; 2597

(372)

¶ " The fadres of hem han in gouernaunce 2598
  ffalisk[1] þe citee, at hir ownë list;
In hy and low, aftir hir ordenance
  Is al þing doon : Whan it is to hem[3] wist,
  That ȝe hir children han vndir your fist, 2602
    Ye schul wel seen, hir children lyf to saue,
    Hem and þe citee schul ye wynne & haue." 2604

(373)

¶ The duke answerde anon to þis traytour : 2605
  " Thogh þou be fals vn-to þyn ownë toun,
And rekkest nat of shame or déshonour,
  But per cas for to gete of me guerdoun
  Desirest ffaliskës[4] déstruccïoun, 2609
    Nat were it knyghtly, me to þè consente,
    That taken hast so traytourous entente. 2611

---

[1] Falex R.   [2] towne R, toun H.   [3] hem R, hym H.
[4] Falexes R.

(374)

¶ " We Romayns kepen riȝtës of bataile   2612   he said Romans didn't fight Children,

As trewëly as þe rightës of pees ;

Our custume is, no children to assayle ;

Thogh we þe toun hadde wonnë, doutëlees

Ther schulde no childe amongës al[1] þe prees   2616

ffor vs han greued be ; we armës bere   but Warriors,

A-geyn the armëd men, hem for to dere,   2618

(375)

¶ " And naght a-geyn children vndéfensable.   2619

In þat in þe is, þi myght hastow do,

Thorgh wicked tresoun, false and déceyuable,

Thi citee to destroyen and for-doo ;

But I, Romayn, agree me nat þerto ;   2623   and he'd have nothing to do with the Traitor.

By vertu of armés wole I it wynne,

ffor al þe myght of men þat ben þerinne."   2625

(376)

¶ The duke comaundeth,[2] schortly for to seyn,   2626   So he sent the false Master back by the children ;

His handës hym be-hindë to be bounde,

And bad þe children lede hym hoom a-geyn

To hir fadres ; whiche, whan þat þey han founde

So greet iusticë in þis duke habounde,   2630

The senat clept, and þis vnto hem tolde ;   and the Senate

The hertës gan to change, of yonge & olde ;   2632

(377)

¶ All þey seiden, of hyë[3] gentillesse,   2633   [leaf 45 *b*]

Groundid vppon iustice, did he þis,

And also of a chiualrous prowesse ;

Thei seiden, " it to vs most sitting is   resolvd to yield the City to him.

Oure ȝatës opne, & offre vs to ben his ;   2637

Is non so good, as lat vs mollifie

Our hertës stoutë[4] to his genterie,   2639

---

[1] amonge all R, among as H.   [2] comaunded R.
[3] hye R, hy H.   [4] stout H, and stonde R.

(378)

¶ " And of his pees, requiren hym & preye."　　2640

The City is
surrenderd
to Camillus. They diden so ; but what was foluynge,

Nou3t haue I red, wher-fore I can nat seie ;

But þis Iust duke, as by my súpposynge,

Was to hem swiche, in wil & in workynge,　　2644

That[1] he hem quittë so as my3te hem queme :

What schulde I elles of suche a lordë[2] deme ?

(379)

Henry I,
Duke of
Lancaster,
did Justice, ¶ Of Lancastre good duke henri also,[3]　　2647　　[R] De nobili
Henrico
quondam
Lancastrie
duce.

Whos Iustice is writén and auctorised,

Whi schulde I nat þè rekene a-mongës þo

That in hir tyme han Iustice excercised ?

3it þat vertu only nat haþ suffised　　2651

and was a
perfect
Knight. To þe, but al þat longith to kny3thode

Was inned in þyn excellent manhode.　　2653

(380)

K. Porus's
doctor offerd
Fabricius ¶ I rede also how þat—hangynge a strif　　2654

Betwixt kyng Porrus and a lord clept ffabrice—　　¶ Nota de
fidelitate
cuiusdam
domini vocati
ffabricius, &
de falsitate
cuiusdam
medici.

The leche of þys kyng, a cursëd caitif

Inuolued and y-wrappëd[4] in þe vice

Of couetisë, schoop hym for to trice　　2658

His ownë lord þe kyng, & hym to kille,

If þat it haddë ben fabricës wille.　　2660

(381)

[leaf 46 a] ¶ This leche vn-to fabrices house by nyght,　　2661

As priuely as þat he coudë, went,

And vnto him ensuryd & be-hyght,

If him list to þe dedë [then] consent, —

He was so glad to plese him & content,[5]—　　2665

to poison
K. Porus. His lorde þe kyng with venym wolde he fede,

So þat ther-þurgh he steruen shuldë nede.　　2667

---

[1] That R, What H.　　[2] lorde R, lord H.
[3] Henry, the first of the Plantagenet *dukes* of Lancaster, and father-in-law of John of Gaunt, one of the greatest men of the reign of Edward III.—T. Wright.
[4] ywrapped R, wrapped H.　　[5] content R, concent H.

(382)

¶ This lorde, w*i*th þat, bad men his handës teye,[1] 2668

    And lede vnto þe kyng þis traytrous[2] wight,

And al þis treson vnto him be-wreye.

    Whan þis was done, þe Kyng seyde anone rigĥt,

        " Se here a trowth and manhode of a knyght ! 2672

        Men may the sonne as lightly his curse[3] reue,

        As þis fabrices make his trowthë[4] leue." 2674

Porus has the Traitor taken back to his King.

(383)

¶ In Perse onës[5] þer was, by Iugëment 2675

    A man to depë[6] dampnyd in wrong wyse,

ffor wrath and hate, & þe[7] irous talent

    þat to þis ilke[8] man bare the Iustice ;

    And whan þe knoulech of þis false iowyse[9] 2679

        Was comyn vnto þe kyngës audience,

        þis dome he ȝafe as blyue, and þis sentence : 2681

¶ Nota de iusticia cuiusdam Regis, qui que*n*dam iudicem ex-coriari fecit, quia falsum reddidit iudici*um* [R. versus quen-dam, causa odij.]

In Persia

a false Judge

(384)

¶ He bad men fla[10] hym quyk out of his skynne, 2682

    And þer-w*i*th keuyr þe iudicial see,

And made his sonë to be set þer-inne,

    That iuge aftir his fadir sholdë be,

    To þis ende and entencio*un*, þat he 2686

        Shuldë[11] be ware how[12] he his domës ȝafe,

        And lene alwey to right-wysenessë staffe.[13] 2688

was flayd, and his skin made into a cover for the Judge's seat.

(385)

¶ Naght ought a iugë, for hatrede[14] or loue 2689

    Othir wey demë þen trouth[15] requirith,

But, at þe reu*e*rence of god aboue,

    Right ay fauoúr, whan þat it apperith.

    Dede of iustice a[16] conciëncë clerith, 2693

        Chasyng a-way thoughtës on wrong I-groundid ;

        Who iuggith wrongfully, is feendly woundid.

[leaf 46 *b*]

A Judge should judge only by rever-ence for God.

[1] teye R, cey H.
[2] lede . . this traiterous R, led . . þeis traytours H.
[3] cours R.   [4] trouthe R, trouth H.   [5] ones R, one H.
[6] dethe R, deþ H.   [7] and R.   [8] ilke R, ilk H.
[9] iewyse R.   [10] flee R.   [11] Shulde R, shuld H.
[12] how R, whow H. " Whow " occurs also in the (? Midland) quaint " Jacob's Well," *Fons Jacobi*, Salisbury Cathedral MS. 103, which explains Prof. Skeat's name. See *The Academy*, Aug. 27, 1892. (The MS. is now at press for the E. E. T. Soc.)
[13] ȝaf rightwisnesses staf R.   [14] hate H R.
[15] than trouthe R.   [16] ay R.

(386)

¶ What Iuge in dome eke ȝeuyth[1] iust sentence,   2696

A-wayting vp-on a golden dragee,[2]

To god he doth displesaunce & offence ;

ffor þe iusticë wich of duëtee[3]

He shuldë[4] do, cursidly sellith he,   2700

ffor loue of mede him prouokiþ þer-to,

And riȝtwysnessë no þing so to do.   2702

(387)

¶ To swich a iugë withdrawë þe hope   2703

Of money, and he fro iusticë flyttyþ ;

Wher he supposith mony [for] to grope,

Iust iugëment he in his hert admittith ;

But who so þat his hand fro ȝiftys shittith,—   2707

As vnto vs wyttenessith ysaye,—

He shal in heuen dwelle, & sitten hye.   2709

(388)

¶ Cristen men, ȝelde oughten iust iugëment   2710

ffrely, for vnleful is it to selle ;

Thogh it be leful and conuenient,

A wyse man for rewarde his reed to telle.

A iuges purs, with goldë noght shulde swelle ;   2714

If one iustice he shape his dome to bilde,

His iugëmentës he ȝiftlés must ȝilde.   2716

(389)

¶ And he þat doth of iusticë rigoure,   2717

Let hym be ware he hauë no delyte

In [þe] punýsshyng of þe óffendoure,

þat haþ I-do þe trespase, or the wyte ;

Ner him reioyse of his anoyance plyte,[5]   2721

Ne þe maner excede in swichë[6] case,

Or quantite of þe gilt, or þe trespace.   2723

---

[1] yeveth R, ȝeuyt H.   [2] draggee R.   [3] duetee R, dutee H.
[4] shulde R, shuld H.   [5] Never ... noiaunce lite R.
[6] suche R, swich H.

(390)

¶ Euen as a soule is bodies lyflynesse,　　　　　2724
　　And when þat it[1] is twynëd from a wight
The hert is dede, so farith right-wisenesse;
ffor whan a reme is reulid by hir myght,
þen may the peple be ful gladde & lyght,　　　2728
　þe londe may bathen in prosperite;
　And lost is al, if þat absent be she.　　　　2730

¶ Egidius in ij^{da} parte primi libri capitulo xj°. Sicut anima est corporis vita, &c.

The Realm ruld by Justice is happy.

(391)

¶ Ther was a lawe I-made vppon a tyme　　　2731
　　At romë, by the consoulës assent,
þat who so werë gilty of þe cryme
　Of áduoutrië, and were þer-in hent.
His eyen bothë shulden[2] out be brent.　　　2735
　　Now fel it so, a man þat sonë was
　To a conseil, was take in þis trespas.　　　2737

¶ Nota bene! qualiter satisfactum erat legi per quondam consulem Romanum.

At Rome, the Consuls agreed that Adulterers should lose their eyes.

(392)

¶ And whan þat þe myshappe of þis persone　　2738
　　Was to þe peple knowën of þe toune,
Thei loueden his fadir so, echon,
　And had him in so chere[3] affeccioun,
þei seyden þat non execucioun[4]　　　　　　2742
　　Shuld on þis sonë for this dedë falle,
　And þe consulës so þei preyden alle.　　　　2744

The Romans wisht to let off a Consul's guilty son.

(393)

¶ To[5] which þe fadir gan replië þo,　　　　2745
　　And þus allegëd he for him, & seyde[6] :—
"Considereth, sires, I am oon of þo
　þat to þis lawe consentid and obeide;
And shulde I now þe samë breke," he seyde,　2749
　"ffor fauour of myself or any of myne?
Nay, sirrës, to þat may I not enclyne.　　　2751

[leaf 47 b]

But the Father refused.

---

[1] it, *om.* H.　　[2] bothe shuld R, both shuld H.　　[3] grete R.
[4] execucioun R, excusacioun H.　　[5] To R, Tho H.
[6] seyde R, leyde H.

(394)

¶ " Maffeith[1] ! þat werë wrong and villonye !   2752

þe lawe shal forthë,[2] thogh it fille on me."

þe peple gan to rumble, & clappe & crye,

And the consulës preyed of þe Citee

The reuers ; and[3] thus ouercome was he ;   2756

So at the last he sye non othir wey,

But in party he must hir lust obeye.   2758

(395)

¶ " Now," quod he, " sithen[4] it may be no bet,   2759

Sum what to yow, me conformë wol I,

So þat þe lawë shal al noght be let,

Thogh þat it myght obseruëd be fully :

Thus wol I, and none othir truëly[5] :   2763

Oon of myne eyen wol I now for-go ;

Mi sone anoþir ; it shal be riȝt so.   2765

(396)

¶ " We two wol hauë but o mannës sight."   2766

Thus was done[6] ; but naght al at the plesaunce

Of þe peple ; but þei none othir myght.

Now if to-morowe fil þer swich a chaunce,

Shulde[7] men fyndë so iust gouernaunce ?   2770

Nay, nay ! þis londe is al to scarce & lyte,

To fynde oon þat so iustly wolde hym quyte.   2772

[§ 4.   *ON OBSERVING OF THE LAWS.*]

(397)

¶ Prince excellent, hauë your lawës chere ;   2773

Obserue hem, and offende hem by no wey !

Bi oth to kepe it, bounde is þe powere

Of kyng ; and by it is kyngës nobley

Sustenëd ; lawe is bothë[8] lokke and key   2777

Of suërtë ; whil law is kept in londe,

A prince in his estate may sikir stonde.   2779

[1] Parde R.   [2] forthe R, forth H.   [3] and R, *om.* H.
[4] sithen R, sen H.   [5] truly H R.   [6] it done R.
[7] Shulde R, Shul H.   [8] bothe R, both H.

(398)

¶ And doutëlesse, if þat fordone be[1] lawe,   2780
   A princes power may goo pley him þenne ;
ffor þei þat nought ne haue, *with* knyfe I-drawe,
   Wol on hem þat of good be myghty, renne,
   And hurt hem, and hir houses fire & brenne, 2784
    And robbe and slee, and do al swich folye,
    Whan þer no lawe is, hem to iustifie.   2786

If Law is not kept, the Have-nots will rob and slay.

(399)

¶ Now in gode feith, I pray god it amende,   2787
   Lawe is nye flemëd out of þis cuntre,
ffor fewë be þat dreden it offende.
   Correccïoun and al is long on the :
   Whi soffrest þou so many an ássemble 2791
    Of armëd folk ? wel ny in eu*er*y shire,
    Partye is made to venge her cruel ire ; 2793

Law is nigh banisht out of England.

Armd folk gather every-where,

(400)

¶ Thei, *with* her hande wrong, to hem done redresse ;
   Hem deyneth naght an accioun attame
At com*un* lawë : swich vnbuxumnesse
   Suffréd, vs makë wol of seuerte lame.
   Who-so may þis correct, is worthi blame 2798
    þat he ne doth naght.   alasse ! þis suffraunce
    Wol vs destroyë by continuance.   2800

and take the Law into their own hands : they won't go to Judges.

(401)

¶ Is ther no lawë þis to remedie ?   2801
   I can no morë ; but, and this forth growe,
This londe shal it repent and sore abye ;
   And al such mayntenance, as men wel knowe,
   Sustenëd is naght by p*er*sonës lowe,[2] 2805
    But Cobbes[3] gretë þis ryot sustene ;
    Correct it, gode is, whil þat it is grene. 2807

[leaf 48 b]

This wrong is done by great high folk, not low ones.

[1] be R, by H.   [2] lowe R, lawe H.
[3] cobbes R, great men, lords. Compare 'wattes,' l. 2816, p. 102.

(402)

If this goes on, England is but lost.

¶ ffor, and it horë, þis lande is but lost;　　　　2808
　　He þat our heede is, sore it shal repent;
And this tamend, axith no gretter cost
　　But to do lawe in no vengeáble entent,
　　Seye I; but for þe better, hem take and hent,　2812
　　　　And punysshe hem by lawful riȝtwysenesse,
　　　　And suffre naght ich othir þus to oppresse.　2814

(403)

Great folk do wrong, untoucht by the Law.

¶ Smal tendirnesse is had now of our lawes;　　2815
　　ffor if so be þat oon of þe grete wattes
A dede do, which þat a-geyn þe lawe is,
　　No thyng at al he punysshid for þat is;

So Spiders catch Little Flies, and let the Big ones go.

　　Riȝt as lop-webbys, flyës smale & gnattes[1]　2819
　　　　Taken, and suffre gretë flyës go,
　　　　ffor al þis worlde, lawe is now rewlyd so.　2821

(404)

If the Rich do wrong, no one speaks.

¶ The riche and myghty man, thogh he trespace,　2822
　　No man seith onës þat blak is his eye;
But to þe pore, is denyed al grace;

But the Poor are snubd.

　　He snybbyd is, and put to tormentrie;
　　He naght a-stirtë[2] may, he shal a-bye;　　　2826
　　　　He caught is in the webbe, & may naght twynne;
　　　　Mochil gode reule is sowe, & spryngith thynne.

(405)

[leaf 49 a] Poor Folk are harried by the Rich.

¶ Of þis groweth strifë, bataille, and discorde,　2829
　　And by þe gretë, poër folk ben greuyd;
ffor he þat noble is of blode, and a lorde[3]
　　In stile, and naght hath, sterid is, and meved
　　Vnto rapynë; þis is often preuyd;　　　　　2833
　　　þe pore it felith.　þus of lawë lak,[4]
　　　　Norysshith wrong, and castith riȝt a-bak.　2835

---

[1] R has in margin, in another hand: "Unde Solon, unus de vij sapientibus. Lex est aranie tela, quia si incideret quid debile, retinetur; grave autem pertransit, tela cissa ∴"
[2] asterte R, astirt H. 　 [3] lordᵈ R, a lorde H. 　 [4] the lak R.

(406)

¶ When a kyng doþ his peyne and diligence, 2836
 His reme by lawë and reson to gye,
He stondith morë in beneualence
 Of god, and more his werk shal fructifie,
 And shal haue gretter mede, it is no lye, 2840
  Than þei þat swich a cure haue none on honde;
  Thus fynde I wretyn, as I vndirstonde. 2842

The King who rules by Law is favour'd by God.

(407)

¶ Who-so þat in hye dignite is sette, 2843
 And may do greuous wrong & cruelte,
If he for-bere hem, to commend is bette,
 And gretter shal his mede and meryte be,
 þen þei þat naght may kithe iniquite, 2847
  Ne naght may done; for were sum man[1] of myght,
  Often wolde he do, grét harme and vnryght. 2849

The High man who can do Wrong, and doesn't, is to be praisd.

(408)

¶ Princi-
patus virum
ostendit.

¶ Hye dignite, the philosofre writeþ, 2850
 Preueth a man, what he is in his dede.
When þat a prince in vertu him delitith,
 þen is his peple warisshëd of drede;
 Then may thei sey and syng alowde, & grede, 2854
  "Honour, long lyfe, ioie, and cristës blyssyng,
  Mot haue oure sustenour, our prince & kyng!"

High place proves a man.

(409)

¶ In vita
l hannis
l lemosinani.

¶ Whan þat an Emperour in dayës olde 2857
 Corownëd was, aftir as blyue anone,
Makers of tounbës cum vnto him sholde,
 And ask him 'of what metal or what stone
 His toumbe shulde ben'; & forth þei gone, 2861
  With swich deuyse as þe lorde list deuyse,
  And vp þei make it in her bestë[2] wyse. 2863

*[leaf 49 b]
Of old, an Emperor, when crownd, had to choose his Tomb.*

---

[1] for if sum man were H, for yf sum man were H.
[2] best H R.

(410)

This, to remind the Emperor that he was mortal,	¶ This was done, for to bring vnto[1] memórie 2864
	That he was naght but a man córuptible,
	And þat þis worldis ioye is transitorie,
	And þe trust on it slippir and fallible;
	And þis considered, ought him be peynyble 2868
and must rule well.	His remë wel for to gouerne and gye;
	ffor who so lyueþ wel, wel shal he dye. 2870

(411)

	¶ Like a bridel is deþës rémembraunce, 2871	¶ *Ecclesiastici* vij° Meditacio mortis est *quasi* frenum homi- *nem* refren- *ans*, ne ex- cerceat vltra.[5]
The just King is the nurse of Peace, Love, &c.	þat mannës hertë[2] réstreyneth fro vice.	
	þat kyng þat knyghtly[3] is of gouernaunce,	
	þat is to seyn,[6] doþ iustly his office,	
	Of loue and pes and rest he[4] is noryce; 2875	
	And whan þat he is out of þis worlde went,	
	Thus seyn[6] men þat goon by his monument:	

(412)

After his death, folk praise him.	¶ " In heuen mote þis kyngës soulë rest! 2878
	þis is a worthy kyng, gret was þe pees
	þat men had in his tyme, he was þe best
	That myght be; he kept his peple harmles;
	In[7] his comyng, glad was al þe pres, 2882
	And sory weren of his départyng."
May you, my Prince, do thus,	O, graciouse princë, swich be your wirkyng!

(413)

[leaf 50 a] and win your folk's good word!	¶ Thus, my gode lorde, wynneth your peples voice;	¶ Vox *populi* vox dei.
The People's voice is God's.	ffor peples vois is goddes voys, men seyne.	
	And he þat for vs starf vpon þe croyse	
	Shal white[8] it yow, I doute it noght certeyne;	
	Your labour shal naght ydel be, ne veyne; 2889	
	" No goode dede vnrewardid is, or quytte;	¶ Nullum bonum irremuneratum. &c.[9]
	Ne euyl vnpunysshid," seith holy writte. 2891	

---

[1] Thus was it done to bryng in R.   [2] hert H R.
[3] knyghtly R, knyght H.   [4] he, *om.* H R.   [5] vicia, &c. R.
[6] seyen H, sey R.   [7] "In" is the first measure or foot.
[8] quyte R.   [9] R adds: "nec malum impunitum.

(414)

¶ In your pro*s*per*i*te and in your welthe,   2892   Remember that you must Die.
  Remembreth eu*er* a-monge, þat ye shul dye,
And wot naght whan; it comeþ in a stelthe;
  Haue often him[1] by-fore your myndes ye;
ffor whan no hertë[2] hydë may ne wrye   2896
  His secre[3] thoughtës, god al wot & weyeth;   Love God,
  Hym, loue & drede; and his lawës obeyeth.   2898   and keep his Laws!

(415)

¶ *Quod elecciones sint in eccl*e*siis cathedrali*bus* libere.*

¶ Now sen a kyng is to his lawës swore,   2899
  And lawë biddeth free elec*ï*oun   Let the Church have her lawful Liberty of Election.
In chirches passe; my godë lorde, þ*er*-fore,
  Let no fauour ne none affecc*ï*oun
So meeue your wysë circums*pe*cc*ï*ou*n*,   2903
  To lette hem[4] of hir laweful liberte;
  Lat hem reioyse hir propre duëte.   2905

(416)

¶ The chapitre of a chirchë Cáthedral,   2906   When a Cathedral Chapter has elected its Head,
  When þei haue chosen hir heed & pastour,
Which as hem thenkeþ sufficiant at al,
  Hem for to rewle, and ben hir gou*er*noure,
Writeþ vnto þe pope in hir fauour,   2910   do you write to the Pope to confirm him.
Bisekyng humble[l]y[5] his fadir-hede
  It to conferme; and þat is a iust dede.   2912

(417)

¶ And if the lawë suffre yow to write   2913   [leaf 50 *b*]
  ffor any man apart, herkenth now me;
Let v*er*tu þennë þ*er*to yow excite;   Don't ask for your own man.
  Lokith þat þe man haue abilite,
þat shal resseyuë þat hy[6] dignite,   2917
  þat is to seyn, he be clene of lyuyng,
  Discrete, iust, and of súffisant konny*n*g.   2919

---

  [1] him R, *om.* H.   [2] hert H R.   [3] secrete R.
  [4] hem R, hym H.   [5] humbly R.   [6] by H, hye R.

(418)

If the Pope adopts your nominee,

¶ If þe pope to þat estate prouyde   2920
    A persone, at your prayer and instaunce,
Your sonde he takeþ to þe better syde;
    He holdeth þe persone of sufficïaunce
    To hauë swich a cure in gouernaunce,   2924
    ffor so wittenessith[1] þe suggestioun
    þat to hym made is for prouisïoun.[2]   2926

(419)

¶ To kynges letters, yeven is credence;   2927
    Beth ware how þat ye wryte in swich matere,
Lest þat ye hurt and maynë concïence.

you shall rue it, if he proves un-worthy.

    ffor if þat execute be your prayere,
    þe persone vnworthy, ye shul ful dere   2931
    Rewe it; no smal charche[3] is the soulës cure
    Of al a diocise, I yow ensure.   2933

(420)

¶ Of swich writyng be of right súffrable,   2934
    And þe man able, swich charge to resseyue,
ffor whom ye writte, þat is comméndable;
    And ellës wol[4] it your soule deseyve.

Help the fit man; shun the unfit, and flatterers!

    Help him þat able is[5]; and tunhable[6] weyue;   2938
    Weyuë fauel with his polýsshïd speche;
    And help him þat wel doth, and wel can teche.

(421)

[leaf 51 a]

¶ But certes, fauel hath caght so sad foote   2941
    In lordës courtës,[7] he may naght þens slyde;
Who com or go, algate abyde he moote;

Flatterers are always on the wrong side.

    His craft is to susteyne ay þe wrong syde,
    And fro vertu his lordë to devide;   2945
    And, for soth[8] sawës ben to lordës lothe,
    Noght wol he soth seyn, he hath made his oth.

---

[1] witnesseth R.   [2] his promocioun R.   [3] charge R.
[4] elles wole R, els wol H.   [5] abl' is.
[6] tunhable H, unable R. The *t* of "th' unable" after *d*, is Midland, like the "qwat" for "what," and "whyte" for "quyte" above.   [7] courtes R, court H.   [8] sothe R.

(422)

¶ Qualiter quidam miles in exilium se posuit, quia leges bonas per se factas[2] vellet obseruari.

¶ Let fauel passë ; foule mot he falle !　　　　　2948
 fforth in iusticë wol I now procede :
þer was a knyght, I not what men hym[1] calle,
A iuste man and a trewe in al his dede,
Which on a tyme, as þought him it was nede,　2952
þe froward peple by sharp lawës bynde ;
lawës ful iust he made, and in streyte[3] kynde.

A Knight once made very strict Laws for his folk.

(423)

¶ And when þei weren byfore hem I-radde,[4]　　2955
þei[5] made hem wondir wroth, & seyden al
þei weren not so nycë ne so madde[4]
To hem assent, for ought that[6] may befalle[7] ;
They wolden nat hem to þo lawës thralle,[7]　　2959
And wold han artyd þis knyght hem repele,
Makyng ageyn him an[8] haynous querele.　　2961

They were wroth, and wouldn't agree to the Laws.

(424)

¶ When he se þis, he blyuë to hem seyde :　　2962
" I[9] mad hem naght, it was god áppollo ;
And on my bak," quod he, " þe charge he leyde
To kepe hem ; sirës, what sey ye here-to ?
As he me chargid hath, riȝt so I do."　　　　2966
And vnto þat, answerd anone þe prees,
" We wol hem naght admitten doutëles."　　2968

He said Apollo made them,

(425)

¶ " Wel," quod[10] he, " þenne is gode, or ye hem breke,
That vnto god apollo I me dresse,
To trete of þis matere, and with him speke,—
With-owtyn him I may it naght redresse,—
Biseche him wol I,[11] of his gentilnesse,　　2973
Repele hem,[12] sen þat þei to streytë be,
And do my deuer riȝt wel, ȝe shul see.　　2975

[leaf 51 b]
and he'd go and ask Apollo to repeal them.

---

[1] hym R, hem H.　　[2] per eum editas R.　　[3] steyte R, sharp H.
[4] hem radde . . . madde R, him I-rad . . . mad H.
[5] þe H, They R.　　[6] that R, om. H.
[7] befalle . . . thralle R, befal . . . thral H.　　[8] an R, and H.
[9] I R, He H.　　[10] koth R (as usual).　　[11] I R.
[12] hem R, him H.

(426)

But the folk
must swear
to keep the
Laws till he
came back.

¶ " But or I go, ye shul vnto me swerᵊ   2976
þe lawës kepë til I agayn¹ come,
And Breke hem naght ; " to which þei gan answere,

They did.

" ȝee, ȝee, man, ȝee ! we graunt it al and summe."
þei made her oth, and he his wey hath nomme.² 2980

The Knight
went to
Greece,

He nought to Apollo, but to grecë went,
And þer abode tyl þat þe deþ him hent.   2982

(427)

and when
nigh Death,
told his men
to throw his
Body in the
Sea, so that
it couldn't be
taken home.

¶ And whan his lastë daye³ gan to appere,   2983
He bad men þrowe his body in þe see,
Lest vpon þe londe made were his bere,
þe peple myghten vn-to hir Citee
His bonës cary, and at hir largë be   2987
Quyte of hir oth, as to hir iugëment ;
Thus he deuysid in his testament.   2989

(428)

¶ Syn I spoke haue of iustice, as ye knowe,   2990

Now I'll turn
to Pity.

Vnto pite—which mot ben had al-gatis,
And namëly in princes ought it growe—
Wol I me dressë : she opneþ the ȝates
Of helth to him þat in sekenesse estate is ;   2994
Sche esith many a wyght þat is distressid,
þat nere hir helpë⁴ shulde be sore oppressid. 2996

[§ 5. *DE PIETATE.*⁵]

(429)

[leaf 52 a]
Pity is good
will to help
all who need.

Pitee, naght ellës is, to vndirstonde,⁶   2997
    But good wille inward of debónair hert,
And outhewarde⁷ spech, and werk of man, to fonde
To help him þat men sen in meschif smert.
Men selde⁸ him seen in-to wykkýd deþ stert,

---

¹ ageyn) R, gayn H.   ² some . . . nome R.
³ that his last day R, his last daye H.
⁴ nere hir helpe R, neuer hir help H.
⁵ R. has in margin : "Scriptum est, Pietas est ex benigne
mentis dulcedine grata omnibus auxiliatrix."
⁶ This page has an illuminated initial letter, which extends
from the top to the bottom, and a heading as above.—G.
England.   ⁷ outward⁣ R.   ⁸ selde R, selden H.

þat pitous is ; but þei han cruel deþ

Often whos cruelte cruelly sleth.[1]   3003

(430)

Whilom þ*er* was a tyraunt dispitouse,   3004

þat so delited him in cruelte,

þat of no þing was he so désirous.

Now shope it so, a man þ*at* to pyte

ffo was, and frende vnto iniquite,   3008

A sotel werkeman in craft of metal,

Wrought in þis wyse as I yow tellë[2] shal.   3010

*Of old, a Ty-
rant delight-
ed in cruelty.*

*To please
him, a work-
man*

(431)

His lorde þe king he þoughtë[3] plese and glade,[4]   3011

And craftëly he made a bol[5] of bras,

And in þe syde of it he slily made

A litel wyket, þat ordeynëd was

To réceyue hem þat stode in depës case,   3015

Vndir þe which men shulden sharpe fire make,

Tho folk to depë[6] for to brenne & bake.   3017

*made a brass
Bull, with a
door in its
side,*

*a fire under,
to burn men,*

(432)

And ȝit more-ou*er*, þe kyng for to meve   3018

The lesse vnto pitee, it made was so

By sotil art[7] þe dampnëd folk to greve

þat whan to crye, hem cómpellyd[8] hir woo,

Hir woys was lyke a bolës eu*er*-mo,   3022

And nothyng lyke a ma*n*nys voise in so*u*n,

As þe scr*i*pturë maketh mencïo*u*n.   3024

*and a device
to turn their
cries into a
Bull's roar.*

(433)

¶ But our lord god, of pite þe auctour,   3025

Displesid w*ith* þis cruel ordinaunce,

Swich rewarde shape vnto this[9] losengeour,

þat it abatid al his countenaunce ;

And for to pr*e*ue his fendely p*ur*ueaunce,   3029

How sharp it was, & coudë folk distreyne,

The first he was þat entryd in þat peyne.   3031

*[leaf 52 b]
(But God
turnd the fell
man's craft
to his own
Death.)*

[1] sleth R, fleth H.   [2] telle R, tel H.

[3] þought H, thought to R.

[4] R. has in margin : " Nota, de crudel, itate cujusdam artificis
subtilis, et qualiter per artem suam propriam puniebatur ; et hoc
refert Horosius."

[5] craftely . . . bole R (bull), craftly . . . bol H.

[6] dethe R, deþ H.   [7] craft R.   [8] compelled hem R.

[9] this R, his H.

(434)

<table>
<tr><td>The Tyrant</td><td>¶ ffor whan þe kyng, his cruel werk had seyne,</td><td>3032</td></tr>
<tr><td></td><td>þe craft of it commenditħ he ful wele ;</td><td></td></tr>
<tr><td>made the
Workman
take the
Maidenhead
of his Bull,
and had him
burnt in it.</td><td>But þe entent he fully helde a-gayne,</td><td></td></tr>
<tr><td></td><td>And seydë, " þou þat art morë cruel</td><td></td></tr>
<tr><td></td><td>Than I, þe maydenhede of this Iuel</td><td>3036</td></tr>
<tr><td></td><td>Shalt preue anone ; þis is my Iugëment."</td><td></td></tr>
<tr><td></td><td>And so as blyue he was þer-in I-brent.</td><td>3038</td></tr>
</table>

(435)

<table>
<tr><td>Flattery
seeks only its
Lord's
pleasure.</td><td>¶ Men may sen here, how fauel hym enclyneth</td><td>3039</td></tr>
<tr><td></td><td>Ay to his lordys lust, what so it be ;</td><td>¶ Contra
blanditores.</td></tr>
<tr><td></td><td>Vnto þat ende he bysieth hym and clynyth,[1]</td><td></td></tr>
<tr><td></td><td>And no consideracïoun hath he,</td><td></td></tr>
<tr><td></td><td>Thogh it be harmë to his lordys degre,</td><td>3043</td></tr>
<tr><td></td><td>Or a-geyn feith, honour, or concïence ;</td><td></td></tr>
<tr><td></td><td>In fals plesaunce is al his diligence.</td><td>3045</td></tr>
</table>

(436)

<table>
<tr><td>It conforms
to whatever
he fancies,</td><td>¶ To what þing it be, if it his lorde lyke,</td><td>3046</td></tr>
<tr><td></td><td>He him conformyth ; he neuer denyeth</td><td></td></tr>
<tr><td></td><td>His lordës resouns, but a þank to pike,</td><td></td></tr>
<tr><td></td><td>His lordys wil and witte he iustifieth ;</td><td></td></tr>
<tr><td></td><td>Whil fauel liueþ, no fals conseil dieth ;</td><td>3050</td></tr>
<tr><td></td><td>ffauel is wedded to plesaunt deseyt,</td><td></td></tr>
<tr><td></td><td>And in þat wedlok trewe is his conceite.</td><td>3052</td></tr>
</table>

(437)

<table>
<tr><td>[leaf 53 a]</td><td>¶ Grounde of treson, o þou cursyd[2] fauel !</td><td>3053</td></tr>
<tr><td></td><td>How longë[3] shalt þou be a potestate ?</td><td></td></tr>
<tr><td></td><td>In lordës courtes þou pleyest[4] þi parcel,</td><td></td></tr>
<tr><td></td><td>So þat it strecchith to þi lordys mate ;</td><td></td></tr>
<tr><td></td><td>ffor þu hast neuer þi lordys estate</td><td>3057</td></tr>
<tr><td>and cares
only for its
own profit.</td><td>To hertë[5] chere, but al þi bysynesse</td><td></td></tr>
<tr><td></td><td>Is for þi lucre, and þi cofres warmnesse.</td><td>3059</td></tr>
</table>

---

[1] pynetħ R.   [2] crueħ R.   [3] longe R, long H.
[4] courtes . . . curt . . . pleyest R, pleyst H.   [5] hert H R.

(438)

¶ Dicit Seneca de quibusdam qui Neronem sequebantur. Mel musce sequuntur,² cadauera lupi; predam sequitur ista turba non hominem.

¶ ffauel was neuer frendly, man vnto ;　　　3060
　lordës, beth ware ! it nedith trewëlye.¹
Senek, by hem þat folweden Nero,
　Seith þus, "a ffyë folweþ the honye ;
　þe wolf, careyn," he seith ; so, wel wot I　3064
　þat companyë folweden her pray,
　And naght þe man ; & so do men þis day.　3066

Lords, beware of Flatterers !

They are only for prey.

(439)

¶ Whil þat þe swetnesse of riches endurith,　3067
　Vnto þe riche is manny man plesaunt ;
Only þe richessë þer-to hem lurith ;
　What he comaundiþ, þei ben obysaunt³
　To do, whil þat he of goode is habundaunt ;　3071
　But whan þe pray, þe ricchesse, is a-goo,
　The man forsaken þei for euermo.　　3073

While Riches last, a man is sought for:

when they go, he is left.

(440)

¶ Ieronimus. Adulator secus est qui pro questu vel gracia transitoria sua & alterius animam interficit.

¶ O ffauel ! a blynde marchant art þou oone,　3074
　That, for wordly goode, & grace and fauoure,—
Which faylë shal & passe, and ouer goone,⁴—
　Swich diligencë dost, and swich laboure,
　þat þou þi soulë fro our saueoure　　3078
　Twynnest, and slest þi lordis soule also,
　And causyst hem to peyne eternel go.　3080

The Flatterer

slays his own Soul, and his Lord's too.

(441)

¶ þer is a long and a large difference　　3081
　Twix vertuous plesaunce and flaterie :
Good plesaunce is of swich beneuolence,
　þat what gode dede he may in man espie,
　He preysith it, and rébukith folye ;　　3085
　But fauel takeþ al on othir parte ;
　In wrong preysyng is al his craft and arte.　3087

[leaf 53 b]

Honest Graciousness praises the Good, but rebukes Folly.

---

¹ trewlye H, truly R.　　² sequuntur R, sequitur H.
³ obedient R.　　⁴ passe in ouer goone H, faile and ouercome H.

(442)

A Flatterer
holds his
tongue even
when his
Lord mis-
takes.

¶ A gloser also kepith his silence   3088

     Often, where he his lord seeth[1] him mystake.

Lest þat his answere myghtë[2] done offence

     Vn-to his lorde, and him displesyd make,

     He holt his pees ; nat a worde dare he crake ;   3092

     And for he naght ne seith, he his[4] assent

     Ʒeueþ[5] þerto, by mannës Iugëment.   3094

¶ Hugo de sancto victore. Adulator est ille qui tacet & dat consensum ne offendat quem optat[3] habere propicium.

(443)

He who
doesn't stop
Evil when he
can, favours
it.

¶ Who-so þat wot þe purpose of a wyght,   3095

     þat is agroundid vppon wykydnesse,

And noght ne lettith it, vnto his myght,

     ffauorith it, as þe boke can expresse ;

     Who-so it[6] lokith, fynde it shal no lesse.   3099

¶ Qui tacet, &c.

¶ Canonum xxiij. q. iij. capitulo. Qui potest.

I now turn to
Pity.

     But of al þis now make I here an ende,

     And to my tale of pite wol I wende.   3101

(444)

A Prince
must be piti-
ful, and re-
strain Anger.

¶ A Princë mot be of condicioun   3102

     Pitouse, and his angir refreyne, & ire,

Lest þat[7] vnavisid commocioun

     Hym chaufë so, & sette his hert on fire,

     That hym to wenge[8] as blyuë he desire,   3106

     And fulfille it in dede : hym owyþ knowe.

¶ Aristoteles, in principum regimine, capitulo de Regis prouidencia.

[leaf 54 a]

     His errour, and[9] qwenche þat firy lowe.   3108

(445)

Aristotle told
Alexander
never to be so
angry as to
kill a man.

¶ Aristotle amonestith wonder faste,   3109

     In his book whiche to Alisaundre he wroot,

If he wolde haue his regne endure and laste,

     That for non ire he neuere be soo hoot,

     Blood of man[10] schede ; and god seith, wel I woot,

     That vnto hym reseruëd is vengeaunce ;   3114

     Who-so þat slep, schal haue þe samë chaunce.

¶ Michi vindictam. (R. adds : Item, Qui gladio percutit, &c.)

---

[1] seeth R, seith H.   [2] myght H R.   [3] optat R, ortat H.
[4] his R, is H.   [5] Yeveth R, þen H.   [6] it R, *om.* H.
[7] þat, *om.* H R.   [8] venge R.   [9] and R, an H.
[10] of man to R, of a man H.

(446)

¶ But this noght ment is by þe cours of lawe,   3116   But to kill
    That put a man to deth for cryme horrible.   murderers is
Whan he a man y-murdred haþ and slawe,   allowable.
    A man to sle by lawe, it is lisible ;

¶ ffacilitas   That slaughtre beforn god is ádmittible,   3120
venie incen-
tiuum *pre-*   And if a kyng do swichë murdrers grace
bet delin-
quendi.   Of lyf, he boldeþ hem eft to trespace.[1]   3122

(447)

¶ *Nota con-*   ¶ kyng of þis lond whilom, herde I seyn,   3123   A King of
tra conces-   England once
siones carta-   ffor mannës deth a pardoun hadde e-graunted[2]   pardond a
rum pardo-   Murderer,
nacionum de   Vnto a man, whiche afterward ageyn   who then
murdris.   The samë gilt hadde in an othir haunted ;   murderd an-
                                                         other man,
    Aftir whos deth, he homly haþ avaunted   3127
       He nas naght so frendlés, he woldë do
       Wel y-now thogh he hadde slayn othir two. 3129

(448)

¶ " Of frendes," quod he, " haue I largë wone,   3130   and said he
    That, for þat they haue had, and schul, of myne,   had friends
                                                      who'd get
Byforne þe kyng for me schal knele echone ;   him off again.
    They at þe fullë kunne his hertë myne ;
    Thidir wil I goo, streght as any lyne,   3134
       And þey þat now annoyen me or greue,
       I schal hem qwite here-aftir, as I leue."   3136   [leaf 54 *b*]

(449)

¶ He cam vnto þe kyng, and axid grace   3137   He went to
    Of þat he wroghtë hadde[3] so synfully.   the King,
The kyng auysëd hym wel on his face,
    And seydë, " frend, me þynketh how þat I   who said he'd
    Haue vnto þe doon grace or þis, soothly ;   3141   forgiven him
       I graunted onës a chartre to þe   once.
       Of mannës deth, as it remembreth me.   3143

---

[1] trespace R, strepace H.   [2] be grauntede R.
         [3] wrought hade R.

(450)

¶ "Hast þou now slayn an othir man also?"   3144

A wise Fool
told the King
he himself
kild the slain
man;
Now stood a foolë[1] sage þe kyng byside;
And or þe kyng spak any wordës moo,
   He to hym seidë, "[Now,] for god þat dyde,
   Whi demen ye þis man an homicide?   3148
      He slow hym naght, for ye your self[2] hym slow,
      And, by your leuen,[3] I schal tellen how: 3150

(451)

for he stopt
the Murder-
er's death;
¶ "If þat þe lawë myghte his cours han had,   3151
   This man here hadde ben, for þe firste man, deed;
and if he
forgave him
again, he'd
slay a 3rd
man.
fforyeue hym now; and yif þat[4] he be drad
   To slee þe thriddë, þan girde of myn heed.
   Now be avisëd wel; it is my reed,   3155
      How ye your pardoun grauntë, leste errour
      Of nycë pitee be your áccusour."   3157

(452)

So the King
¶ This kyng wel þoughtë þat he seide hym trouthe,
   And chartirles gooþ þis man ful of drede;
   And aftirward, of whos dissert was routhe,
let the Mur-
derer be
executed.
   The lawe hym yaf þat longëd to his mede.
      My tale is doon; now sooþly it is nede   3162
      To grauntës to wiþstondë, þat procure
[leaf 55 a]
      Meschévous deth to many a crëature.   3164

(453)

Don't pity
Murderers;
slay em!
¶ Pitee auailith mochil, but naght þere;   3165
   ffor bet it is to sle þe mordreman,
   Than suffre hym regnë, for he haþ no fere
   His hand to vsë forth as he by-gan;
      And in my cónceit, feelë wel I can,   3169
      That of suche pitee, is þe abstinence
      Of gretter pite, for þe consequence.   3171

---

[1] foole R, fool H.
[2] self R, *om.* H (*with a later 'selfe' overline*).   [3] leve R.
[4] þat, *om.* H R.

(454)

¶ If right-ful deth of oo man, kepe and saue   3172
    Two innocentës lyuës, þinkeþ me
By resoun morë merit oghte hym haue
    That cómandith his¹ gylty man deed be,
    Than he þat lif hym graunteþ : why lat se,   3176
      The gylty man is no wrong doon vnto,
      But wrong is doon vnto² thise othir two.   3178

Better kill one Murderer than let him slay two Innocents.

(455)

¶ Euery man woot wel, fór to saue tweyne   3179
    Is gretter gracë þan to³ saue but on.
Of murdre, is cause gret for to⁴ compleyne ;
    Tho pardons alle to lyghtly passe and goon ;
    Auyse hem þat fauoúre hem, by seynt Iohn ;   3183
      Who so it be that þerto þe kyng meeveth,
      Wel morë þan he woot, his soulë greeveth.   3185

Pardons for Murder are too lightly given.

(456)

¶ Avise a kyng eek, for any requeste   3186
    Vnto hym maad, by greet estat or mene,
That he fauoúre it noght ; it is þe beste
    Tho réquestës to werne and voydë clene,
    Of swiche in sothe as murdrers ben, I mene ;   3190
      But and⁵ on be by malice of his foos
      Endited, pardoun be to hym noght cloos.   3192

A King should never grant any.

But if a man is maliciously accused,
[leaf 55 b]

(457)

¶ If þat be sooth, lat pitee walk at large,   3193
    ffor sche and mercy þerto wil assente ;
It is a parcel of hir either charge ;
    Routhë were it þe giltëles turmente ;
    Pitee schal soul of man to god presente,   3197
      And god, þat yaf vs ensample of pitee,
      To pitous folk sauacïoun schal be.   3199

let him be forgiven.

---

¹ this R.   ² vnto R, to H.   ³ to R, *om.* H.
    ⁴ grete to R.   ⁵ and, an, if.

(458)

When Mar-
cellus

¶ The pitous herte of Marcus Marcellus   3200

Wele worthy is, be drawen in memórie ;

¶ De pietate
Marci Mar-
celli.

He may ensample and mirrour be to vs ;

ffor, as Valerie writith in a storie,

had won
Syracuse,

Whan þis Marc obtened hadde[1] þe victórie   3204

By segë leyde to men of siracuse,

As I schal seyn, he heuyly gan[2] muse.   3206

(459)

¶ He wente hym vp on hy vppon a toure,[3]   3207

Where he byholdë myghte al þe citee,

And how fortune hadde schape hym þat honoure.[4]

With hertë tendre than considered he,

he wept over
the folks'
deaths,

And hadde of folkës dethës suche pitee,   3211

That from wepynge he myghte hym not restreyne ;

Al his tryumphë was to hym but peyne.   3213

(460)

¶ Who-so hadde stonden by hym in þat tyde,   3214

And hym avisëd on his contenaunce,

as if he had
been con-
querd, and
not the Con-
queror.

Wolde han supposëd that þat othir side

Rathir hadde I-putte hym to þe outraunce,

Than he hadde had of hem so fair a chaunce :   3218

O worthy knyght ! who schal þi steppës sue ?

[leaf 56 a]

Thi súccessour halt hym to longe in mue.   3220

(461)

Syracuse had

¶ O citee ! syn fortune was contrarie   3221

To the in o part, yit hir gentilnesse

a kindly foe.

Purveyëd þe a bénigne aduersarie.

Thanke hir of þat, for thy disese is lesse,

ffalle in þe daunger of lambës humblesse,   3225

Than he with cruel woluës al to-frete ;

A lamb is naght so gredy on hir mete.   3227

---

[1] opteynede R (? hadde obtened).   [2] gan R, *om.* H.
[3] tree R.   [4] that he did see R.

(462)

¶ Ther nys no þing, as witnessith a[1] storie,   3228   Mercy to
    Makyth a knyght so schynynge in renoun,   conquerd foes
Whan þat he of his foos hath þe victórie,   gives the Vic-
   As rew on hym þat throwen is a-doun,   tor renown.
   And of his blode eschue effusioun.   3232
      A bestes kynde is, þat is wilde and wood,
      Victórie naght desire, but þe blood.[2]   3234

(463)

¶ Also, whan þat þe kyng of hermenye   3235   Pompey
    Venquysshet was in batayle by pompeye,   lifted up the
This kyng fel doun vnto his foot in hye,   King of Ar-
   And from hym caste his dyademe aweye ;   menia, who
   But pompeyus, as blyue, of his nobleye   3239   fell at his
      Stirte vnto hym, and vp hym lifte & hente,   feet.
      And many a word benigne on hym dispente. 3241

(464)

¶ He dide his myght hym to conforte and qweeme ;
   And right anon, with-oute any delay,
Vpon his heed bad sette his dyademe
   Ageyn ; and so[4] was doon, it is no nay.
   Whan Cesar, emperour, eek on a day   3246   Cæsar wept
      Pompeyë saw biforn hym lad & bounde,   when he saw
      Cesar in terës saltë gan habounde.[5]   3248   Pompey pris-
                                           oner.

(465)

¶ Whan Alisaundre eek, as Vallerie haþ told,   3249   [leaf 56 b]
    Was, in a tyme, in þe feld wiþ his host,   Alexander
An agëd knyght of his, for verray cold,   took an old
   His lyfly myght he loren hadde al-moost,   knight,
   So greuous tempest tho fil in þat coost ;   3253   nearly dying
      And whan þis worþy kyng þis hadde aspied,   of cold,
      Out of his see he roos, and to hym hied,   3255

---

[1] the R.
[2] R. has in margin : Scriptum est, Ferarum genus est non
victoriam sed sanguinem sitire.   [3] benignitate & pietate R.
[4] so R, *om.* H.   [5] abounde R, hobunde H.

(466)

¶ And by the hand þis oldë knyght he took,   3256
  Confortynge hym [right] in his ¹beste manere,

to his own tent, and sat him in his Royal chair.

And ledde hym to his¹ tente, as seith þe book,
  And in² his real seege and his chaiere
As blyue hym settë : þus may kyngës leere,   3260
  Distressëd knyghtes to helpë and releeue :
  To take ensample of þis, it schal noght greue.

(467)

No wonder that Knights longd to serve such a noble King.

¶ What wonder was it, thogh þat knyghtës tho   3263
  Desirëden so noble princë serue,
Syn þat hym leuer was for to for-go
  His dignite, and hir helþë³ conserue,
Than his estat keepe, and hym suffre sterue ?   3267

May you, Prince Henry, be his heir!

  Yit hoope I seen his heir in þis prouince ;
  And þat schal ye be, my good lord þe prince. 3269

(468)

A knight, under trial, cald to Cæsar for help.

¶ Before a iuge, eek in poynt to be deed,   3270
  Of Iulïus Cesar þer was a knyght,

¶ De Pietate Iulii Cesaris.

Whiche, wiþ an hye voys, for to saue his heed,
  To his lord Cesar cryde a-lowdë ryght,
By-sechynge hym þat, of his gracious myght,   3274

Cæsar sent him an Advocate.

  He wolde hym helpe and rew⁴ on his estat ;

[leaf 57 a]

  And Cesar sente hym a good aduocat.   3276

(469)

¶ And vnto þat, þis knyght as blyuë þus   3277
  On heightë wel, þat al þe peple it herde,
With manly cheerë spak to Iulius,
  His lorde, and in þis wisë hym answerde :—

The knight reminded him of the Asian war.

  " Han ye for-gote how scharp it wiþ yow ferde,   3281
    Whan ye were in þe werrës of asie ?
    Maffeith ! your lif stood þere in iupartie ;   3283

----

¹⁻¹ best manere And ledde hym vnto his R, *om.* H.
    ² in R, *om.* H.   ³ helthe to R.   ⁴ rewe R.

(470)

¶ " And aduocat ne sente I non to yow,
    But my-self put in prees, & for yow faght ;
My woundës beren good witnesse y-now
    That I sooth seye ; and, lest ye leeue it naght,
I schal yow schewe what harmë haue I[1] caght, 3288
    The doute out of youre hertë for to dryue."
He nakid hym, and schewëd hym as blyue. 3290

3284   *He sent no Advocate to help Cæsar, but fought himself, as his Wounds witnest.*

(471)

¶ Of whiche, Cesar ful sorë was aschamed,   3291
    And in his hertë sorwe made, and moone ;
He heeld hym selfen worthy to be blamed.
    " My freend," [2] he seidë, " let me now allone ;
Aduócat wole I be in my *persone*   3295
    ffor þe ; I am wel holden to do soo."
And þus, þis knyght, his deth he saued fro. 3297

So Cæsar went himself, and saved the Knight's life.

(472)

¶ He dredde hym, if he naddë þus y-wroght   3298
    The peple hym wolde han[3] for a proude man deemed,
And vngentil, and þat he cowdë noght,
    As that it scholde eeke haue vnto hym seemed,
Thanke hem þat worþy[4] werë to be qwemed ;   3302
    " What princë," q*uoth* he, " peyneth hym naght wynne
His knyghtës[5] loue, his loue is to hem þynne."

3298   *He feard being thought ungentle, if he hadn't done so.*

[leaf 57 *b*]

(473)

¶ Out of pitee, growith mercy and springiþ,   3305
    ffor piteelés man cán do no me*r*cy ;
What prince hem lakkith, naght aright he kyngeth ;
    And, for þat þei ben neghëboures so nygh,
To pitee, mercy ioynë now wole I.   3309
    Excellent prince haue in hem good sauour,
    And ellës al in waast[6] is your labour.   3311

Mercy springs from Pity.

---

[1] I haue R.   [2] frend R, feend H.   [3] wold*e* hym haue R.
[4] worthy R, worþ H.   [5] knyghtes R, knyghes H.
[6] all in veyne R, in waast H.

[§ 6.] ¶ De Misericordia.

(474)

¶ *Augustinus* dicit, quod *misericord*ia est aliene miserie ex corde vera com-passio, & hec vertus consistit in duo-*bus, scilicet,* dando & dimittendo.

Mercy, aftir þe worde of seynt Austyn,[1]   3312
    Of herte is a verray compassïoun
Of othir menys harm, and þat comth yn
    By gyfte of god, and by remissïoun ;
As, if[2] iniúrie or oppressioun   3316
    Be doon to vs, þat gilt for-yeue vs oghte,
ffor loue of crist, þat, by deth, our lif boghte. 3318

Mercy is compassion for others' harm.

(475)

¶ *Matthaei* vij°. Qui *enim* dimittit iniuriam, & si peccauerit ipse, dimittetur ei. ¶ *Vnde domi-nus* in euan-*gelio:* Date & dabi*tur* vo-bis; dimitte & dimite*tur* vobis; sed qui dimittit & non dat, & si plene non operatus est, eam meliorem tamen par-tem tenet misericordie.

Who-so, wronge to hym doön, wole for-yeue,   3319
    His synnë schal to hym for-yeuen be ;
Thogh þat he no þing of his goodës yeue,
    The better part yit of mercy halt he ;
Thus fynde I writen of auctorite :   3323
    but fully may þere no man do mercy,
But if þat he releuë þe nedy.[3]   3325

He who for-gives, shall be forgiven.

(476)

¶ *Ambrosius.* Quis fidelis sit, sobrius & castus & aliis vertuti-*bus* oneratus, si *tamen* mis-ericors non est miseri-*cord*iam non meritur. *Di-cit* enim Apos-*tolus* Iacobus ij°. Iudicium sine *miseri-cord*ia illi qui no*n* facit misericor-diam.

Thogh þat a man be sobre, chaast, & trewe,   3326
    And be wiþ many an hy vertu endowëd,
And yeue, and naght for-yeue, it schal hym rewe :
    Where as oure werkes mostë ben avowëd,
The vnmerciáble schal be disallowëd :   3330
    Who naght forȝeueth, mercy dooth he non ;
And mercyles man, mercy schal for-gon.   3332

Without Mercy, other virtues are worthless.

[leaf 58 a]

(477)

¶ Mercy, crist causëd to ben incarnate,   3333
    And humbled hym to take oure breþerhede.
God in-mortel, rewynge oure seek estate,
    Mortel be-cam, to purge oure synful dede ;
Hym lothid naght his precious body sprede   3337
    Vpon þe croys, this lord benyngne and good ;
He wroot oure chartre of mercy with his blood.

Christ incar-nated Mercy, and sufferd on the Cross for us.

---

[1] This page has an illuminated border and initial.
        [2] if R, of H.
[3] R. has the lines of this stanza wrong : 3319, 3324-5, 3320-1.

(478)

¶ Of hym, his handwerk and his crëature,   3340 From Christ,
    ffor to be merciable, aright may lerne ;   all should
This lyf present schul but a whilë dure,   learn to be
    And lastynge it, your mercy naght ne werne,   merciful.
    O worthy princë, for to god eterne   3344
        It ful plesant is ; dooth your mercy here ;
        ffor to late is, aftir ye goo to beere.   3346

(479)

¶ De miseri-
cordia Iohan-
nis ducis
lancastrie,
(cuius anime
propicietur
deus!) & de
misericordia
dómini nostri
Regis hen-
rici, filii sui.

¶ Take hede, excéllent prince, of your graunt-syre,   Prince,
    How in his werkës he was merciáble ;   recollect your
He þat for mercy dydë, qwyte his hire !   Grandfather,
    He neuere was, in al his lyf, vengeáble,   John of
    But ay for-yaf the gylty and coupáble.   3351 Gaunt, and
        Our ligë lord your fadir, dith[1] þe same ;   your Father,
        Now folwe hem two, my lord, in goddis name ! Henry IV.

(480)

¶ They often haddë gret cause hem to venge,   3354 They forbare
    But hir spiritis bénigne and pesible   to take venge-
Thoghten þat craft vnlusty and alenge,   ance.
    And fórbaar it ; þei knewe it vnlisible.   [leaf 58 *b*]
    To mercy were hir hertës ay flexible ;   3358

¶ Beati
misericordes
&c.

        ffor-why with mercy god schal qwyte hem wel,
        Aftir þe wordës write in þe gospeH.   3360

(481)

¶ It is to leue and deme, if a kyng schyne   3361 The Son of
    In vertu, þat his sonë schuldë sue,   a virtuous
And to his fadris manerës enclyne,   King should
    And wykked teichës and vices eschue :   follow his
    Thus oghte it be, this to natúre is due.   3365 Father's way.
        He mot considre of whom he took hys kynde,
        And folwe his vertu, as men writen fynde.   3367

---

[1] doth R.

(482)

¶ He moost is like to god, as seith Bernard,   3368

    þat holdeth no þing morë precious

Than to be merciful; it is ful hard

    To lakkë mercy and ben vnpitous.

    "Mercy wole I," seith oure lord glorious;   3372

        He þat denyeth god, þát he wolde haue,

        God nayte[1] hym schal, þat he wil axe or craue.

(483)

¶ Senek seith how þe kyng and þe ledere   3375

    Of bees is prikkëles; he haþ right non

Wherwith to styngen, or annoye, or dere;

    But othir bees, prikkës[2] han euerichon;

    Natúrë woldë sche schulde it[3] for-goon,   3379

        And do no cruelte vnto þe swarm,

        But mekely hem gouerne, & do non harm.   3381

(484)

¶ Of þis, ensample schuldë kyngës take,   3382

    And princes, þat han peple for to gye;

ffor to hem longith it, for goddës sake,

    To wayuë cruelte and tyrannye,

    And to pitee, hir hertës bowe & wrye,   3386

        And reule hir peple esily and faire:

        It is kyngly, be meeke and debonaire.   3388

(485)

¶ I rede of á kyng, þat Pirus was named,   3389

    Whan hym was tolde, how þat men of Tarente

Hadde, at a festë, his estat diffamed,

    He for þe samë folkës blyuë sente;

    And whan þey cam, axid to what entente   3393

        They of hym spak so, and so foulë ferde;

        And oon of hem, as ye schulle here, answerde:[5]

---

[1] nay R.   [2] prikles R.   [3] hir R.
[4] De misericordia R.   [5] answerde R, answere H.

(486)

¶ " My lord, if þat þe wyne noȝht faillëd hadde,   3396
Al þat we spak, nerë but game and play,
Hauynge rewardë[1] to þe wordës badde
That we thoghte haue I-spoken in good fay."
   The kyng took a laghtre, and wente his way,   3400
     And of al þat, he heeld hem[2] ful excused :
     He seide it wás wyne, þat so hem accused.   3402

he accepted at once a witty excuse for it.

(487)

¶ Wengeance, in þis good lord, haddë no stide ;   3403
Mercy and humble disposicïoun
Dispensid[3] with tho men, and grace hem dide,
And thriste vndír foote cruelte adoun.
   O myghty princë ! this condicïoun   3407
     To your highnessë is ful ácordant,
     And vnto god al-myghty ryght plesant.   3409

He had no desire for Vengeance.

(488)

¶ Power withouten mercy, a kyng tourneth   3410
Into a tyraunt, war þat feendly spek !
ffor in what man þat cruelte soiourneth,
Vnto his soule it is an odious spek.
   Tho men of god han nouthir look ne bek,   3414
     But if þat it be bekkës of manace,
     Where as his[4] mercy folweþ mochë grace.   3416

¶ *Potestas sine miseri- cordia vertit Regem in tirannum : ita scriptum est.*

Power with- out Mercy makes a King a Tyrant.

[leaf 59 *b*]

(489)

¶ Salomon in his prouerbis expressith,   3417
' Mercy and trouthë,[5] wardeynes ben of kyngës ;
And with iustice also,' as he witnéssith,
' His trone is strengþed :' what man þat a kyng is,
   But if þat he, amongis oþir thyngës,   3421
     Endowëd he wiþ allë þisë thre,
     Men seyn he halteth in his hyge[6] degre.   3423

¶ *Prouerbi- arum capitu- lo xxº. Misericordia & veritas Regem cus- todiunt ; & roboratur clemencia thronus eius.*

Solomon says that Mercy and Truth are a King's Keepers.

---

[1] rewarde R, reward H.   [2] hem R, hym H.
[3] Dispendede he R.   [4] his R, is H.
[5] trouthe R, trouche H.   [6] hye R.

(490)

¶ A noble and glorious kynde of vengeance[1] is,   3424
  A knyght to spare, whan þat he sleë may.

Pisistaris
had a fair
young
Daughter.

Ther was a duc callid pisistaris,
  þat a yong doghtir haddë, a fair[2] may,
  Whiche with hir modir walkid on a day—   3428
    Naght seith the book whider, ne what to done,
    But þus it schoop, as I schal tellë sone.   3430

¶ De *miseri-cordia* ducis Pisistaris.

(491)

A young
Lover of hers

¶ A yong, fresche, lusty, wel by-seyën man   3431
  So brente in loue, he wentë for to dye,
Rauyssht of þe beauté of þis womman,
  This tendir[3] yong morsel, þis doghter, I seye.
  And as þis yong man mette hir in þe weye,   3435

rusht at her
and kist her.

    He at a leep was at hir, and hir kyste :
    The modir, angry wood, whan sche it wiste,   3437

(492)

Her mother
wanted him
kild.

¶ Sche right[4] anon hir lord, þe duc, be-soghte[5]   3438
  To putte hym to þe deth for his trespas.
He seydë nay ; to do þat neuere he þoghte :

[leaf 60 a]
Pisistaris
said No :
if we kill
Friends, what
shall we do
to Foes ?

  "Schulle[6] we sleen hem þat louen vs ? allas !
    What schuld we þanne in the contrárie cas,   3442
    That is to seyn, do[7] to our enemys ?"
  Thus seide þis duc, merciable and wys.   3444

(493)

The Mother
lackt Wo-
manhood.

Allas ! whi was þis womman so vengeáble ?   3445
  Certes, in þat sche lakked wommanhede.
This louer hadde ben deede, it is no fable,
  If þis duc hadde ben like[8] to hir in dede ;

Pisistaris
had Mercy.

  But mercy hym for-bad, any blood schede ;   3449
    Sche and pitee weren of oon accord,
    And senten paciënce vnto þis lord.   3451

---

[1] signe of mercy R.   [2] faire R.   [3] tendre R, tedir H.
[4] right R, righ H.   [5] besought R, be-soghe H.
[6] Shulde R, Schullen H.   [7] done to R, to do H.
[8] like R, *om.* H.

(494)

And for as mochil as þat pacïence 3452
    To mercy as in lyne of blood atteyneth,
Now wole I do my payne and diligence,
    To telle how hir benignyte restreyneth
The feruent hetë þat þe hertë pyneth 3456
    Wrechë cruel to take, and scharp vengeaunce,
    Of þat þe herte of man felith greuaunce. 3458

As Patience
is allied to
Mercy, I'll
treat of it.

[§ 7.] ¶ De Paciencia.

(495)

Gregórie seith, pacïencë verray [1] 3459
    Is, of harm doon to man, softë souffraunce,
And naght be wrooth, by no manere of way,
    With hym þat hath y-doon a man nusance.
Socrates seith, no mannës gouernance 3463
    Is wys, but it be by suffrancë preeued ;
    A good man souffrith wrong, and is not greued.

¶ Gregorius
dicit, paci-
encia vera est,
aliena mala
equanimiter
pati, & contra
eum qui mala
irrogat, nullo
dolore mori.
¶ Socrates
dicit, Nemo
bene sapiens
est qui paci-
enciam non
habet ; viri
enim boni est
scire[2] pati &c.

Patience is
gentle suffer-
ance of
wrongs.

(496)

¶ The kynde of pacïence is to sustene 3466
    Myghtily wrongës, and hem neuere wreke,
But hem for-yeue, and wratthe & irous tene
    Out of þe hertë for to spere and steke.
Hir kynde is noght to lete a word out breke, 3470
    That harmful is ; for hertë voyde of ire
    Hath naght wherwith to sette a tonge afire. 3472

[leaf 60 b]
It never re-
venges them,
but forgives.

(497)

¶ O pacïent, o humble kyng benyngne ! 3473
    O kyng Dauid ! þi pacïent meeknesse
Naght meeued was ageyn Semey maligne,
    Whos hy malice and crabbid wikkidnesse
Yaf greet enchesoun to thy worthynesse 3477
    To vengë the ; but þi benyngnite
    ffor-bad þyn hand to kythë cruelte. 3479

O patient
David ! Thou
wast not
moved by
curser Shi-
mei.

---

[1] This page is illuminated with an initial G, and a scroll work
border on three sides.—G. England.   [2] scire R, fore H.

(498)

Shimei curst ¶ As this kyng onës cam to bahurim,   3480 ¶ Regum 2⁰.
    Out cam þis man, malicïous Semey,   *Capitulo* 16.
    Sone of Gera, and swiche despite dide hym   Venit *ergo*
    And to his men, as by hym wenten they,   Rex Dauid
and cast   Castyngë stonës vnto hym alwey,   3484 vsq*ue* bahu-
stones at   rim & ecce
David, who   That wondir was; for which, on Abusay   egrediebat*ur*
wouldn't   &c.
have him   Wolde haue hym slayn; but þe kyng seidë, "nay!   ¶ Dixit au-
slain.   tem Abusay
            fil*ius* Saruie:
            Quare male-
            dicit canis
            iste? &c.
            Vadam & am-
            putabo [ca-

(499)   put ejus R],

            ¶ Et ait Rex:
    ¶ " Lat hym curse, aftir þe comau*n*dëment   3487 ' dimitte eum
David hoped   Of god; whan he seeth myn afflicciou*n*,   vt maledicit
God would   iux*ta* prece*p*-
see his suffer- And my disese, and my grevous turment,   tum dom*i*ni.
ing, and help   He wole, for þis dayës malicïou*n*,   Si forte respi-
him.   ciat domin*us*
    Par áventurë, do me som guerdou*n*."   3491 affliccionem
      Thus vndirstonde I, write is in þe bible,   meam, &
      Whiche is a book autentik and credible.   3493 reddet[1] mi*h*i
            bonum p*ro*
            male*diccione*
            hac hodierna
            &c.

(500)

[leaf 61 *a*] ¶ The pacïence of Iob, men may nat hyde,   3494 ¶ De pacien-
    The comou*n* voys wole algate it by-wreye;   cia Regis
Alexander   And Alisaundre, whos fame is sprad ful wyde,   Alexa*n*dri.
    fful pacïent was, as þe bookës seye.
    A sad wys knyḡt of his witħ lokkës greye,   3498
      Grucchynge ageyn his fleschely lustës, seide
      Vnto his lord, and þus he hym vp breyde :   3500

(501)

was fiercely ¶ " O Alisaundre! it is vncouenable,   3501
reproacht
for his Lust   The for to haue of peple regyment,
by a Knight. Syn þi lust, bestial and miserable,
    Hath qweynt thy resou*n* and entendëment
    So ferforth, þat the hetë violent   3505
      Of leccherye is in þe, lord and sire ;
      Repreef, I dredë, qwytë schal þin hire.   3507

---

[1] reddet R, reddit H.

(502)

¶ "ffy! schamëles vnworthy gouernour!" 3508
And whan þe knyghtës talë was al endid,
The kyng answerde, " I knowë myn errour;"   *He confest his sin, and said he'd amend.*
And pacïently seide, " I haue offendid;
I woot it wel; and it schal be amendid." 3512
¶ De paciencia Iulii Cesaris.   A man also to Iulius Cesar onës   *Julius Cæsar was rebuked*
Crabbidly seid, and schrewdly[1] for þe nonës, 3514

(503)

¶ And among othir wordës þat he speek, 3515
" Iulius," quod he, " make it noght so tow,[2]   *for his pride,*
ffor of thy birthe art þou noght wort a leek:
Whens þat þou cam, men knowen wel I-now:
Wenest þou naght þat[3] I can tellen how 3519   *and told he was only a Baker's son.*
Thy fadir was a bakere? o, lat be!
Ne make it nat so qweyntë, I pray the!" 3521

(504)

¶ Smylynge, vnto hym spak þis Emperour: 3522   [leaf 61 *b*]
" Whethir supposist þou bet, þat noblesse   *He gave a gentle answer,*
Begynne in me, or noblesse and honour
Deffaile in þe?" this questïoun, I gesse,
Was, in swiche cas, but answer of softnesse; 3526
ffor þat was seide in repreef of his name,
His pacïence, as who[4] seith, took[5] in game. 3528   *as if in joke.*

(505)

¶ De Paciencia Scipionis affricani bellicosissimi. ¶ To þe chiualrous worþy[6] Scipio 3529   *Scipio Africanus was told he fought but little.*
Of Aufrik, also speek onës a wight,
And seide, " in armës durste he but smal do;
He faght but smal whan he cam to þe fight."
And pacïently answerde he anon right, 3533
" My modir me bare, a childe feeble and smal,   *He said, when he was born, he couldn't fight at all.*
And forth me broghte, and no fightere at al." 3535

[1] sharply R.   [2] tough R (*rymes:* ynough, hough)
[3] that R, þan H.   [4] who R, swo H.   [5] took it R.
[6] Chyualerous worthy R, chiualours worþ H.

(506)

¶ Senek seith, how þe kyng Antigone   3536

Herde onës folk speke of hym wikkedly,

ffor ther nas[1] but a curtyn, as seith he,

Twixt hym and hem ; and whan hys tyme he sy,

Aside he drow the curtyn sodenly,   3540

And seidë, "gooth hens, lest þe kyng yow here,

ffor þe curtyn haþ herde al your matere."   3542

(507)

¶ Of duc Pisistaris eek wil I telle :   3543

He hadde a freend, arispus was his name,

Whiche onës hastily, with wordës felle

Rebukid so þis duc, þat it was schame

To heren it ; and yit, with sorwe and grame,   3547

He in despyt spette in þis dukës face ;

And he þerto no word spak in þat place.   3549

(508)

¶ He had him so in port & word and chere,   3550

Ryght as hym hadde be do no vilenye,

But luked forth in a freendely manere.

Now ther were in this dukës companye

His sonës two, that busked hem in hye   3554

To this Arispus, and wolden ful[2] fayn,

Nad hir fadir hem let, haue hym Islayn.   3556

(509)

¶ The nextë day after, this Arispus   3557

To takë gan consideracïoun

How that he to þe duke mys-bare hym thus,

And madë morë waymentacïoun

Than I can make of nominacïoun[3] ;   3561

He wolde han slayn himselfe, it is no lese,

But that this duke broughte al to rest & pees.

---

[1] nas R, nat H.   [2] full R, su H.

[3] now mensioun R.

(510)

¶ Whan he knew how it with Arispus stood, 3564
  He dressid him to him, and þat as swithë,
And bad him to be glad of cheere and mood ;
  He seide, and swoorë[1] to him oftë sithë,
" As freendly wole I be, and stande as ny the 3568
  As I dide euere ; " and thus his paciencie
And meknesse hath qwenchid al[2] þis offence. 3570

(511)

¶ Salomon seith, in him is sapience 3571
  That is indewed with benyngne humblesse.
Grace of þe holy goost, no residence
  Holdith in þat man þat lakkéth meeknesse.
God took vppon him humble buxumnesse 3575
  Whan he him wrappid in our mortelᵭ rynde :
That oughte a myrour be to al man-kynde.[3] 3577

¶ Salomon. Ubi est humilitas, ibi sapientia. Origines: si humilis non fueris in te non potuit habitare gracia spiritus sancti.

Solomon says, where Humility is, Wisdom is.

(512)

¶ Plesant to god was þe virginite 3578
  Of his modir ; but verray god & man
Conseyued was thoruȝ þe humilite
  Whiche he be-heeld in þat blyssed woman.
O humble maidë ! who is it þat can 3582
  The debonaire humblessë tellen al,
Restynge in þy clennessë virginal ? 3584

¶ Bernardus dicit, Beata maria, ex virginitate placuit deo, sed ex humilitate concepit deum. [Written over stanza 512.]

Christ was conceivd thro Mary's humility.

(513)

¶ Thogh þat þe humble were a foul habyt, 3585
  Ȝit in vertuës glorious is he ;
But þe proud man stant in anoþer plyt ;
  Thogh his array be fair & fresche to se,
His dedës and his werkës foulë[4] be. 3589
  What hyȝe estate þat a man represente,
Humble to be, let hym sette his entente ! 3591

¶ Basilius. Humilis licet habitu vilis sit, gloriosus tamen est virtutibus. Superbus autem si decorus videatur aspectu tamen operibus vilis est. ¶ Isodorus. Quamuis summus es humilitatem tene. Salomon. Quanto maior, &c.

[leaf 62 b]
The ill-clad humble man is Glorious in Virtues.

---

[1] swore R, swoor H. [2] alᵭ R, as H.
[3] At the bottom of this page is the figure of a man in a pink jacket, lying on his back upon a patch of grass, and holding in his hands the end of a rope noose, with which he is pulling into its place stanza 512, left out at first, and then written in the margin opposite st. 511.—G. E. [4] foule R, foul H.

(514)

¶ Humylite verray, as seith Cesárie,
   May neuere be with-outen charite ;
And sche is a vertu most necessarie :
   Amongës allë vertuës þat be,
   Sche on hem alle opteeneth dignite.
     They fro þe regne of god hem-self dyuyde,
     That charite wayven and caste a-syde.

3592
3596
3598

¶ Cesarius.
Nunquam
sine caritate
vera humili-
tas aut fuerat
aut poterat
esse.
¶ Ysodorus.
Nullum pre-
mium cari-
tati equatur,
caritas enim
virtutum om-
nium optinet
principatum.
A regno dei se
separant qui
semetipsos
a caritate
dissociant.

(515)

¶ Right as a man ne may nat thider goo
   Where he purposeth hym, but if a way
Be thiderward, seint Amselm seiþ, right so,
   With-outen charite, men goo ne may
   Aryght vnto godward : men mowen ay
     Doon as him list, if þei ben charitable ;
     But lakkynge it, is no þing profitable.

3599
3603
3605

¶ Anselmus.
Et sicut sine
via nullus
peruenit quo
tendit, Ita,
sine caritate
que dicta est
via ab aposto-
lo, non recte
ambulare
possumus in
via dei.
¶ Augustin-
us. Habe
caritatem &
fac quod vis,
&c.

(516)

¶ Only keepyng of charitee vs preeveth,
   That we disciples ben of god almyghty.
What þing it be þat harmeth man or greueth,
   By goodnesse ouercome it paciently ;
   No seint to heuene comyth, as rede I,
     But by kepynge of paciënce, and how
     Men may it lerë, wole I schewë yow.

3606
3610
3612

¶ Gregorius
in moralibus.
Omnipoten-
tis eterni dei
nos esse dis-
cipulos sola
custodia cari-
tatis probat.
¶ Scriptum
est, Nemo
quidem sanc-
torum ad
celestem glor-
iam, nisi
paciënciam
seruando
peruenit.

(517)

Take heede how, whan þat crist oure sauëour
   Was bobbid, and his visage al be-spet,
And gret despit doon him, and déshonour,
   Bounden and scourgëd & greuoúsly bett,
   Crownëd with thorne, naylëd to þe gybett,

     Ʒit, for al this tormént, no word he speeke,
     So was he paciént, benigne, and meke.

3613
3617
3619

(518)

And syn our lord god was of swiche suffránce,   3620
  Thanne is it to his crëaturë schame,
On greef to hym doon, take any vengeánce.
  Man oghtë rathir sorowe for the blame
  That god schal konne him þat hath done þe grame,
    Than for þe harme þat þe greuéd haþ hent :
    So doth þe charitáble and pacïent.   3626

It is shame-
ful to take
Vengeance
for Wrongs.

[§ 8.]   **De Castitate.**

(519)

To chastite purpóse I now to haste,[1]   3627
  Whiche couenable is, and conuenient,
Vn-to a kyng for to sauoure and taaste.
  What princë þat with vnclennesse is brent,
  And ther-in settith his luste and talent,   3631
    No perfyt dede or werk him folwe may :
    Mochil, is hertë chaast, to goddys pay.   3633

Chastity is
right for a
King.

¶ Scriptum est, Nisi pudicitia sedeat in mente, nulla perfectio sequitur in opere.

(520)

Right as þe persone of a prince outward   3634
  Honúred is wiþ clothës precïous,
So aughte his hertë cloþid ben inward
  With vertu, and hym kythë vertuous.
  ffresche apparaile and hertë leccherous   3638
    Unsittynly ben in a Princë ioynt,
    Namëly in a cristen kyng enoynt.   3640

His heart
should be
clad with
Virtue.
[leaf 63 b]

(521)

¶ In as mochel as dignite of a kyng   3641
  Excedith othir folk in reuerence,
The more hym oghtë peyne hym, lest al þing
  Othir folk passe in vertuous excellence.
  Honour noȝt ellës is in éxistence   3645
    Than reuerencë ȝeuen in witnesse
    Of[2] vertu, as þe scripturës[3] expresse.   3647

He should
strive to be
better than
other folk.

---

[1] This page, 63 a, has an illuminated initial T, and scroll
bordering on three sides.—G. E.
[2] Of R, Or H.   [3] scripture doth R.

(522)

Honour is got by Virtue, not by high place.

¶ Honur, whiche was goten vertuously,   3648   [R, *om.* H]
Boecius dicit,
Honor vir-
tuose adqui-
situs, non
primo *per*
dignitatem
adquirebatur,
sed dignitatis
honor *per*
virtutem ad-
quisitus erat,
&c.

Ne was naght first by dignite *p*urcháced,
As þat Boecë telleþ éxpresly,
But dignitees honour was émbraced
   With *ve*rtu ; dignite had ben vnlaced   3652
      And vngirt of honour, nad *ve*rtu be ;
ffor *ve*rtu hath hir *p*ropre dignite.   3654

(523)

¶ Aristotle coun*n*seilled Alisaundre,   3655
To leccherye he noght enclynë scholde,

Lechery is a Hog's life.

ffor it [is] hoggës lif, whiche were esclaundre[1]
To him, if he tho weiës takë wolde
   That beestës resonles vsen and holde ;   3659
      ffor of body it is destruccïoun,
      And eek of al *ve*rtu corrupcioun.   3661

(524)

As Heathens shund it, Christians ought to.

¶ Syn thei, þat naght were[2] of cristen bapteme,   3662
Coun*n*seillëd men eschuë leccherie,
Than oghte vs cristen men þat vicë fleeme,
And swichë lustës in vs mortifie.

[leaf 64 *a*]

   Who so entendeth in-to blisse stye,   3666
      That firy sparkle algate he moste qwenche,
      And lustës leue, of lady and of wenche.   3668

(525)

No Forni-cator shall inherit the Kingdom of God.

¶ The scripture seïþ, no fornicatour,   3669   ¶ Ad Ephe-
sios. v°. ffor-
nicator non
*ha*bebit here-
ditatem in
regno *chris*/i
& dei.
Ad Ebreos,
iijo. fforni-
catores &
adult*er*os
iudicabit
deus.

The regne of crist and god shal énherite ;
It seith eek, that him and þe aduoutour
God demë shal ; he can hir labour qwyte
   fful scharply, that in tho tweynë delite,   3673
      And so he wolë, but[3] correccïoun
      Be mannës scheeld, & his *p*roteccioun.   3675

---

[1] disclaundre R.   [2] were R, neu*er* H.   [3] but yf R.

(526)

¶ Affrican Scipio, þat noble knyght,   3676

  Whan he was xx^{ti} and iiij of age,
And by prowesse, and by manhode & myght
  Cartágiens putte hadde into seruáge,
  Ther was a mayde sent him into hostáge,   3680
    Of yeerës ripe I-now, and of beaute
    Most excellent that men myghte owher se.   3682

To Scipio Africanus, when 24, was sent a beauteous maid.

(527)

¶ And whan þis worthi ȝong prince honurable,   3683
  This woman sigh, of hir he took good ȝeme,
Thynkynge þat she was of beaute able,
  The worthieste on lyuë for to queeme ;
  And in him multiplied thoughtës breeme ;   3687
    But nathëles, for al þis besy þought,[1]
    Enquere he gan, if she wyf were, or nouȝt. 3689

He askt if she was a wife.

(528)

¶ Sche trouthëd was to Iudibal, men seide,   3690
  A lord of þat Citee ; and Scipio,
On a mynystre of his þe chargë leide,
  ffor hir fadir and modir blyuë goo.
  Thei at his[2] hestë cam vnto him tho ;   3694
    And in hir clenë virginal estat,
    Restorëd he þis mayde inuiolat.   3696

She was be-trotht to Judibal.

[leaf 64 b]

So Scipio sent her back a virgin,

(529)

¶ The gold eek þat for hir redempcioun   3697
  Purveyëd was, for-ȝaf he vtterly,
In help and increes and promocïoun
  Of hir wedlok.   and whan Iudibal sy
  And knewe how scipio thus nobl[el]y   3701
    Demenëd him, he was ful wel apayed
    Of þat he grucchid first, and was affrayed. 3703

with her ransom-money as a portion.

---

[1] thought R, þough H.   [2] his R, *om.* H.

(530)

¶ He went vnto testatës[1] of þe toun,   3704
　　And tolde hem al þe cas, as it befil;
And thei þis lord yaf loude[2] and hy renoun
　　ffor þat; and allë,[3] with oon hert and wil,
　　　Submitted hem to þis princë[4] gentil;   3708
　　　Thus hertë[5] chaast and tendre gentillesse
　　　Conquéreth hertës, rather þan duresse.   3710

(531)

¶ Or marcus marcellus had þe citee   3711
　　Of Ciracusë taken or y-nome,
He leet do crye amongës his meyne,
　　That whan þe citee he had ouercome,
　　And his folk ther-in entred[6] were & come,   3715
　　　Noon be so hardy, þe wommen oppresse,[7]
　　　Ne touche hem by no wey of vnclennesse.   3717

(532)

¶ Ther was also a seemly fresshe yong man,   3718
　　To whom naturë swiche fauour had lent
Of schap and beaute, þat þer nas womman
　　That onës had a look on hym dispent,

　　But þat hir hertë[5] yaf flesshely consent;   3722
　　　And nathëles eschuëd he þe taast
　　　Of vnclennesse, and kepte his body chaast.   3724

¶ De casti-
tate cuiusdam
iuuenis.

(533)

¶ By toknës knew he hire vnclene entente,   3725

　　And with his naylës cracched he his face,
And scocched it with knyuës, and to-rente,
　　And it so wonderly þus[8] gan difface,
　　That his beaute refusëd hadde hir place :   3729

　　　Al þis dide he, hir hertës[9] to remewe
　　　ffrom him, and make hem vnclennésse eschue.

---

[1] thestates R.   [2] laude R.   [3] alle R, al H.
[4] (? vnto þis prince) to this prynces wille R.   [5] hert H R.
[6] entred R, entreted H.   [7] to oppresse R.
[8] þus, *om.* H R.   [9] hertes R, hert H.

(534)

¶ De castitate cuiusdam femine Vlie numcupate.

¶ Ierom tellith, agayn Iouinian,   3732   An old Roman with a young wife
   A faire womman, a maidë clept Vlie,
Y-wedded was vnto an agëd man,
   A Romayn, smyten *with* þe pallësie ;
But sche in chastite was sette so hye,   3736
   That an ensaumple *v*errayliche was sche
   To allë tho þat louëd chastitee.   3738

(535)

¶ Hire housbonde herde onès[1] an enemy,   3739
   Whiche þat he haddë, spoke[2] in his repreef,   *was told that his breath stank.*
That.his breth stank, as þat he stode him by ;
Wher-of he toke gret heuynesse and greef ;
He goth hoom to his wyf, and þis mescheef   3743
   fful heuely to hire he gan compleyne,
   And þus of hire he gan to aske and freyne : 3745

(536)

¶ "Whi, wyf," quod he, "han ye noght or this tyme
   I-warnëd me how þat it wiþ me stood ?"
"Sire, it was nought," quod sche, "aspied by me ;   *His wife said she didn't know it;*
   I held your breth ay also suete and good
As other mennës ben ; I vnderstood   3750   [leaf 65 *b*]
   Non othir, ne yit do in sothfastnesse."   *she'd smelt no other man's.*
   fful fewë men had sche kist, as I gesse.   3752

(537)

¶ She hily was to preyse and to commende,   3753
   That naght ne knewe by othir mennès mouthes
Hir makis vice : it[3] was al wel, sche wende.
To fyndë many swiche ful vnkouthe is ;   *There are few such wives now.*
Lat vs awayte wel when þe wynd south is   3757
   And north at onès blowynge on þe sky,
   And fyndë swiche an hepe þan hardily.   3759

---

[1] ones hade R, herde oned H.
[2] that said and spake R, þat he hadd spoke H.   [3] it R, at H.

(538)

Plato livd in
the wilder-
ness to curb
his lust.

¶ Plato, his patrimoygne and his contree   3760   ¶ De Platonis castitate.
    Lefte and for-sook, and dwelte in wildernesse,
ffor to restreynë fleschely nycete ;
And his disciples louëd so clennesse,
And for to fallen hadden swiche gastnesse,   3764
    Hir eyën they out of hir heedës brente,
    Lest sighte of hem, spottë myght[1] her entente.

(539)

Demosthenes
wouldn't pay
a woman 40d.
to enjoy her.

¶ Demostenes his handës onës putte   3767   ¶ De Domes-tenes[2] casti-tate.
    In a wommannës bosom iapyngly,
Of facë faire, but of hir body a slutte :
"With yow to delë," seide he, "what schal I
Yow yeuë ?" "xl pens," quod sche, soothly.   3771
    He seydë nay, so dere he byë nolde
    A thyng for whiche þat him repentë[3] schulde.

(540)

A Duchess's
daughters
let meat rot
under their
breasts, to
keep men off.

¶ I fynde, how two doughtres of a duchesse,   3774   ¶ De casti-tate duarum filiarum cuiusdam ducisse.
    The fleschely touches of men for to fle,
When men of Hongary hem wolde oppresse,
In cónseruynge of hir virginite,

[leaf 66 a]

    Thei hem purveyded a good sotilte :   3778
    Thei chiknës flesche putte vndirneþe hir pappes,
    Hem to defendë from vnclenly happes.   3780

(541)

¶ Be-holde, of wommen here a noble wyle !   3781
    In schort avisëment, who can do bet ?
Bi that þis flesche þus hadde leyen a while,
And þat it was y-chaufëd wel and hete,

It stank so
that the men
went away.

    It stank so foulë, þat it haþ I-lette   3785
    Tho men, þat wery þei were of hir pray,
    And fórsook þe wommen, and went hir way. 3787

---

[1] myght spotte R.   [2] Demostenis R.   [3] repent H, R.

(542)

¶ O wommanhode! in þe regneþ vertu   3788
  So excellent, þat to[1] feble is my witt
To éxpresse it; wherefor I am eschu
  To melde[2] or make a long sermoun of it.
    Som mannës mouth yit wolde I were I-schet,   3792
      That vice of wommen spareþ nought[3] bywreye,
      ffor allë[4] soothës ben nought for to seie.   3794

My wit is too weak to say enough of Women's Virtue.

(543)

¶ But for to talkë forth of contynence   3795
  Or chastite,—who-so chaast lyuë schal,
Moot scourge his fleschely lust with abstinence,
  Thristë him dowyn, yeue him no place at al:
    Metës & drynkës make a soulë thral,   3799
      If þe body be reulëd by excesse;
      ffor-thi it nedeth take of hem þe lesse.   3801

Lust must be kept down by Abstinence.

(544)

¶ Excesse of mete and drynke is wombës frende,   3802
  And wombe is next to oure membres priue;
Glotonye is ful plesant to þe fende,
  To leccherië redy path is sche.
    The fend lyth in a-wayte of oure freelte,   3806
      And stireth a man to drinkës delicat,
      To make agaynës chastite debat.   3808

Gluttony is the easy way to Lechery.

[leaf 66 b]

(545)

¶ A man schulde ete and drynke in swiche a wise 3809
  As may be to his helthës sústenynge,
Aftir þe doctrine of Senek þe wise.
  Sum man drynketh the wyn þat is wenynge;
    Than[5] he drynkeþ his witt: more is preysinge 3813
      And honurable, a man compleyne of[6] thrist,
      Than dronken be, whan he þe cuppe haþ kist.

Eat and drink only for Health,

---

[1] to R, so H.   [2] medle R.   [3] not R, nough H.
[4] alle R, al H.   [5] When R.   [6] of R, or H.

(546)

¶ Thus seidë Ierom vn-to a virgyne :   3816

How can a girl be continent .

" O doghter, syn thapostle sorë dredde

Lust of his flesche, and dide his body peyne,

And heeld it lowe, and symplëly it fedde,

Wherthoruȝ þe vice of vnclennesse he fledde,   3820

who indulges in delicacies,

Of continence how maist þou siker be,

Of foodë delicat þat hast plente,   3822

¶ Ieronimus ad filiam virginem. 'O filia,' inquit, 'si apostolus castigauit corpus & in seruitutem redegit.'

(547)

and is young? ¶ And specialy now in þi youthës hete [1] ? "   3823

ffor who so wilneth to be contynent,

Superfluous pleasures must be given up. Many a lust superflu mot he lete,

And lykerous ; by mesure, his talent

Mesúre he moot ; whan resoun is regent   3827

Of man, þan regneþ no delicacie ;

Resoun, a man defendeth fro folye.   3829

¶ Seneca. Si continenciam diligis, circumcide superflua & voluptuosa.

(548)

Wine buries Wit, ¶ The wynës delicat, and swete and strong,   3830

Causen ful many an inconuenience ;

If þat a man outrageously hem fonge,

Thei birien [2] wit, and fórbeden scilence

[leaf 67 a] Of conseil ; thei outraien pacience,   3834

fires Lechery, and kills Body and Soul. Thei kyndlen ire, and firen liccherie,

And causen both body and soulë dye.   3836

(549)

It is very dangerous for a Prince. ¶ And trewëly [3] it is ful perilous   3837

Vnto a princë, whiche þat hath a land

In gouernance, in þat be vicïous ;

It nedeth him take heede vnto his hand,

þat that vicë him combre not ; for and   3841

It do, he schal noght regnë but a throwe :

fful many a man haþ éxcesse ouerthrowe.   3843

---

[1] hete R, hede H.   [2] birien R, biren H.
[3] trewly H, truly R.

(550)

¶ Daniel*is*
vi°. Eadem
nocte inter-
fectus est
Baltasar, Rex
Caldeus, &
Darius med*us*
successit in
regno, &c.

¶ Of babiloynë, þe kyng Baltasar,   3844 Drunkenness cost Belshazzar his life.
  Nat haddë ben I-pryuëd of his lyf,
If he of dronkenessë[1] hadde be war ;
  But for þat he þerin was défectyf,
  It of his deth was *ve*rray causatyf ;   3848
    By nyghtertale he was slayn by kyng dárie ;
  Thus payeth gloto*u*n éxcesse hir salárie.   3850

(551)

¶ Reg*um* I.
capitulo xxv°.
Cor Nabal
iocundum
erat ebrius
enim nimis,
&c.
Machabeo-
r*um* xxviij°.
¶ Et c*um*
inebriatus
esset Simon
& filii e*ius*,
surexit tholo-
meus, &c.

¶ Thorugh drunkenesse, how took his deth Nabal ?
  And how slow Tholome also Symoun ?
Allas ! þat drynkë so man seruë schal !
  How leidë Lothës doghtres hem a-down It let Lot's daughters lie with him,
  By hir fadir ? whan his discrecïoun   3855
    Was dreynt with wyn, he with hem fleschely delte,
    And þerof no thing ne wistë nor[2] feelte.   3857

(552)

¶ Genes*is*
xix°. Veni,
inebriem*us*
eum vino,
dormiamus-
q*ue* cum eo,
vt reser*u*are
possim*us* ex
patre n*ostro*
semen, &c.
Iudith. *capi-*
tulo 22°.

¶ How was eek Oloférnë, by Iudith   3858 and Judith slay Holofernes.
  The wo*m*man slayn, but þorugh his drunkenesse ?
What prince it be, þat spotted is þer*with*,
  His welthe haþ but a brotil stablenesse :
  Of swichë stories mo wolde I expresse,   3862 [leaf 67 *b*]
    But for I noght ne can, I lete hem passe ;
    I am as lewed and dulle as is an asse.   3864

(553)

¶ With litel foodë,[3] cóntent is natúre ;   3865 Nature is content with little.
  And bet þe body farith wiþ a lite,
Than whan it charged is out of mesúre.
  Lookë what þing may þe body profite,
  And þe soule in þe samë schal delite ;   3869
    What þing þat it distempereth & dissesith,
    The soule it hurteth, for it god displesith.   3871

---

[1] drunkenesse R, dronkenes H.   [2] nor R, or H.
[3] foode R, food H.

(554)

The evils of
Wrath,
Envie, and
Lechery.

¶ Wratthë, þe body of man inward fretith,   3872
    And god þer-wiþ displesid is ful sore ;
  Envie also of god and man hir getith
    Lik thank and ese, and schal do euermore ;
    And leccherie, as techiþ smertës lore,   3876
      The body wastith, and þe soulë grevith,
      And foodë delicat þerto man meevith.   3878

(555)

A full belly

¶ Be-holde also, whan þat þe paunche is ful,   3879
    A fumë clymbith vp in-to þe heed,
  And makiþ a man al lustles and al[1] dul ;

makes a man
as heavy as
Lead.

  He vexith[2] heuy as a peece of leed.
    Who-so þat þan woldë yeue him reed   3883
      To looke in a book of deuocïoun,
      I trowe in ydel were his mocïoun.   3885

(556)

Yet, ask him
to drink :
he will, and
go to women
too.

¶ But conseil him to trotte vnto þe wyn,   3886
    And, for al his excesse and his outrage,
  He þerto wole assentë wel and fyn,
    And þerë wole he outen[3] his langáge,

[leaf 68 a]

    And do to Bachus and Venus homáge ;   3890
      ffor non of hem two can be wel from othir,
      Thei loue as vel[4] as doth sustir & brothir.   3892

(557)

  And aftir moot he rownë with a pilwe,   3893
    His lyfles resouns þerë to despende.

Why will we
rational
creatures
war against
Reason ?

  We beestës resonable, allas ! whi wil we
    Ageyn resoun werrye, and hir offende ?
    O goodë[5] god ! thy gracë to vs sende,   3897
      That we may fle suche superfluite,
      And al þing that is foo to chastite !   3899

---

[1] aﬁ R, *om.* H.   [2] wexeth R.   [3] uttre R.
[4] wele R.   [5] goode R, good H.

[§ 9.] De Regis Magnanimitate.

(558)

Off magnanimite now wole I trete,[1]
  þat is to seyn, strong herte or grete corage,
Whiche in knyghthode haþ stablisshed hir sete.[2]
  Ye, gracious Prince, of blode and of lynage
  Descendid ben, to haue it in vsage ;
    Mars haþ euer ben frend to ȝour worþi lyne ;
    Ye moot of kyndë to manhode enclyne.

3900   Magnanimity is great-heartedness.

3904

3906

(559)

He þat is strong of corage and of herte,—
  Yf he lordschipës haue, or grete richesse,
Or þat fortunës stynge hym ouerthwerte,[3]—
  Is alwey on[4] in welthe and in distresse ;
  He, lucre and los, weyeth in euenesse ;
    He settiþ litel by good temperel ;
    How þe worlde schape, he takiþ it ay wel.

3907   The strong man

is ever one, in weal or
3911   woe.

3913

(560)

¶ But for to speke of corage of a kyng,
  he of his peple oweþ be so cheer,
That hir profet he moot for any þing
  Promotë wit his myght and his power.
  ¶ And for his reme and him take him so neer,
    That vnto þe perilës of bataille
    He moot him puttë, and in hem trauaylle,

3914   [leaf 68 b]

A King should

3918   put himself in Peril for his Realm,

3920

(561)

¶ And in diffense of holy chirche also,
  And for oure feith putte him in iupartye[5] ;
Othir causes ben ther but fewë mo,
  Whi a kyng aughte to bataylë hym hye,
  And in tho causes drede him not to dye,
    But kythe hym a good knyght a-mong his foos :
    Thus wonne is magnanymyteës loos.

3921   and to defend Holy Church.

3925

3927

---

[1] This page is illuminated.—G. E.   [2] sete R, fete H.
[3] fortune . . ouerthwert R, fortunes . . ouerthwete H.
    [4] one R.   [5] iuperdie R, partye H.

(562)

As one Limb defends the whole Body,

¶ Rigĥt as we seen by reson and natúre,   3928
 Part of mannys body diffendetĥ al ;
As an arme putteþ him in áuenture
 ffor þe body, þat nat *perische* it schal,

so a King must his folk.

Right so a kyngës chertë special,   3932
 If he god loue, and his peple, & his[1] land,
Whan nede is, mot diffende hem wiþ his hande.

(563)

¶ Thoruӡ grete[2] emprises wonne is hy reno*un* ; 3935
 Renoun is callëd glorie & honour ;

Greatheart faces Death,

Magnanim*ite* haþ þis condicïoun,
 That in bataile, how scharp þat be þe stour,
Hym leu*ere* is to suffre dethës schour, 3939

and does not flee.

 Than cowardly and schamëfully flee,
 So manly of euráge and herte is he. 3941

(564)

[leaf 69 *a*] It deals only with high and virtuous things.

¶ He medleth neu*ere* but of þingës grete, 3942
 And hye, and v*ertuous* ; he neu*ere* is meeved
With smalë thingës, as the bookës trete ;
 And swiche a drede haþ for to be rep*reued,*
That vnto þing þat may be knowe or p*reued* 3946
 ffor vilonous, or foul, or répreeuáble,
He neu*ere* obeieþ, þis knyӡt honuráble. 3948

(565)

The Athenian general, Codrus,

¶ Thane I rede of oon clepet[3] Coadrus, 3949
 That was prince of þe oost of Athinyens,
How in þe feeld a lawë made was þus
 Twixt his host and hem of Polipolens—
With triumphë schuldë[4] þat part go þens, 3953
 Whos duc or Princë were vnarmëd slawe
In habit straungë ; lo ! swiche was þe lawe. 3955

¶ De magnanimitate Coadri Principis excercitus atheni*sis.*

---

   [1] his, *om.* R. [2] grete R, *om.* H.
[3] I haue yredde of one clept R. [4] shulde R, schuld H.

(566)

¶ Him leuer was him selfen for to dye,   3956 would sooner die than see his men suffer.
  And his men liuë, þan se hem be-stad
So streitë, þat by violent maistrie
  His foos hadde hem venqwissht or ouer-lad.
A-dayës now is non swiche chierte had ;   3960
  Algatës I ne can nat seen it vsid,
Knyghtës ben loth þerof to ben accused.   3962

(567)

¶ O worthi Prince ! I truste in ʒour manhode,   3963 Prince Henry, I trust you will humble our Foes' Pride.
  Medlid wiþ prudence and discrecïoun,
That ʒe schulle makë many a knyʒtly rode,
  And þe pride of oure foos thristen adoun.[1]
Manhode and witt conquéren hy renoun ;   3967
  And qwo-so[2] lakkiþ outhir of þe tweyne,
Of armës wantiþ þe bridél and reyne.   3969

(568)

¶ Yf[3] þe ordre of knyghthode be resceyuëd,   3970 [leaf 69 b]
A Knight must be prudent.
  fful nedeful is a man to be prudent,
Ellës þat host may lightly be disceyuëd
  That is vnto his gouernance I-bent ;
Presumpcïon[4] is disobedient   3974
  Al day, and by wisdom not wiłł him gie,
Ałł iustifieth his obstýnacie.   3976

(569)

¶ Ofte in batailës hath be seen or this,   3977 An unwise leader has often ruind an army.
  A sydë suffred hath discomfiture,
Whiche an vnwys heed gïed hath amys.
  What knyght on hym takith þat charge or cure,
If he in knyghtly honur schal endure,   3981
  Him oghte endowëd ben of sapience,
And haue in armës greet experience.   3983

---

[1] Hoccleve's trust was fulfild at Agincourt, &c.
[2] who so R.   [3] Yf R, Of H.   [4] Presumptuous R.

(570)

Skill in Battle is worth more than Hardihood.

¶ Experience and art in a[1] bataille,　　　　3984
　　Of þe prudent knyght morë may profite,
Than hardinesse or forcë may auaille
　　Of him þat þerof knoweþ noght or lite.
Hardinesse, in effecte, nat worth a myte　　3988
　　Is to victorious conclusïoun,
　　But wiþ hym medle art, wit, and resoun.　3990

(571)

Knowledge and Bravery joind bring Victory.

¶ Whan reueled wit and manly[2] hardynesse　3991
　　Ben knytte to-gidre, as ȝok of mariage,
Ther foloweþ of victórie þe swetnesse ;
　　ffor to sette on hym whettith his coráge,
And wit restreyne his wil can & aswage　　3995
　　In tymë duë, and in[3] couenáble ;
　　And thus tho two ioynt ben ful profitable.　3997

(572)

[leaf 70 a 4] But be a knyght wys or coragëous,　　3998
　　Or haue hem bothe at onès at his lust,

But Love of Good must be with em. If þat his herte of good be désirous,
　　On his manhode is ther but litel trust.
God grauntë knyghtès rubbe away the rust　4002
　　Of couetise, if it hir hertës cancre,
　　And graunte hem picche in souffisance hir ancre.

[§ 10.] **Quod rex non debet felicitate**m **suam pon**ere in diuiciis.

(573)

Now, for as moche as magnanymyte　　　　4005
　　May no foot holde, if þat þe herte of man
Gretly vnto richesse enclynëd be,

A King must not delight in Riches. Than is þe bestë reed þat I see can,
　　A kyng þer-in delyte hym naght ; for whan　4009
　　His herte is in þat vicë ficched hye,
　　Smal prowesse in hym wole it signifie.　　4011

---

[1] a R, *om.* H.　　[2] reuled . . manly R, reueled . . namly H.
[3] due and R.　　[4] This page is illuminated.

(574)

And if a kyngës honour schal be queynt[1] 4012   Folk won't trust a covetous King.
  With a foul and a[1] wrecched couetise,
His peples trust in hym schal be ful feynt[1] ;
  A kyng may naght gouérne hym in þat wise ;
The coueitous may do no gret emprise ; 4016
  ffor whan his hertë lurketh in his cofre,
  His body to batayle he dar not profre. 4018

(575)

If þat a kyng[1] sette his felicite 4019   A money-grasping King ruins his people.
  Principally on rychesse & moneye,
His peple it torneþ to aduersite,
  ffor he ne rekkeþ in what wise or weye
He pile hem : allas ! þat kyngës nobleye 4023   [leaf 70 *b*]
  Turnë schulde into style of tirannye !
  Allas ! the peril, harme, and vilenye ! 4025

(576)

¶ God I byseeche, your hert to[2] enlumyne, 4026   I pray God that you, Prince Henry, may not be devild so !
  Gracïous princë, þat þe feend our foo
No power hauë so your hertë myne,
  But of his gracë kepë yow ther-fro,
And grantë yow to gouernë yow so 4030
  As most holsom is for bodý and soule ;
  That desire I, by God and by seynt Poule. 4032

(577)

¶ Whan that Marcus Curcius, a Romeyn, 4033   Marcus Curtius, when offerd money to raise a siege,
  Vnto þe Beneventans seegë leide,
ffor he was poore, as þat þey herdë seyn,
  They a grete somme of gold hym sente, & preyde
Withdrawe his seege ; and he answerde and seide,
  " To hem retourneth / þat yow hider sente,   sent it back.
  And thus to hem declareth myn entente : 4039

¶ Qualiter Marcus Curcius dixit, *quod* mallet diuites ha-bere suo mandato obedi-entes, *quam* diues ipsemet esse.

---

[1] a R, *om.* H.   [2] hert to R, herte H.

REGEMENT.   L

(578)

¶ " Seye hem, Marcus Curcïus leuer is   4040
   Richë men haue at his commandëment,
Than to be riche hym-self ; tellë hem this :
   He may with gold not be corrupt, ne blent ;
   Of force of men eek, þey ben impotent   4044
      To venqwisshe hym ; for þere hir art schal faile,
      Hir blyndë profers schal hem noght auaile." 4046

(579)

¶ To Alisaundre, as I schal tellen here,   4047
   A knyght, whiche was vnto hym specïal,
Thus spake, and blamed hym in þis manere :
   He seide, " if oure goddës[1] thy body smal,
   To thi gredy desire had maad egal,   4051
      Al þe world haddë nouȝt be súffisant
      To han receyuëd so large a Geaunt.   4053

(580)

¶ "ffor with þi riȝt honde, thow þe orient   4054
   Shuldest han touchid, I am sure of þat ;
And with þi lift honde, eke þe occident ;
   Now, syn þat þy[2] body answérith nat
   Vnto þi willë, what may[3] I sey, what?   4058
      Ethir þou art a man, or god, or nouȝt ;
      Mechil of þe, merueyle I in my þought.   4060

(581)

¶ " If þou be god, thow folow most his trace,   4061
   And nouȝt men of her gode robbe or be-reue,[4]
But hem releue, & do hem ese and grace.
   If þou be man, considere eke, by thy leue,
   þou art mortél, þou mayst be dede or eue.   4065
      If þou be no þing, þe putte out of mynde,
      Os[5] he þat is of no nature or kynde.   4067

---

[1] goddes R, gooddes H.   [2] þy R, *om.* H.   [3] shaﬅ R.
    [4] nor reue R.   [5] As R.

(582)

¶ " Ther is no hye estate so sadde and stable, 4068 No King is so stable that he may not fall.
Remembre wele,[1] lat it nat be for-ȝete,
But he to falle in perile is ful able.
By deeth, a leon maad is briddës mete,
And bestës also his flessh gnawe & frete." 4072
þe answere of þe kyng, naught haue I herde ;
My booke not telleth how he was answerde. 4074

(583)

¶ Pauper diogenes dicior erat Alexandro.

¶ Senek seith, the poër[2] Diogenes, 4075 Diogenes was richer than Alexander.
Kyng Alisandre in richessë past,
ffor he ne myȝt, as he seith doutëles,
Ȝeue hym so mochil golde, ne on hym cast,
¶ As he refusë wolde : O ! at the last, 4079 [leaf 71 *b*]
Men þinke shullen þei to mochil[3] haue had,
And of þis worldys muk be ful vnglad. 4081

(584)

Desire of good, a king mot leye apart, 4082 A King must not desire property, but a good Name.
And peyne him to purcháse him a good fame ;
Ther-in lat him laboure, and doon his art ;[4]
Ther nys no þing vnto[5] a worthi name ;
And if a kyng it lakke, it were his shame, 4086
And shame is contrarie vnto worthynesse ;
Gode lose desserued,[6] is grettest richesse. 4088

(585)

¶ And for largessë[7] wynneþ gode renoun, 4089 And as Bounty wins good renown, I'll treat of it.
Ther-of[8] þink I now, to trete a litil stounde ;
A prince & kyng of al a regioun
Mot avaricë thrist a-doune to grounde ;
To hym þat lith in hellë depe I-bounde, 4093
The,[9] auarice, by-takë I to kepe ;
Thow pynëpeny,[10] ther ay mot þou slepe ! 4095

---

[1] wele R, wile H.   [2] poore R.   [3] moche R.   [4] part R.
[5] vnto = comparable to.   [6] loos decerued R.
[7] largesse R, larges H.   [8] Therof, *pron.* throf.
[9] Or is 'the' an article ?   [10] pynchepeny R.

(586)

¶ Golde wolde, for[1] false enprisonyng,[2] a writ   4096
   Sue agayn þe, if he at largë were ;
But he so fast is in þi cofre shit,
   He may not out.   O fals enp*ri*sonere,

Largessë woldë be w*ith* shelde & spere   4100
   Euen in þi berde, if he brake out to-morwe,
   And for his sakë do thë care and sorwe.   4102

(587)

¶ Þou to largessë dost ful muchil wronge,   4103
   Þat haþ[3] hir s*er*uant vndir þi s*er*uage ;
On the, and noght on hir, is it a-longe
   Þat golde is lette to goon on hir message.

She haþ hym sent in many a viage   4107
   Or this, & that was the como*un* p*ro*fyte,
   The whiche to lette, is eu*er*e þi delyte.   4109

(588)

Largesse only noght list golde s*er*uant be   4110
   Vnto hir self ; but the peple, she wolde
Had as gode part of hir s*er*uyce as she ;
   To hir is al the como*un* peple I-holde,
   But þou makest þe peplës[4] hertës colde ;   4114
   Þou slest an hepë which þat she wolde saue ;
   Þou no wyte helpest, [5]þow he þi help[5] craue. 4116

(589)

Me list no morë speke of þe this tyme,   4117
¶ But of myne helply lady souereyne
Largessë, my ladý, now wil I ryme,
   And aftirward of þi cursëd careyne
I spekë shal ; nought o worde wol I feyne,   4121
   But as scripturës treten of the, wrecche,
   I touchë shal ; þe feende[6] the hennës fecche ! 4123

---

[1] for R, *om.* H.   [2] fals prisonyng R.   [3] hast R.
[4] peples R, peple H.
—[5] though he þyne help R, þow he þi peple H.
[6] deuell R.

[§ 11.] De Virtute Largitatis, & De Vicio Prodigalitatis.

(590)

¶ *Aristoteles de regimine principum, capitulo de largitate.* 'Si vis virtutem largitatis adquirere, considera posse tuum, tempora necessitatis & merita hominis,' &c.

Aristotil, of largesse, telleth this : [1]   4124
  Who vertuously largë list to be,
Concider first of what power he is,
And eke the tymës of necessite ;
And as þe men disseruen, so be fre ;   4128
  Yif in mesure vn-to þe indigent
  And the worthi, and þat is wel dispent.   4130

The right giver gives as he can,

and as men deserve.

(591)

[R, *om.* H] Qui al*iter* dat, reg*u*lam excedit largita*tis.* Q*ui* lar*giter* bona sua *hominibus* non indigentib*us* nulla ; et quicq*uid* dat*ur* indignis p*er*dit*ur* ; *et* qui fundit ult*ra* modum diuicias suas, cito veniet ad amara litora pa*u*p*er*tatis, *et* assimilat*ur* illi qui victoriam sup*er* se dat inimicis suis &c.

¶ And who doth othir wyse in his ȝeuyng,   4131   [leaf 72 *b*]
  Largesses rulë passith and excediteh ;
He nouther worthi is þank ne p*r*eysyng,
  That to hym þat no nede hath, ȝiftës bedith.
Of v*er*ray folye also it p*r*ocedith   4135
  To ȝeuë the onworthi ; for þat[2] cost
  Aħ mysse dispendid is, for it is lost.   4137

It's folly to give to the unworthy.

(592)

¶ And he þat díspenditeh out of mesúre   4138
  Shal tast a-none pouértes bitternesse ;
ffoole largesse is ther-to a v*er*ray lure.
  Of hem also he berith the lyknesse,
  That on him self, as þe booke berith witnesse,   4142
    Victórie ȝeueth to his enemys ;
    And he þat so dispendith, is not wyse.   4144

Immoderate giving ends in poverty.

(593)

¶ Largessë stant noght in mochil ȝeuynge,   4145
  But it is aftir þe wille & þe myght
Of hym þat ȝeueth aftir his hauyng*e* ;
  ffor it may som tyme happë þat a wigħt,
  Which of richessë berith nat but light,   4149
    ȝeueth but smal ; & ȝit larger is he
    Than he þat ȝeueth gretter quantite.   4151

Liberality depends on the will, not on amount.

---

[1] This page is illuminated, like the other section-head ones are.   [2] þi R.

(594)

¶ Aftir his goode, man may ȝeue & dispende   4152

Wher as nede is; but he þat al[1] dispendith,

And wastith al, shal him-selue first offende.

ffoolë largesse al day wrycchédly endith[2];

Many a man hir foule outragë shendith;   4156

But of largesse is goode þe[3] gouernaunce;

Bothë to god and man[4] it is plesaunce.   4158

(595)

¶ Evene as a mannës blood is norisshyng   4159

To his body, if it corrupt naght be,

So ben richesses to soulës feedynge

Holsom, if þei, were-as necessite

Axith, despent ben, and also if he   4163

Whiche þat hem wan, gat hem with riȝtwisnesse;

ffor heuene and helle is gotë[5] by richesse.   4165

(596)

¶ A crookid hors neuere is the bet[6] entecched,   4166

Al-þogh his bridel glistre of gold, and schyne;

Right so a man þat vicious is, & wrecched,

And his richésses gote haþ of rapyne,

And also euele as man can ẏmagyne,   4170

Despendith hem / naght for hem þe bet is,

But mochil wers; good is[7] take hede of þis.   4172

(597)

¶ He þat his flesche dispendith, and his blood,   4173

Mi lorde, in ȝour seruice, him ȝiftës bede;

There is largessë mesuráble good;

A kyng so bounde is, he moot doo so nede;

Seruice vnquyt and murdre, it is no drede,   4177

As clerkes writen, and desheritaunce,

Bifore al-mighty god auxen[8] vengeaunce.   4179

[1] aH R, hath al H.
[2] Foole large . . . wrecchedly endith R, Fool largesse . . .
wrycchedly enditith H.   [3] of largessés goode R.
[4] Bothe . . . to man R, Both . . . man H.   [5] ben goten R.
[6] the better is R.   [7] gode is to R.   [8] axen R.

(598)

¶ Of fool largessë wole I talke a space;   4180
   How it befil, I not in what contree,
But þere was oon named Iohn of Canace,[1]
   A richë man, & two douȝtres had he,   The rich John of Canace had 2 daughters.
That to two worthy men of a Citee   4184
     He wedded[2] leet; and þerë was gladnesse
     And reuel, morë than I can expresse.   4186

(599)

¶ The fadir, his doughtres and hir husbondes   4187   [leaf 73 *b*]
   Loued ful wele, and had hem leef & dere;
Tyme to tyme he ȝaf hem with his hondes   He gave them money freely.
   Of his goode passyngly; & þei swich chere
Him made, & were of so plesant manere   4191
     þat he ne wist how be bettre at ese,
     þei couden hym so wele cheryssh & please.   4193

(600)

¶ ffor he as mochil hauntid in partie   4194
   Hir house, as þat he did his ownë house;
þei held hym vp so with her flaterye,   They flatterd him.
   That of dispens he was outragëous,
And of goodë þei were ay desirous;   4198
     Al þat þei axed, haden þei redy;   He gave them all they askt,
     þei[3] euer weren on hym right[4] gredy.   4200

(601)

7 þis sely man contynued his outráge,   4201   till all his money was gone.
   Tyl al his goodë was disshid[5] & goone;
And when þei felt his dispenses a-swage,
   Thei wax to him vnkyndë right[6] anone;   Then they were unkind
   ffor after haddë[7] he cherishing none,   4205 to him.
     Thei wery weren of his companye:
     And he[8] was wyse, and shope a remedye.   4207

---

[1] This story, under different forms, was a very common one in the Middle Ages. One version will be found in my Latin stories, p. 28 . . . . the story of King Lear and his daughters is another version.—T. Wright, *De Reg.*, p. 199.   [2] wedden R.
[3] And they R.   [4] right, *om.* R H.   [5] wasted R.
[6] right R, *om.* H.   [7] hade R, had H.   [8] And he R, He H.

(602)

John of
Canace
borrows
£10,000,

¶ He to a marchaunt goose, of his notise,   4208
 Wich þat his trusty frende had be ful ʒore,
Besechyng hym, þat he wold hym cheuyse
 Of *ten thousand*[1] pounde, ne lenger ne more
 Than dayës thre, and he wolde it restore   4212

and takes it
home.

 At his day; þis was done; þe summe he hent,
 And to his ownë house þer-*with* he went.   4214

(603)

[leaf 74 *a*]
He asks his
Daughters
and their
husbands to
supper,

¶ And on the mornë, prayde he to soupere   4215
 His sonnës both & his doughtres also.
Þei to him cam, *with*-owten any daungere :
 How þat þei ferden, lat I passe and goo ;
 Thei ferden wel, *with*-outen wordës moo ;   4219
  To his konyng, he grete disport hem made,
  He did his myght to chere hem, & to glade. 4221

(604)

¶ Aftir souper, whan þei hir tymë sye,   4222
 Þei toke her leue, & home þei wolde al-gate ;
And he answerd, and seyde hem sekirly,

and makes
them stay the
night with
him.

 "This nyʒt ye shul nat passe out of the gate ;
 Your house is fer, and it is dyrke and late ;   4226
  Neuen it nat, for it shal nat be-tyde ;"
  And so al nyʒt he made hem to abyde.   4228

(605)

He puts them
next him,
with only
a chinky
partition
between.

¶ The fadir logëd hem, of sly purpóse,   4229
 In a chambre next to his ioynyng ;[2]
ffor by-twix hem nas þer but a *par*close
 Of bordë, nauʒt but of homly[3] makyng ;
 þurgh out þe which, at many a chynnyng,   4233
  In echë chambre þei myghten[4] beholde,
  And see what othir dyden, if þat þei wolde. 4235

---

[1] 'x. Mł.' H, ten thousand R.   [2] ioynyng R, ionyng H.
[3] bord . . . homely R.   [4] myghten R, myght H.

(606)

¶ I kan nat sey how þei slepten þat nyȝt ; 4236
 Also it longith[1] nat to my matere ;
But on þe morwë, at brodë day liȝt   Next morn-
 The fadir roose ; and for þei shulden here   ing
What þat he dyd, in a boystous manere 4240
 Vnto his chist, which þat[2] three lokkys hadde, he unlocks
 He went, and þer-at wrested he ful sadde. 4242 his chest of
                 gold,

(607)

¶ And when it was I-opned & vnshytte, 4243 [leaf 74 *b*]
 þe bagged gold by þe marchaunt hym lent
He hath vncofred, and streyte forþ wi*th* it
 Vnto his beddis feete gone is & went.
What doth þan þis fel[3] man & right[4] prudent, 4247
 But out þis golde on a tippet hath shotte, and shoots it
 That in þe baggës leftë[5] þere no grotte. 4249 all out on a
                 cloth.

(608)

¶ And al þis did he noght but for a wyle, 4250
 As þat ye shul wel knowen aftirwarde ;
He shope his sonnës & doughtres begile.[6]
 His noysë made hem dressen hem vpwarde ; His Daugh-
 þei cast her erës to his chambre-warde, 4254 ters and Sons-
                in-law hear
 And herd of golde þe russhyng and the so*u*n, him,
 As that he rudëly threwe hem ado*u*n. 4256

(609)

¶ And to þe p*ar*clos þei hem hast and hye, 4257 and thro' the
 To wyte and knowë what her fadir wrouȝt. chinks see
In at þe chynnës of þe borde þei prye,   him handling
 And sigh how he amonge þe nobles sought the gold,
 If défectif were any, as hem þought ; 4261
 And on his nayl he threwe hem oft & cast, which he
 And baggëd hem and cofred at the last ; 4263 coffers again.

---

[1] longeth R, logith H. [2] þat, *om.* H R. [3] felle R.
[4] right, *om.* H R. [5] left H R. [6] to begile R.

(610)

¶ And opned his dore, & dounë goth his wey.   4264

The Daughters come down,

And aftir blyue, out of hir bedde þei rise,
And cam doune eke : hir fadir þanken þey
Of his gode cherë, in hir bestë[1] wyse,—
And al was for þe goldës couetyse,—   4268

and set off home.

And to gon hoom, þei axid of hym leue ;
Thei ben departyd, and þei þere hym leue.   4270

(611)

[leaf 75 a]
They talk of their Father's gold.

¶ Walkyng homward, þei iangeld fast, & speeke   4271
Of þe golde which þei sey hir fadir haue.
Oon seyd, " I wondre ther-on ; " "and I eke,"
Quod a-nothir, " for, also god me saue,
ȝistir-day, thogh I shuld in-to my graue   4275
Haue crept, I durst on it haue leyde my lyfe,
That golde with hym nought haddë[2] ben so ryfe."

(612)

¶ Now lat hem muse on þat, what so hem list ;   4278

He, John of Canace, takes the Gold back to the man who lent it him, and goes to his Sons-in-law.

And to hir fadir now wol I me dresse.
He al þis golde takith out of his chist,
And to þe marchaunt payde it more & lesse,
þankyng hym often[3] of his kyndënesse ;   4282
And þennës goth he homë to his mete,
And to his sonnës house when he had ete.   4284

(613)

They make much of him,

¶ When he cam thidir, thei made of hym more   4285
þan þat þei werë wont, by many folde ;
So gret disport þei made hym noȝt ful ȝore.

and say everything of theirs is at his command.

" ffadir," quod þei, " þis is your owne housholde ;
In feith, þer is no þing within oure holde,   4289
But it shal be at your comandëment ;
Wolde god þat ye weren at[4] oure assent,   4291

---

[1] best H R.   [2] hade R, had H.   [3] ofte R, oft H.
[4] werest H, were of R.

(614)

¶ þennë[1] we shulden ay to-gedir dwelle."   4292   They ask him
Al what þei menten, wist he wel I-now :   to live with
"Sonnës and doughtres," quod he, " soth to telle,   them.
Mi wille is goode also to be with yow.   He agrees
How shuld I myrier be? nat wot I how,   4296   to do so.
Than with yow for to be continuel ;
Your companyë liketh me ful wel."   4298

(615)

¶ Now shope it so, þei helden house in fere,   4299   [leaf 75 b]
Sauf þe fadir ; and as þei lough & pleyde,
His doughtres bothë with a[2] lawghyng chere   His daugh-
Vn-to hir fadir spake, and þus þei seyde,   ters ask him
                              how much
And to assoile hir questïoun hym preyde :[3]   4303   he has in his
                              Chest.
   " Now, godë fadir, how mochil monye
   In your strong bounden chist is, we yow preye?

(616)

¶ " *Ten thousand*[4] pounde," he seide, & lyëd lowde,   £10,000 he
   "I told hem," quod he, " nat ful long agoo,   says;
And þat as redely as þat I cowde.
ʒif ye wil aftir þis do to me so   and he'll
                              leave it them
As ye haue done by-fornë, þan al tho   4310   if they keep
   I in my testament disposë shal   kind to him.
   ffor your profytë ; yours it shal ben al."   4312

(617)

¶ Aftir þis day, þei all in oon house were,   4313   So they live
Til þe day com of þe fadirs deying.   together.
Goode mete and drynke, and clothës for to were
He had, and payëd nat to his endyng.
When he sey þe tyme of his départyng,   4317   His death
His sonës and his doughtres did he calle,   draws nigh.
And in this wise he spakë to hem alle :   4319

---

[1] þen H, Than R.   [2] bothe with R, both with H.
[3] As lines 4304-5, MS. Reg. 17 D vi, has :
     " What so euer it be, koth the fader, now
       And I kan or may, I shaƚƚ it telle yow."
And for lines 4310-12 it has—
     "As ye haue done, ye shuƚƚ haue alle tho."
[4] 'X^{m.}' H, Ten thousand R.

(618)

He'll be-
queath the
money (not)
in his chest:
¶ " Nat purpose I make othir testament,   4320
  But of þat is in my strong chist I-bounde ;
And riȝt anone, or I be hennës[1] hent,

£100 to
Preachers,
£100 to Grey
Friars,
£50 to Car-
melites.
  An *hundred pound*[2] of nobles gode and rounde,
  Takith to *pre*chours ; tarryeth it no stounde ;   4324
    An *hundred pound*[2] eke to þe frerës grey,
    And carmës *fifty*[3] : tarrye it nought, I sey.   4326

(619)

[leaf 76 *a*]
The keys of
the chest
are with the
Friars.
¶ " And when I buried am, of hem the keyes   4327
  Of my chist takith, for þat[4] þei hem kepe ;
By eu*er*y keyë[5] writen ben the weyes
  Of my wille." þis golde was nat suffred slepe ;
  It was anone dalt, for hir hertis depe   4331
    Stak in his bounden cofre, and al hir hope
    Was godë bagges þerin for to grope.   4333

(620)

His Daugh-
ters and
Sons-in-law
pay these
and other
bequests.
¶ To eu*er*y chirche and recluse of þe toune,   4334
  Bad hem eeke of golde ȝeue[6] a quantite :
Al as he bad, þei weren *pr*est and boune,
  And did it blyuë ; but, so mot I the,
  ffful slily he disceyuyd þis meyne,   4338
    His sonnës and his doughtres boþ, I mene ;
    Hir berdës shauëd he right smothe & clene.   4340

(621)

They bury
John's
corpse,
¶ When he was dede, and his exéquies do,   4341
  Solenily[7] þei to þe frerës ȝide,
And bad þo keyes delyu*er*e hem vn-to ;
get the keys
of the chest,
  And as þat[8] þei hem beden, so þei dide.
  Tho ioyful sonës dresse hem to þe stide   4345
    Wher as þis strongë bounden chistë[9] stoode ;
    But or þei twynned þens, þei pekkid moode. 4347

---

[1] hens H R.   [2] 'C.ħ' H, hundred pounde R.
[3] *MS.* 'l,' fifty R.   [4] þat, *om.* H R.   [5] key H R.
[6] yeue eke of golde R.   [7] Solempnely R.
þat, *om.* H R.   [9] strong . . . chist H (chest) R.

(622)

¶ Thei opneden þe chist, & fonde riȝt nought   4348   open it,
But a passyngly greet sergeántës mace,   and find only
In which ther gaily made was and I-wrought   a mace
This samë scripture: "I, Iohn of Canace,
Makë swhich testament here in þis place;   4352
Who berith charge of othir men, & is   and a mock
Of hem despisëd, slayn be he with this."   4354   for them-
selves.

(623)

¶ Among folïes aH is noon, I leue,   4355   [leaf 76 *b*]
More þan a[1] man his gode ful largëly   Gifts in hope
Despende, in hopë[2] men wol hym releue   of future help
Whan his gode is despendid vtterly[3];   are a great
The indigént men setten no þing by.   4359   folly.
I, Hoccleue, in swich[4] case am gilty, þis me touchith,[5]   I, Hoccleve,
   am guilty
So seith pouert, which oon foole large him vouchith.   herein;

Hoccleve de
seipso.[6]
(*In a later
hand.*)

(624)

¶ ffor þogh I neuer were of hy degree,   4362   for tho' I
Ne haddë[7] mochil gode ne gret richesse,   never was
Ȝit hath þe vice of prodigalite   prodigal,
Smerted me sore, & done me hevynesse.
He þat but litil hath, may done excesse   4366
In his degree, as wel as may þe riche,
Thogh hir dispenses werë nat elyche.[8]   4368

(625)

¶ So haue I plukked at my pursë[9] strynges,   4369   and have
And made hem often for to[10] gape & gane,   beggard
þat his smal stuf hath take hym to his wynges,   myself,
And hath I-sworne to be my welthës bane,
But if releef a-way my sorowe plane;   4373
And whens it comë shal, can I nought gesse,   unless you,
Mi lorde, but it procede of your hynesse.   4375   Prince, help
me.

---

[1] a R, *om.* H.   [2] hope R, hop H.   [3] vttirly R, viterly H.
[4] suche R, swich H.   [5] See "am gilty / þis me touch / ith."
[6] R. has Nota de prodigalitate Occleve.   [7] hade R, had H.
[8] be not eliche R, were not lyche H.   [9] purses R, purs H.
[10] for to R, for H.

(626)

I, Hoccleve,
repent my
evil life.

¶ I me repent of my mysrewly lyfe[1];   4376
    Wherfor, in þé wey of sauacïoun
I hope I be ; my dotage éxcessyfe
Hath put me to swich castigacïoun,

Poverty now
sways me.

þat indigence hath dominacïoun   4380
    On me ; o ! had I help, now wolde I thryue,
    And so ne did[2] I neuer ʒit in my lyue.   4382

(627)

[leaf 77 a]
My Annuity
is in arrear.

¶ My yeerly guerdoun, myn annuite,   4383
    That was me graunted for my long labóur,
Is al behynde, I may naght payëd be,
    Whiche causeth me to lyuen[3] in langour.

Prince
Henry,
help me !

O liberal prince ! ensample of honour !   4387
    Vnto your gracë lyke it to promoote
    Mi poore estat, and to my woo beth boote !   4389

(628)

¶ And, worþy prince, at cristës reuerence   4390
    Herkeneth what I schal seyn, and be noght greued,
But lat me stande in your beneuolence ;
    ffor if myn hertës wil wiste were, and preeued,

I love you,
and desire
your well-
being.

How yow to loue it stirëd is and meeved,   4394
    Ye schulden knowe, y your honour and welþe
    Triste and desire, and eek your soulës helþe. 4396

(629)

¶ In al my book[1] ye schul naght see ne fynde,   4397
    That I youre dedës lakke, or hem despreise ;
But for I woldë þat ye hadde in mynde

I write only
for your
renown,
and in good
faith.

Swich thyng[1] as your renoun myghte vp areyse,
    I write as my symple conceyt may peyse ;   4401
    And trustith wel, al þat my pennë seith,
    Proceedith of good herte and trewe, in feith. 4403

---

[1] See Hoccleve's 'Male Regle' in his *Minor Poems*, I, p. 25.
    [2] so did R.   [3] lyue H, liue R.

(630)

¶ *Aristoteles de regimine, capitulo de vicio super-fluitatis.* "O *Alexander, firmiter dico tibi, quod quis rerum superflue con-tulerit domi-naciones, vl-tra quod reg-num suum possit suffi-cere, talis Rex procul dubio destruit & destruitur.*'

¶ What kyng þat dooth more éxcessif despenses   4404

    Than his land may to suffice or atteyne,

Schal be destruëd, after þe sentences

    Of Aristotle ; he schal naght fle þe peyne.

ffoolë[1] largésse and avarice, þo tweyne,   4408

    If þat a kyng eschue, & largë be,

    Reioyse he schal his rëal dignite.   4410

The king who spends unduly shall be destroyd.

(631)

¶ How fool largesse a kyng destroyë may,   4411

    As blyuë wole I vnto yow declare :

ffool largessë yeueþ so moche a-way,

    That it þe kyngës cofres makeþ bare,

    And þanne awakiþ poorë peples care ;   4415

    ffor al þat sche dispendid haþ & wastid,

    They moot releuë, therto be þey hastid.   4417

[leaf 77 b] Foolish giving beggars a king, and troubles his folk.

(632)

¶ The Tylere[2] witħ his porë cote and land,   4418

    That may vnnethës gete his sustenance,

And he þat naght haþ but labóur of hand,

    Ben often put vnto ful smert nusance.

    Good is be-ware of goddës long suffrance ;   4422

    Thogh he to venge hym tarie, & be suffráble,

    Whan his strook cometh, it is importáble.   4424

The poor Tiller and Labourer

are often distrest.

(633)

¶ Naght speke I ageyn eidës[3] vttirly,   4425

    In sum cas þey ben good and necessárie ;

But whan þey goon to custumáblely,

    The peple it makiþ for to curse and warie :

    And if þey ben despended in contrárie   4429

    Of þat þey graunted of þe peple were,

    The morë grucchen þey þe cost to bere.   4431

I don't object to all Aids ;

but when they're too frequent, they make folk curse.

[1] Foole R, Fool H.   [2] tilyer R.
[3] dysmes (tenths) R.

(634)

When folk
have emptid
purse and
back, they
grumble.

¶ The pot so longë to þe watir gotħ,   4432
    That hoom it cometh at þe laste y-broke.
Whan þat þe peple, with a cherë loth,
    Hir purs y-emptid[1] haue, & eek hir poke,
Hem þynkith þat þey ouer nyh ben soke.   4436
        What harm of þat to kynges haþ be-tid,
        Scripturës tellen; it may nought[2] ben hid.   4438

(635)

[leaf 78 a]

Flatterers
hide Lords'
soul-salve
from them,

¶ But fauel naght[t] reportith tho scripturis ;   4439
    His lordës soulë salue, he from hym[4] hydith ;
He besieth hym so in sly portraituris,
    þat homly trouthë naght with hym abidith ;
The swetë venym of his tongë gydeth   4443
        His lord vnto þe valeie of dirknesse,
        If he gouérne hym by his fykilnesse.   4445

¶[3]*Aristoteles
eodem capit-
ulo.*[3] Subditi
vero propter
iniuriam cla-
mauerunt
ad deum ex-
celsum &
gloriosum.

(636)

¶ The trewë man, if he may apparceyue   4446
    A défaute in his lord, as othir while
It happith, he his lord it redith weyue,
    And bit hym to *ver*tu hym reconsile ;

and get
thanks, while
the true man
is snubd.

And yit fauel, þe net of fraude and gile,   4450
        The þank hath, and þat othir þe maugree :
        O god! þat *ver*ray trouþe art for to see.   4452

(637)

The hider of
truth trom
lords, pro-
vokes God.

¶ Who þat, fro[5] drede of any lord or syre,   4453
    Hydeth þe trouthe, and naght wil it out seie,
He vppon hym pr*ou*okith goddës yre,
    ffor þat he more of man than god[6] hath eye.
They þat þe trouthë of hir hertes bywreye   4457
        To lordës, and telle hem hir wicked lyf,
        No grace in hem fynden for hir motyf.   4459

¶ *Augusti-
nus.* Quis-
quis metu
alicuius po-
testat*is* veri-
tatem occul-
tat, iram dei
super se pro-
uocat, quia
magis timet
hominem
quam deum.
¶ libere veri-
tatem *pre*-
dicantes &
praue vite
gesta argu-
uentes, non
habent gra-
tiam apud
homines, &c.

---

[1] purses empted R.
[2] nough H.   It may not be be heled in no wise ne hidde R.
[3]–[3] For this, R. has : Deficient*ibus* redd*itibus* et expen*sis*,
Reges extenderunt manus suas ad res et redd*itus* alienor*um*.
[4] soules salve fro hym he R.   [5] for R.
[6] of man than god R, of god and man H.

(638)

¶ But bet, for trouthe is to suffre turment,   4460

Than richëly enhauncëd be for glose.

If þis lyf herë be naght wel dispent,

¶ Augusti-
nus. Melius
est *pro* veri-
tate pati sup-
plicium,
quam adula-
cione bene-
ficium, &c.

I wot it wel, I wele it naght suppose,

God wole his regnë from vs schitte[1] & close.   4464

Here is þe way to peynë, or to blisse ;

Who so wel dooth, of yoye[2] he may naght misse.

(639)

Eternel god, the blessid trinite,   4467   [leaf 78 *b*]

Whiche þat[3] euery man of cristen byleeue

Knoweth an vndyuyded vnite,

His me*r*cy and his gracë kythe & preeue

In yow, my lord ; þat so your dedës cheeue   4471

As þat your soule, aftir þis lyf *present*,

To heuene blisse vp may be take & hent.   4473

[§ 12.]   **De Vicio Auaricie.**[4]

(640)

N ow go[5] we to þe Auericïous,[6]   4474

To whom non hábundancë may suffice.

A chynchë neu*ere* can be plentevous

Thogh al were his ; swiche is his couetise ;

To thriste ay aftir more, it is his gyse ;   4478

He is þe swolwe þat is neu*ere* ful :

At Auericë now haue here a pul.   4480

(641)

Sche may, as god forbede, vndo a[7] kyng   4481

Thurgh hire insaciable gredynesse.

Hire herte is sette vppon non oþer þing

But how sche may golde hepe ; al in dirknesse

Lurkith þe purchas of hire egrenesse ;   4485

In bagges vndir lok, hir gold sche thristeth ;

Al to þe cofre it[8] goth, and al sche chistith.   4487

[1] hide R.   [2] ioye R.   [3] that R, þa H.

[4] 'De vicio auaricie' is also in black in the margin, as a direction to the rubricator.   [5] go R, ga H.

[6] This page is illuminated.   [7] a R, *om.* H.   [8] it R, sche H.

(642)

A miser's
gold is
hidden,
and denied
to every one.

There is it hidde ; no sonne it seeþ, ne moone ;   4488

Thogh al þe world steruë schulde on a day

ffor lak of good, naght were it for to done

To borwe of hire ; euere is hir answere nay ;

That sche naght haþ, also sche swerith ay.   4492

[leaf 79 a] Hir nature is to kepe, and naght despende,

And hir desir of good ne hath non ende.   4494

(643)

Avarice is
immoderate
love for
riches,

¶ Auarice is a loue inmoderat,   4495

Richésses temporel for to purcháce ;

Sche besieth hir[1] in euerych estat ;

Sche shapith[2] hir al þe world to[3] embrace

ffro[4] þe morë to þe lessë ; hir trace   4499

To suë, studien men, seith Ysaye,

And sche þe thraldom is of Maumetrye.[5]   4501

¶ Scriptum
est, Auaricia
est amor im-
moderatus
adquirendi
temporalia, &
est pestis fere
omnes homi-
nes solicitans.
Vnde reg-
pheta ait
Ieremie vj°
A maiori vs-
que ad min-
orem omnes
student
Auariciam
&c.[6]

(644)

an excessive
covetousness
for others'
goods.

¶ Sche is a couetysë éxcessyf   4502

Of othres good ; & of hire ownë, sche

So streit and hard is, and so rétentyf,

That it profytë may in no degree.

O auericïous, what eilith þee ?   4506

þe goodës whyichë[7] ben vnto þe lent,

Why hydest þou ? I-wis þou wilt be schent.   4508

(645)

A miser is
wicked to
keep so many
men's living.

¶ Weenest þou þat þou doost naght wickedly,   4509

þat so many a manys sustenance

Thi self wiþ-holdest soul[8] ? yis, hardily.

Thow þat of richesse hast greet habundaunce,

And to þe nedy yeuest no pitaunce,   4513

No lesse offendist þou than he þat schakith

Men out of hire good, and from hem it takith.

¶ Iterum
scriptum est
Neque enim
minus est
criminis ha-
benti tollere,
quam cum
possis & ha-
bundans sis,
indigentibus
necessaria
denegare.

---

[1] desireth hye R.   [2] shapeth R, shapit H.   [3] to R, *om.* H.
  [4] For R, Fro H.   [5] mawmetrie R, Maumetye H.
  [6] R. adds : Avaricia est ydolorum *servitus.*   [7] which þat R.
  [8] so R.

(646)

¶ Thus may thy stylë liknëd be to thefte ;   4516
 As a theef in þis world is hangid here,
ffor good whiche þat he of þe peple refte,
 So schalt þou honge in helle, and bye it deere,
  But if so be, or þou goo to þi beere,   4520
  Thow córrectë thy greedy appetyt,
  And of streit kepynge emptë þy delyt.   4522

The Miser shall hang in Hell as a Thief hangs here.

[leaf 79 b]

(647)

¶ The breed of hungry peple þou with-holdist,   4523
 And schutest vp the nakid mennës cloth
That keuere hem sholde ; if þou oght of god toldist,
ffor to doo so, þou woldest be ful loth.
 Al þat þou getist, to hid place it goth.   4527
  As many men, hir good þow hem byreuest
  As þou releuë myghtest, and[1] it leuest.   4529

He keeps back men's bread and clothes.

¶ Item scriptum est. Esuriencium panis est quem tu detines ; nudorum vestimentum est quod tu recludis.
¶ Iterum scriptum est, Tantorum ergo te scias inuadere bona, quantorum de possessione tua poteris subuenire, & non vis. Prouerbiarum xxvij. Qui odit auariciam, longi fient dies eius.

(648)

¶ Who so þat fro þe poorë mannës cry[2]   4530
 Stoppith his erës, þogh he lowdë crye,
Schal naght be herde ; and more ouer, rede y,
 His dayës schulle encresse & multiplie
  That auerice hatith, þis is no lye.   4534
  Werse is no þing þan[3] to loue moneye,
  As þat Ecclesiasticus can seye.   4536

¶ Ecclesiastici x. Nichil iniquius quam amare pecuniam.

Nothing is worse than the love of Money.

(649)

¶ Ambrosë seith, war, man, þat þou ne schitte   4537
 With-in þi purs þe nedy peples[4] hele,
And to þe buriellës naght committe
 The lyf of poorë men ; ȝeue hem, & dele
  Part of þi good ; o, þy baggës vnsele ;   4541
  Opne hem ; hir knyttynge al to sore annoyeth ;
  Thy pynëd stuf, many a man destroyeth.   4543

¶ Ambrosius de officiis. Caueas ne intra loculos tuos includas salutem inopum, & tanquam in tumilo ne sepelias vitam pauperum.

Give to the poor!

---

[1] and thou R.
[2] R. has "Prov. xx°. Qui obturat aurem suam ad clamorem pauperis, ipse clamabit, et non exaudietur."
[3] than R, þat H.   [4] peples R, peple H.

(650)

¶ Thow seist per cas, "yf I no man byreue   4544
  His good, what wrong, myn owne is it to hyde

And multiplie?" o, chynchë! by þi leue,
  What seist[1] þou is þin? what was þin, þat tyde
  Thow cam in-to þis world, þou homycide?   4548

   Thow broghtist naght; claymë no propertee   *Scilicet* tem-
   Of thing þat oghtë communë[2] to be.   4550   pore necessi-
                                                              tatis R.

(651)

¶ Thi talkinge and þi clap is al of erthe,   4551   ¶ *Ysaie* xix°.
  And þe ground for-þi schal answere the,   de terra lo-
ffor þat þe loue of muk sittith so neer þe.   queris & de
  Of him þat hath of goodës gret plentee,   humo audie-
  Of god and man mochil axid schal be;   4555   *tur* eloquium
                                                           tuum *propter*
                                                           amorem
                                                           quem habes
                                                           ad sordes.
                                                           Luce xij. Cui

   Thow schalt be rekned with, heer-aftir,[3] chynche,   multum da-
   Where as þou schalt not at þe acountës pynche.   tum est mul-
                                                              tum queretur
                                                              ab eo a deo &
                                                              hominibus.

(652)

¶ By what[4] title þat þou getist þi good,   4558
  Thow countist naght þe value of a myte;
Thyn hert is euermore on gold so wood,
  That no thing ellës canst þou in[5] delite;

  Of consciencë rekkist þou so lite,   4562
   What goodis þat þou getist of rapyne,
   þou hem affermest by good title þyne.   4564

(653)

¶ ffeith and prowessë, leist þou vndir foote,   4565   ¶ Salustius
  And techist folk to haue in hem-self pride;   dicit: Aua-
And cruelte hath caght in þe swiche roote,   ricia fidem &
  That sche noght slippë may fro þe, ne slyde;   probitatem
                                                          subpeditat,
                                                          & docet homi-
                                                          nem in se

  And euery vertu throwest þou a-syde.   4569   habere super-
   O, euery prince and[6] kyng moot ben eschu,   biam & cru-
   In al maneere, of þi lym and þi glu.   4571   delitatem.

---

[1] seyest R.   [2] oght comon R.   [3] there as a R.
[4] what R, þat H.   [5] in, *om.* H, That in no . . . thow R.
[6] and R, or H.

(654)

¶ ffor ellës is it light to vndirstonde,   4572
  To euery man þat wit can & resoun,
It is nat likly, á kyng for to stonde   A king may
destroy his
folk by
Avarice.
  In his welthë but a litil sesoun,
ffor Auaricë may ben énchesoun   4576
  His peple to destroyen[1] and oppresse ;   [leaf 80 *b*]
And, as I saydë, so may fool largesse.[2]   4578

(655)

¶ ffool largesse is a sekenesse curable,   4579 Prodigali!y
is curable ;

¶ Dicit idem
philosophus,
quod prodi-
galitas est
morbus cura-
bilis, ab
egestate vel
etate.

  Outhir of indigence, othir ellës[3] age ;
He þat fool large in ȝouthe is, is ful able
  In eldë to abate it and aswage,
ffor agid folk ben more in þe seruage   4583
  Of auaricë þan ben folk in yowthe ;
And what I schal eek seyn, herkneth wel nowþe.

(656)

¶ Auaricia
est morb*us*
incurabilis,
vt idem dicit.

¶ Of nede eek may it curid ben, and helid ;   4586
  A man may so largë despenses make,   when all is
spent,
poverty
comes ;
Til al is good be díspendid and delid ;
  And whan his purs y-emptid is, and schake,
Than, begynneþ indigence a-wake,   4590
  By whiche he cured is of þe seekenesse
Of prodigalitee, or fool[4] largesse.   4592

(657)

¶ But auarice, he seith, incurable is ;   4593 but Avarice
is incurable :
it grows with
age.
  ffor ay þe more a man þerin procedith
And wexith olde, so mochil more I-wys,
  He auaricious is ; in him naght breedith
But thoght[5] and woo, for ay his hertë dreedith   4597
  His good to leese ; and morë for to hepe   [leaf 81 *a*]
His thoghtës stirten heere & þere, and lepe.   4599

---

[1] distroien R, destoyen H.
[2] H. wrongly puts st. 659 here, before sts. 655-8. R. puts st. 659 in its right place.
[3] or elles of R.   [4] foole R, ful H.   [5] thought R, toght H.

(658)

For a King,

¶ Now if þe heed of al a regioun,   4600
By whom þat al gouérned is and gyed,
Be of so seekly a condicïoun,
That it may by no curë be maistryed,
Thanne is he to þe wersë part applied ;   4604
And as the philosofre seith vs to,

Avarice is
worse than
Prodigality.

The lessë wikke is fool largesse of two.   4606

(659)

Worse,

¶ The philosofre preeueth Auarice   4607
Wel wersë þan is prodigalite :
By thre causes he halt it gretter vice :

1. because
a man can
recover from
it ;

ffirst, he seith, it is better seek to be,
Of a sekenesse or infirmite   4611
Of whiche a man may haue rekeueryng,
þan of swiche on as þer is non helyng.   4613

¶ Respice in
Egidio de
regimine
principum :
' probat phi-
losophus iiij⁰
ethicorum,
iij⁰ racione,
quod auaricia
peior est *pro*-
digalitate.
[R adds]
primo enim
melius est
infirmari
morbo cura-
bili *quam*
incurabili.

(660)

2. because it
is nigher to
Virtue :

¶ The seconde cause is, prodigalitee   4614
Is morë ny to vertu many del
Than Auerice ; and why, ye schul wele see :
He þat is liberal, naght list so wel
ffor to receyue any good or cateħ   4618
As yeuë, but what man þat is fool large
To take and yeuë, yeueth he no charge.   4620

[lf. 83 (81) *a*]
¶ *Secundo,*
probat *quod*
prodigalitas
est magis
propinqua
virtuti *quam*
Auaricia,
nam libe*ralis*
non libent*er*
recipit, sed
libent*er* dat,
quorum
vtrum*que* fa-
cit prodigus ;

(661)

¶ Wherfore he seiþ, þere is no difference   4621
Twixt[1] fool largesse and liberalitee,

and only
differs from
Liberality
because it is
too lavish,

Sauf þe fool largë, óf his imprudénce,
Of his dispenses is to dislauee,[2]
And yeueth there as oghtë naght to be ;   4625
And for what cause also, and for what skile
He yeuë schal, non hede he takë wile.   4627

non ergo
differt prodi-
gus a liber-
alitate, nisi
quod prodi-
gus non dat
vt debet, &
quib*us* debet,
nec cuius
gratia debet,

---

[1] Twixit H, Betwixt foole large R.   [2] See Hoccl. *Min. Poems* I.

(662)

quare cum prodigus non sit amator pecunie sicut nec liberalis, de facili prodigus fieri possit liberalis &c.

¶ And syn fool large, on gold settiþ his herte   4628   *so that it*
  No morë þan þe liberal, þan may   *can easily turn into*
ffool large into liberalite[1] sterte   *Liberality ;*
lightly ynow.[2] for *ver*tu is kynges pray,
He Auerice eschuë mot alway,   4632
  By causë sche more is contrarious   *[leaf 81 b]*
  To *ver*tu, þan the large outragëous.   4634

(663)

[R] Tercio, *quia* rex est positus in regno prop*ter* salut*em* regni, & vt prosit hijs qui in regno sunt ; auarus autem nulli prodest.

¶ The þriddë skile is, for a kyng is set   4635   *3. because a*
  In his remë for his peples[3] releef,   *King is bound to*
ffor þey schulden for hym fare þe bet ;   *relieve his folk,*
But þe streyt chynchë qwencheþ neu*ere* greef ;
His gold is neu*ere* saluë to myschef ;   4639
  Only to gadre and kepe, he hym delititħ ;   *and a Miser*
  But þe fool largë, many man *pro*fititħ ;   4641 *keeps all to himself.*

(664)

[R] Idem *dicit quod* largitas est ad sim*i*litudinem vaso*rum* ; vasa enim habencia os larg*um*, abunde emittunt quod in eis est.

¶ Yit vices ben þey gretë bothë tweyne.   4642
  O ! worþy princë, take on yow largesse ;   *Prince*
Dooth so, o gracious lord, for goddës peyne !   *Henry, be liberal!*
Largesse I-put is vnto þe liknesse
Of vessels, whos mouthës han gret wydnesse, 4646
  And hilde out hir lic*ó*ur habundantly ;
  Thus seith þe philosofre trewëly.   4648

(665)

[R] Cum *ergo* tanto deceat fontem ha*bere largum* os, quanto ex eo plures participare debent, tanto decet regem largiorem esse, &c.

¶ And in as mochil as a welle also,   4649
  At þe whiche many folk hir wat*er* fecche,
Nedith to han the larger mouth ; right so
The largesse of a kyng moot ferþer strecche,   *A King should give*
If he of his estat any þing recche,   4653 *more than other folk.*
  Than oþer mennës ; for hir[4] impotence
  Strecchiþ naght so fer as his influence.   4655

---

[1] liberalitee R, liberte H.   (Scan 'libér / ali / te').
[2] ynough R, now H.   [3] peples ese and R.   [4] hir, *om.* H R.

(666)

¶ Largesse is ' liberalitee' y-callid,   4656
 And likned is vnto hem þat ben free;
But he þat auaricious is, is thrallid
 To moneie. a kyng moot algatës flee
A chynchës hertë, for his honeste   4660
 And for þe profyte, as I seide aboue,
 Of his peple, if he þynke wynne here loue.   4662

(667)

¶ Victorie and honour, he schal hym purcháse   4663
 That is of yiftës fre ; but war alway
That he naght tarye ne delaye his grace ;
 Dryue it noght forth vnto anoþer day,
 Whan, if hym list, anon he yeuë may ;   4667
  Yeue it as blyue, hys þank is wel þe more ;
  This vouche I on holy scripturës lore.   4669

(668)

¶ The vertu is of liberalitee,   4670
 Yeue and dispende, in place and in tyme[1] due ;
Right as largessë dooth in swiche degree,
 They bothë moot in hir conseytes chue
 Where is good yeue,[2] and wherë to eschue,   4674
  The persone, and þe somme, and causë why :
  What þey[3] yeuen, yeue it vertuously.   4676

(669)

¶ But it naght longeth to þe liberal   4677
 To yeue hym good þat vseþ flaterie ;
His menynge and his éntencïoun final
 On fals plesance, is set for briberie ;
 He is þe verray cofre of treccherie ;   4681
  His doublenesse his lord doun ouerthroweþ ;
  The seed of his confusïoun he soweþ.   4683

---

[1] n tyme and place R.   [2] to yeue R.   [3] ye R.

(670)

¶ Nota quod laudandus est ille quem pietas mouet reuelamen prestare indigenti : nota bene hic !

¶ That man I-born is in a blissed hour,   4684   He was born
    Whom þat pitee, dissert, or kyndënesse,   in a blessed
Stiren to yeue, or mynystre hym socour,   hour who
    That infortunës strokës bitternesse   helps the
unfortunate :

    I-woundid hath wiþ pouertes scharpnesse[1] :   4688
      Nat mene I hem þat[2] hire, and fees and wages,   [leaf 82 b]
      Hath[3] at þe dees loost, and[4] hir heritáges ;   4690   not gamblers,

(671)

¶ But þo þat men welthy han[5] ben byfore,   4691   but honest
    And vertuous ben, and han hir goodë[6] lost,   poor.
And can not beggë, to be deed þerfore ;
    On hem ful wel bystowëd is þe cost.
    But welaway ! as harde as is a post—   4695   Hearts are
      A post ? nay, as a stoon—ben hertës now !   now as hard
      Lordës, for schamë ! what þing eyleth yow ?   4697   as stones.

(672)

¶ A gentil hertë, for to begge haþ schame ;   4698   A gentle
    His rody schamfastnessë dar not preye.   heart is
Ye þat of gentillesse han stile & name,   ashamed to
    Lat nat your poorë bretheren by yow deye !   beg.
    Se vnto hem, thogh þey nat speke or seie.   4702
      Is pitee fro yow fled ? calle hir agayn !
      ffor hir absence haþ many good man slayn.   4704

(673)

¶ Senek seith, hé haþ nat þat þing for noght,   4705   A gift is not
    That byeth it by speche and by prayere.   a gift if it has
There is no thyng þat is in eerthë wroght,   to be won by
    As þat he seith, þat is y-bought so deere ;   begging.
    It standith streytë, whan it schal apere,   4709
      ffor it is vois of wrecchidnesse and sorwe,
      Whan þat a man schal praye, or begge, or borwe.

---

[1] sikenesse R.   [2] Nought yeue hem R.   [3] Hat H, That han R.
    [4] dice lost.   [5] han R, and H.   [6] goode R, good H.

(674)

¶ Allas! þogh[1] þat a man disceu*ere* & pleyne   4712

Many Lords don't care a blackberry for folk's misfortune.

   To many a lord his méscheuous myserie,
The lord naght deyneth vndirstonde his peyne;
   He settith noght þerby a blakberie.

[leaf 83 *a*]

   Welthe in þe lordës sayl bloweþ ful merye;   4716
But the nedy berith his sail so lowe,
   That no wynd of comfórt may in hit blowe. 4718

(675)

¶ Of liberalitee yit forthermore   4719
   I tellë wole, as þat I haue herd seyn
Amongës wysë folk, gon is ful yore.

¶ Hic caueant capitanei, quod non retineant vadia.

A Leader's labour is vain, who is not liberal to his soldiers.

   What man a ledere is, or a chiefteyn
Of peple, his labour is al wast and veyn,   4723
   But he be fre vnto his sowdëours,
   If þat he sekë conquest of[2] honours.   4725

(676)

He mustn't cut down their wages.

¶ And specialy þat he hir duëtee   4726
   Abriggë naght, ne naght syncope hir wages
That hem assigned ben: in certeyntee,
   Peril of schamë folwen swiche vságes.
   Whan al a-counted is, tho auantáges   4730
   That founded ben of wrong and on repreef,
   Ben naght but auantáges of mescheef.   4732

(677)

Avarice is the root of all Harms.

¶ This makith couetise or Auarice   4733
   Roote of al harmës, fo to conscïence;
Of wikked purchas is sche Emp*er*ice,
   And mochil hath, and ay haþ indigence.
   Sho rather wil lyuen[3] in abstinence   4737
   Of mete and drynkë, for hertës scantnesse,
   Than for þe soule or bodyes holsu*m*nesse.   4739

[1] though R, þoght H.   [2] or R.   [3] live R, lyue H.

(678)

¶ Prince excèllent ! so moot ye wirke and wilne[1] 4740

As may your soulës helthë[2] edifie ;

And a-mong othir þingës, þat your wilne[1]

Be infecte wiþ no wrecched chyncherie.

Largesse mesúrable vnto yow tye, 4744

And fool largessë voydeth fro yow clene

ffor free largessë is a vertuous mene. 4746

Prince Henry, may you not be miserly, but liberal!

[leaf 83 b]

[§ 13.] De regis prudencia.

(679)

N ow, gracious princë, lyke it yow to wyte[3] 4747

That touche I thynke of a kyngës prudence,

As þat I ther-of fynde in bookës write.

Prudence is callid wit and sapience,

And needës moot rëal magnificence 4751

Be prudent, as þat þé scripture vs lereth,

If he schal ben as his estate[4] requerith. 4753

I'll now treat of how a King should be Prudent.

(680)

Prudence, attemperancë, strengthe, and right, 4754

Tho fourë ben vertuës principal[5] ;

Prudencë gooth by-fore, and ȝeueth light

Of counseil, what þo other thre do schal,

That þey may wirkë, be it greet or smal, 4758

Aftir hir reed, wiþ-outen whom no man

Wel vnto god, né þe world lyuë can. 4760

Prudence, Temperance, Strength, and Right are 4 chief virtues.

(681)

Prudence is vertu of entendëment ; 4761

She makith man by resoun him gouérne.

Who-so þat list to be wys and prudént,

And þe light folwe wole of hir lanterne,

he mostë castë his look[6] in euery herne 4765

Prudence makes man rule himself by Reason.

Of þyngës past, and ben, & þat schul be :
The endë seeþ, and eek mesúreth, sche.   4767

(682)

There is no wight þat sche schapiþ disceyue,   4768
   And, thogh men casten hem[1] hire to begile,
Naght' wole it be ; by wit sche wole it weyue.
Eek sche obserueth so wele trouthës style,
And þerto can so wel her tonge affyle,   4772
   That, lest' þe fauour of frendschipës corde,
   Othir þan trouthë can sche not recorde.   4774

(683)

¶ Sche bý-heetith by good avisëment,   4775
   And ȝeueth morë þan hir list *pro*mette ;
Scho yeueth tó men eek commandëment

'Naght in fortune truste, or by hir sette ;
And al þe truste, out of hir hertë schette,   4779
   Of myght of worldly dominacïou*n* :'
   Vertu gyeth hir ope*r*acïou*n*.   4781

(684)

¶ Prudence hath leuer louëd be þan drad ;   4782
   Ther may no prince in his estate endure,
Ne ther-yn any whilë standë[2] sad,
But he be louëd ; fór loue is armure
Of seurëte.   o ! take on yow þe cure,   4786

   Excellent princë, louë to embrace,
   And þan your herte is sette in siker place.   4788

(685)

¶ Now, if þat ye graunten by your patente   4789
   To your seruauntës a yeerly guerdou*n*,
Crist scheeldë þat your wil or your entente
Be sette to maken[3] a restricciou*n*[4]
Of paiëment ; for þat condicïou*n*   4793
   Exileþ þé peples beneuolence,
   And kyndeleþ hate vndir p*r*iue scilence.   4795

---

¹ men casten hem R, man cast hym H.   ² endure R.
³ make H R.   ⁴ retraccïou*n* R.

(686)

¶ Beeth wel avisëd, or your graunt out go,   4796
  ¶ How ye þat chargë may performe and bere ;   [leaf 84 *b*]
Whan it is past, obserue it wel also,
  ffor ellës wole it yow annoye and dere ;
ffor your honur it muchel bettre were,   4800
  No graunt to graunt at al, þan þat your graunt
  Yow preeue a brekere of a couenaunt'.   4802

You'd better not grant the Pension at all, than not pay it.

(687)

¶ He þat is louëd, men drede hym offende ;   4803
  But he þat drad, & naght by-louëd is,
As Tullïus seith, lightly may descende,
  And þe lordschipë leesë þat was his ;
And Senek also seith as[1] touchyng þis,   4807
  The sogett hateth whom he haþ in drede ;
  And hate is hard, if it his venym schede.   4809

Men fear to offend those they love.

(688)

¶ Was neuere dredë yit a good wardeyn,   4810
  To holdë lordschepe in his sikernesse,
But only loue is þing most souereyn ;
  Loue is norice of welþe and of gladnesse,
  But out of louë spryngeþ ferdfulnesse,   4814
    And feere is good, whiche þat on loue hym
      groundeth,
    But othir feerë naght heliþ, but woundeth.   4816

Fear was never a good keeper of a king's estate.

(689)

¶ Louë, withouten a good gouernaille,   4817
  A kyng haþ non ; for thogh men no word seye,
If he his peple oppresse, it is no faile
  They loue hym noght, in no manere of weie ;
They may his hestës outward wel obeie,   4821
  But in hir hertes is smal obediaunce,
  And vnto god þey cómpleyne hir grevaunce.   4823

If a king oppresses his folk, they hate him.

[1] as, *om.* H R.

(690)

¶ And swich a kyng is naght prudent ne wys, 4824

   ¶ That of his peple purchaseth hym hate,

ffor loue excedith al tresour in prys ;

   So hath it ben, and so be wole algate.

   Whan þat richésses ebben & abbate, 4828

    If loue endurë, it may hym restore,

    And loue is goten by prudénces[1] lore. 4830

(691)

¶ By wise conseil, settith your hy estat 4831

   In swhiche an ordre as ye lyuë may

Of your good propre, in reule moderat ;

   Is it knyghtly lyue on rapynë? nay !

ffor Cristës sakë, so yow gyeth ay, 4835

   As þat may strecchë to your peples ese,

   And þerwith-al ye schul god hily plese. 4837

(692)

¶ It apparteneth a kyng for to be 4838

   A kyng in verray soth and éxisténce.

A kyng, of office and of dignite

   The name is ; he moot don his diligence

His peple for to gyë by prudénce ; 4842

   ffor þat he rule hem schuldë duëly,

   The stile of a ' kyng ' he berith certeynly. 4844

(693)

¶ As an archer may naght his arwe schete 4845

   Euene at a merk, bút he þe merk see,

No morë may a kyng, I yow byhete,

   Gouerne his peple in rigth[2] and equitee,

   But by prudénce he reule his hyghe degree ; 4849

   If þat be wel, his peple hath sikernesse

   Of reste and pees, welþe, ioyë, and gladnesse. 4851

---

[1] prudences R, prudentes H.   [2] right H.

(694)

¶ Inicium
sapiencie,
timor domini.

¶ Bygynnynge of wisdom is, god to drede;   4852

What kyng þat dredith god, is good and iust

To his peple; beeþ swiche, my lord, I rede!

In[1] loue and in awe of god, ficcheþ your lust;

Than be ye wys, and þan yow needës must,   4856

Aftir your worldly sceptre transitórie,

In heuene regne in pérpetuel glorie.   4858

The fear of
God is the
[leaf 85 *b*]
beginning of
Wisdom.

[§ 14.] **De consilio habendo in omnib*us* factis.**

(695)

Now purpose I, to trete how to a kyng[2]   4859

  It nedeful is to do by consail ay;

With-outen whiche, good is he do no þing';

ffor a kyng' is but a man soul, p*ar*fay!

And be[3] his witt neuere so good, he may   4863

  Erre and mistake hym oþer while among',

Where-as good counsail may exclude a[4] wrong.

A King must
do nothing
without tak-
ing Counsel.

(696)

Excellent princë, in axynge of reed,   4866

  Descouereþ naght your wille in no maneere;

What þat ye þinkë doo, lat it be deed

  As for þe tymë, lat no word appere;

But what eu*er*y man seith, wel herkne & here; 4870

  And yit whan good counsail is yeuen yow,

What ye do wolë, kepe it close y-now   4872

Prince
Henry, when
you ask for
advice, don't
express your
own opinion.

(697)

Til þat yow lykë párforme it in dede;   4873

  And if it schal be don, lat it noght tarie,

ffor þat is p*er*illous with-outë drede;

  Ther is no þing may make a lond myscarie

Morë than swiche delay; ful necessárie   4877

  It is, a gode purpos parforme as bliue,

As, if it naght be,[5] out of mynde it dryue.   4879

When you've
to act, act at
once.

[leaf 86 *a*]

(698)

¶ And if þat á man of symple degree,   4880
    Or pore of birth, or ȝonge, be wel conseile,[1]
Admytte his resoun and take it in gre :
    Why naght, my godë lorde? what shuld yow eyle?
    But men do naght so; where-of I meruyele;   4884
    þe worlde fauórith ay þe richës sawe,
    þow þat his conseil be noght worth an hawe. 4886

(699)

¶ What he seith, is vp to þe clowdës bore ;   4887
    But and þe porë spekë worth þe twey,
His seed naght spryngë[2] may, it nys but lore ;
    Thei seyen, " what is he, þis? lat hym goo pley !
    O ! worthi princë, beth wel ware, I prey,   4891

    þat your hye dygnite and sad *prudénce*
    No desdein haue[3] of þe porës senténce.   4893

(700)

¶ Thogh men contrárie eek your óppynyoun,   4894
    þei may, *per cas*, conseilë[4] yow þe best ;
Also ye ben at your eleccioun
    To doo or leuë, as your seluen lyst.

    If it be gode, impresse it in þe chest   4898
    Of your memórie, and excusith it[5] ;
    If it naght be, to leue it, is a wyt.   4900

(701)

¶ And if yow list your cónseilere to preue,   4901
    Ye feynë mot ye haue necessite
Of golde ; and if he sterë yow, and meeue,
    Your Iewels ley in weddë,[6] certeyn he
    Loueth your éstate and prosperite ;   4905

    But he þat redith yow, your peple oppresse,
    He hatheth[7] yow, certéyne, it is no lesse.   4907

---

[1] be, goode counseile Yow yeve R.   [2] spryng H R.
[3] haue R, *om.* H.   [4] counceile R, conseil H.   [5] execute R
[6] wedde R, wed H.   [7] hateth R.

(702)

¶ And if a man, in tyme of swich a nede,   4908

   Of his goode ӡeuë yow a goode substaunce,

Swich oon cherich, and ellës[1] god forbede,

   Konneth hym þank of his goode cheuesaunce,

ffor him is leuer to suffre penaunce   4912

    Him-self, þan þat your peple shuldë[2] smeıt;

    Ther is a preef of trewë louyng hert.   4914

If a man helps you in the time of need, cherish him.

(703)

¶ In auxenge[3] eeke of reed, ware of fauel;   4915

   Also ware[4] of þe auaricïouse;

ffor none of þo two can conseilë[5] wel;

   Hir reed & conseil is envenymouse;

þei bothë[6] ben of golde so dësirous,   4919

    þei rekkë naght what bryge[7] her lorde be Inne,

    So þat þei mowen golde & siluyr wynne.   4921

¶ *Non exigatur consilium ab adulatore nec de auaro.*

Beware of flatterers and avaricious folk: their advice can't be trusted.

(704)

¶ And if your conseil which þat ye haue take,   4922

   Vnto þe knowlech or þe audience

Of your foos comen be, þan lat it slake,

   And witterly putte it in abstinence;

ffor execute it were an[8] inprudence;   4926

    In swich a caas, is wisdam it to chaunge;

    Goode is, your conseil·be to your foes straunge.

If your counsel gets known to your foes, don't follow it.

(705)

¶ Conseil may wel be likend to a bridil,   4929

   Which þat an hors vpkepeth fro fallyng,

If man do by conseil; but al in Idel

   Is reed, if[9] man naght folwe it in wirkyng.

Do no þing redeles, do by conseylyng   4933

    Of hedës wyse, and than[10] noo répentaunce

    þer folwe yow schal in your gouernaunce.   4935   [leaf 87 *a*]

¶ *Scriptum est, quod consilium bene potest freno comparari.*

¶ *Sine consilio nichil facias, & post factum non penitebis.*

Counsel is like a bridle, that keeps a horse from falling.

---

[1] Suche non cherissheth and elles R, els H.
[2] shulde R, shuld H.   [3] axyng R.   [4] beware R.
[5] counceille R, conseil H.   [6] bothe R, bot H.   [7] brike R.
[8] and H (it / it were grete prudence R !).   [9] yf R, of H.
[10] than R, *om.* H.

REGEMENT.   N

(706)

¶ Comméndable is, conséil take óf þe wyse,   4936
    And noght of foolës, for þei may noght loue
    But[1] swich þing as hem likyth. in al wyse,
    Your conseiler, chesith our lorde god a-boue;

Chesith eke godë men; ánd awey shoue   4940
    The wykkyd, whos conseyl is déceyuáble;
    Þus byddyth holy writ, it is no fable.   4942

(707)

¶ Chesith men eke of olde experience;   4943
    Hir wit and intellect is gloriouse;
    Of hir conseil, holsome is þe sentence;
    Þe oldë mannës rede is fructuouse;
    Ware of yong cónseyl, it is perilouse;   4947

    Roboas fonde it so, whan he forsoke
    Oldë conseil, and to þe yong hym toke.   4949

(708)

¶ The éntente, wot I wele, of þe yong man   4950
    As louyng is and trewe, as of the olde,
    Þogh þat he noght so wele conseilen can.
    Yong men, strong ben, hardy, and bolde,
    And more weldy to fight, if þat þei sholde;   4954

    But aske[2] þe olde in tyme of pees or werre
    Rede & conseil; it schal naght be þe werre.   4956

(709)

¶ He þat is fressh and lusty now þis day,   4957
    By lengthe of yerees shal no þing be so;
    ffresshnesse & lust may naght endure al-wey;
    Whan age is comen, he commaundeth, ho!
    But lat see, who considereth þis two,[3]   4961

    Goode is þat agë sette a gouernayle,
    And youthe it sue: thus may al avayle.   4963

[1] But R, And H.   [2] aske R, þow H.   [3] who R.

(710)

¶ Mandatum est, sabata sanctifices.

Excellent prince, eeke on the holydayes 4964
  Beth warë þat ye nat your conseilles holde ;
As for tho tymës,[1] put hem in deleyes ;
  Thenketh wel this, ye wel apayed be nolde
    If your soggettes not be your hestës[2] tolde, 4968
    Right so our lorde god, kyng & commaundour
    Of kynges al,[3] is wroth with þat errour. 4970

Prince Henry, don't hold your councils on holy days;

(711)

¶ In þe longe ȝere be werkë daye[4] I-nowe, 4971
  If þei be wel despent, for to entende
To conseilës[5] : to god your hertë[6] bowe,
  If ye desire men hir hertës bende
To yow. What kyng nat dredeth god offende, 4975
    Ne naght rekkéth do hym desóbeisaunce,
    He shal be disobeïëd eeke perchaunce.[7] 4977

there are plenty of workdays for em.

(712)

¶ The firstë fyndere of our faire langáge, 4978
  Hath seyde in caas sembláble, & othir moo,
So hyly wel, þat it is my dotáge
  ffor to expresse or touche any of thoo.
    Alasse ! my fadir fro þe worlde is goo— 4982
    My worthi maister Chaucer, hym I mene—
    Be þou aduóket for hym, heuenes[8] quene ! 4984

My Master Chaucer has treated this.

Mary ! be his advocate.

(713)

¶ As þou wel knowest, o blissid virgyne, 4985
  With louyng hert, and hye deuocïoun
In þyne honour he wroot ful many a lyne ;
  O now þine helpe & þi promocïoun,
    To god þi sonë make a mocïoun, 4989
    How he þi seruaunt was, maydén marie,
    And lat his louë[9] floure and fructifie. 4991

In your honour he wrote many a line. Help him now with your Son !

[leaf 88 a]

---

    [1] the tyme R.   [2] by your hest R.   [3] alle R.
[4] ben werke dayes R.   [5] counceiles R, conseils H.   [6] hert H R.
[7] perchaunce R, perchaunche H.   [8] heuen R.   [9] soule R.

(714)

Tho' Chaucer
is dead, I've
had his like-
ness put here
that men
who've for-
gotten him
may find him
again.

¶ Al-þogh his lyfe be queynt, þe résemblaunce[1]   4992

Of him haþ in me so fressh lyflynesse,

þat, to putté othir men in rémembraunce

Of his persóne, I haue heere his lyknesse

Do makë, to þis ende in sothfastnesse,   4996

þat þei þat haue of him lest[2] þought & mynde,

By þis peynturë may ageyn him fynde.   4998

[Grass-green
background,
black hood
and gown,
gray hair,
hazel eyes,
red lips,
paleish face
and hands ;
black beads
and penner
on red
strings.]

(715)

Images in
church make
folk think on
God and his
Saints.

¶ The ymages þat in þe chirchë been,   4999

Maken folk þenke on god & on his seyntes,

When þe ymáges þei be-holden & seen ;

Were oft vnsyte[3] of hem causith restreyntes

Of þoughtës godë : whan a þing depeynt is,   5003

Or éntailëd, if men take of it heede,

Thoght of þe lyknesse, it wil in hem[4] brede. 5005

---

[1] In the MS. Chaucer's carefully drawn and colourd likeness
is in the right margin.   At the top of the much commoner full-
length figure in the left margin of MS. Reg. 17 D 6, is " ¶ Chau-
cers yn age."   [2] lost R.   [3] Wher as vnsight R.
[4] hem R, hym H.

(716)

¶ Yit somme holden oppynÿoun, and sey,   5006   Images may rightfully be made.
þat none ymáges schuld I-maked be :
þei erren foule, & goon ont of þe wey ;
Of trouth haue þei scant sensibilite.

Passe ouer þat : now, blessid trinite,   5010   May the Trinity and Mary have mercy on my Master's soul !
   Vppon my maistres soulë, mercy haue,
ffor him, lady, eke þi mercy I craue.   5012

(717)

¶ More othir þing, wolde I fayne speke & touche   5013   I'd like to treat of other things, but my power is empty, and my spirit heavy.
Heere in þis booke ; but such[1] is my dulnesse—
ffor þat al voyde and empty is my pouche,—
þat al my lust is queynt with heuynesse,
And[2] heuy spirit cómaundith stilnesse.   5017

And haue I spoke of pees, I schal be stille ;   [leaf 88 b]
God sende vs pees, if þat it be his wille.   5019

[§ 15. *OF PEACE.*]

(718)

¶ Scriptum est, Qui amplectitur pacem in mentis hospicio [4]mansionem preparit Christo, &c.[4] Ieronimus: Qui sine pace est, christum non habet. apud christianos non qui patitur sed qui facit contumeliam miser est.

Prouerbiarum 12º. Qui pacis ineunt consilia, sequitur eos gaudium. Ciprianus dicit, Sacrificium deo est pax nostra & fraterna concordia.

Touche I wol heere, of pees, a worde or two,[3]   5020   I'll speak of Peace.
   As þat scripturës maken mencïoun,
And[5] þan my boke is endid al, and do.
To crist ordeyneþ he a mancïoun,
Which in his hertës habitacïoun   5024
   Embraceth pees. wher pees is, crist is there,   Where Peace is, Christ is.
ffor crist nat lyst a-byden ellës-where.[6]   5026

(719)

A-mongës cristen folk, wreche is he none   5027
   þat pacïéntly suffreth a duresse ;
But sikirly a wrecchë[7] is he one   He who makes strife is a Wretch.
   þat makiþ strife ; & hym sueth gladnesse
Which þat of pees conséilith þe suernesse.[8]   5031
Our pees also and concorde brothirly
Is sacrificë to god ál myghty.   5033

---

[1] such R, schuch H.   [2] An R.
[3] This page is illuminated   [4-4] added in R.
[5] And R, An H.   [6] elleswhere R, els where H.
[7] wrecche R, wrecch H.   [8] swetnesse R.

(720)

Thyngës þat leden men to pees be thre :   5034

Conformyng in god ; in our self humblesse ;

And with[1] our neighëboures *tranquillite.*

ffirst seye I þat we moot our willës dresse,

And hem conformen allë more & lesse   5038

To goddis wil ; al þingis[2] is in his myght,

Sauf only þat he máy done non vnright.   5040

(721)

Euene as a man is eu*er* in werre and strife,   5041

þat besieth hym withstande a man, which he

¶ Nat may ; right so hathe he peisible[3] lyfe

Continuelly, whos willës fully be

To goddës wille conformyng : o, pardee !   5045

A-geyn god helpeth þere no résistence,

So strong and myȝty is his excellence.[4]   5047

(722)

¶ Humilite, to pees eke may men lede ;   5048

Men say two gretë may nat[5] in o sak ;

But symple humblesse is of such[6] godely-hede,

þat she of troubly hatë haþ no smak ;

She stryueth nat ; of discorde hath she lak ;   5052

She voyde and empty is of cruelte :

Humble spirit desirith vnite.   5054

(723)

¶ The thrid is eke *tranquillite* of þougħt,   5055

þat gydeth man to pees ; for as a wight

May in a bedde of þornës restë[7] noght,

Riȝt so, who[8] is w*ith* greuous þoughtës twight,

May w*ith* himself nor[9] othir folk a-riȝt   5059

Hauë no pees ; a man mot nedys smert

Whan irous þoughtës occupye his hert.   5061

---

[1] with R, wit H.   [2] aꝉ thyng R.
[3] pesible R, preisible H.   [4] residence R.
[5] grete may eviꝉ R, gret may nat H.   [6] such R, schuch H.
[7] rest H R.   [8] who þat H, he that R.   [9] nor R, non H.

(724)

¶ And euene as vppon a pillow softe, 5062
 Man may him restë[1] wele, and take his ese,
Riȝt so þat lorde þat sittith in heuen a-lofte,
Hertë[2] peisible can so like and plese,
þat he wol entre þér-in, and it sese, 5066
 And occupie it as iust póssessoure ;
 In place of pees, resteth our saviour. 5068

(725)

¶ But al an othir pees þer is also, 5069
 Which is naght worth ; it is envenymouse ;
ffor it is vnto verray pees a foo ;
Whan[3] men in a purpós malicïouse
Acorden, þát pees is to god greuous : 5073
 Swich pees was twix Heródes & pilat ;
 And in swich caas, pees is wers þanne debat. 5075

(726)

¶ A feynëd pees, eeke is to pees verray, 5076
 A foo ; and swich was þe pees of Iudas
Kissyng crist. Lord ! whedir þat þis day
Any swich pees vsëd is as[4] þat was !
ȝe, so I drede me, by seynt Thomas, 5080
 The kus of Iudas is now widë sprad,[5]
 Tokenes of pees ben, but smal loue is had.[5] 5082

(727)

¶ Men contrefete in wordis Tullïus, 5083
 And folwe in werke Iudas or Genyloun[6] ;
Many an hony[7] worde and many a kus
Ther is ; but wayte on þe conclusïoun,
And pryue galle all turnyth vp-so-doun ; 5087
 Ther leueth naght of pees, but contenance,
 ffor al þe peyntyd chere and daliance. 5089

[1] rest H R. [2] Hert H R. [3] Whan R, Wham H.
[4] as R, os H. [5—5] spradde . . hadde R, sparde . . had H.
[6] The traitor at Roncesvalles. See Chaucer's *Monk's Tale*,
Pedro of Spayne. [7] hony R, heny H.

(728)

¶ Ther is also a pees inordinat,   5090
    Whan þe grettér obeith to þe lesse;
As[1] þus, whan to his soget a prelat
    Obeyeth; and whan reson, þe blyndnesse
Sueth of sensualitees madnesse,   5094
    Obeying it: al swich pees is haynous,
ffor it is goodë[2] pees contrarious.   5096

Peace is ill-orderd when

Reason obeys Sensuality,

(729)

¶ Right swich a pees, Adam had with Eue,   5097
    Whan þat he vnto hir desire obeyde;
He was, per caas, adraddë[3] for to greue;
    Where-for he did as þat she to[4] hym seide:
In þat obediencë he foleyde,   5101
    ffor god hir him bytoke him to obeye;
But I a-drad am þat I þus fer seye[5];   5103

as Adam did Eve.

[leaf 90 a]

He obeyd her, and playd the fool.

¶ Contra talem pacem loquitur christus, Matthaei 10. Non veni, inquit, pacem mittere, sed gladium. &c.

(730)

¶ If þat þis come vnto the audience   5104
    Of women, I am sure I shal be shent:
ffor þat I touche of swich obedience,
    Many a browë shal on me be bent;
Thei willë wayten been[6] equipollent,   5108
    And sumwhat morë, vnto hir housbondis,[7]
And sum men seyn swich vsage in þis lond is.[8]

If Women hear this, they'll pay me.

They're equal to their husbands here now.

(731)

¶ And it no wonder is, as semeth me,   5111
    Whan þat I me be-þought haue al aboute,
þogh þat womén desiren souereynte,
    And hir housbondës makë to hem loute;
Thei made ware of a ribbe, it is no doute,   5115
    Which more strong is, and súbstancial,
þan slyme of eerthe, & clenner þer-with-al.   5117

And no wonder they desire Sovereignty: the Rib they were made of is solider and cleaner than the slime Man was made of.

¶ Genesis 2º. Mulier facta fuit de costa Ade; homo vero de limo terre, &c.

---

[1] As R, And H.   [2] to god. R.   [3] adredde R, adrad H.
[4] as that she R, at þat she H.   [5] ferre sey R, fer seide H.
[6] wolden waite to ben R, wil . . . H.
[7] husbondis R, housbond(es *scratcht out*) H.
[8] lond is R, lond(es *scratcht out*) H.

(732)

¶ Wher-for it semeth þat þe worthynesse   5118
    Of women, passyth mennës encerteyne ;
And ȝit sum nysë men, of lewdënesse,[1]
    In répref of hem holden ther-a-geyn,
    ffor crokid was þat ribbe ; and speke & seyne,   5122
      That also crokid is hir curtaisie ;
      But a-gayn þat, strongly wil I replie ;   5124

Yet some foolish men say the rib was Crooked, like women's Tempers.

(733)

ffor in the writyng and in þe scripture   5125
    Of Philosophers,[2] men may see & reede,
¶ Cercly[3] shap is most perfite figúre,
    Bi-tokenyng, in gémetrie, onhede ;
    And crokydnesse a part is, þat may lede   5129
      Sumwhat vnto[4] cercle or a cumpas :
      What so men seyen, women stonde in gode caas.

¶ Secundum omnes philosophos, ffigura circularis est perfectissima figura, & significat in geometria vnitatem.

But all Philosophers say [leaf 90 b] that a circle is the perfect figure; and that's crooked.

(734)

¶ ffor ther-by shewith it, þat crokydnesse   5132
    Streccheth vnto þe gretter perfeccioun,
þan doth a þing þat is of euenesse ;
    Of þis helpith no contradiccïoun,
    ffor it soth is ;[5] it is no ficcïoun ;   5136
      Euery perfit body þat man kan neuene,
      Is rounde and crokyd, and noght[6] streghte ne euene.

Crookedness approaches perfection.

Every perfect body is round and crooked :

(735)

¶ By-gynnë first at heuen, & rounde it is ;   5139
    þe sonne and mone, & þe sterrës also ;
Hed of man, þen mouth, & hert, I-wisse,
    Ben allë[7] rounde ; and othir ben þer moo
    Than I expresse as[8] now ; but or I goo,   5143
      ȝit shal I bet wommannës part sustene ;
      So biddeth pees, & þat to folwe I mene.   5145

the Heaven, Sun, Moon, Stars, man's Head, Mouth, Heart.

---

[1] lewdenesse R, lewenes H.
[2] Philosofres R, Philosophes H.   [3] Cerclelyk R.
[4] vnto (*overline, ? later*) R, *om.* H.   [5] is R, *om.* H.
[6] not R, nogh H.   [7] alle R, al H.   [8] as R, os H.

(736)

Moreover,

¶ Now for to speke or touchen of þe place   5146

In which þat man & womman [1]fourmed were :

God made Woman *in* Paradise,

Almyghty God to womman[1] shope swich *grace*,

That she was formëd in the worthier ;

In *pa*radys men wot wel he made here ;   5150

and Man *out* of it.

But man ymade[2] was out of *pa*radys,

In place of lessë worthinesse & prys.   5152

¶ Mulier fuit formata in paradiso, & homo in agro damaseeno, qui locus est extra paradisum, &c.

(737)

¶ And of þe maner of formacïoun   5153

Of bothë[3] two herkenþ now wel I prey ;

[leaf 91 *a*] And Adam's creation signified less than Eve's.

The token or þe significacioun

Of making of Adám, may be no way

Strecchë[4] to so *per*fyte a goode, I say,   5157

As didë[5] þe formacïoun of Eue ;

And þat as swithë here I schal it preue.   5159

(738)

¶ ffor morë haue I for hir partye ȝit :   5160

The making of Eve tokend that of Holy Church and its Sacrament.

Making of Euë tokned þe makyng

Of holy chirche, and sac*ra*mentes of it ;

As of þe syde of Adam, him slepyng,

Euë vas[6] made, so our lorde crist deyeng   5164

Vpon þe crois, holý chirche, of his syde,

And þe sac*rá*mentes made were in þat tyde.   5166

¶ Secundum *augustinum* & omnes doctores catholicos, fformacio Eue significauit formacionem ecclesie & sa*cramentorum* eius ; Nam sicut, Adam dormiente, formabatur Eua & membra eius de latere ips*ius* Ade, sic *christo* dormiente in cruce, forma*batur* de latere &c. [R eius ecclesia et eius sac*ra*menta.] Beatus ber*nardus dicit.

(739)

Christ, from 12 to 30, servd his Mother, who was his Wife too.

¶ ffro tyme eeke crist was of xij ȝerë[7] age   5167

Vnto þritty, he w*ith* his modir ay

Was seruyng hir w*ith* right[8] plesant coráge ;

To teche humilite, he tooke þe way

ffro heuen hiddir, and mekënesse v*er*ray   5171

Tauȝt he, þe mostë[9] *pa*rtie of his lyf,

Whil he was w*ith* his modir & his wyfe ;   5173

¶ A tempore quo *christ*us erat duodennis, v*s*que ad annum xxx[ti].

[1]—[1] H *om.*   [2] ymade R, made H.
[3] bothe two herkeneth R, both . . . H.
[4] Strecche R, Strecch H.   [5] did H R.   [6] was R.
[7] twelve yere of R.   [8] right, *om.* H R.   [9] most H R.

(740)

¶ ffor she was bothe[1] two ; and syn she had   5174
   So long of hir housbonde þe maystrie,
Women, I trowe,[2] be nat now so mad
   þat style to for-go ; nay, swich folye,
     What man þat can in a woman espye,   5178
       Is worthi shryned be ; god saue hem alle,
       And graunt hir hye corage nat to palle![3]   5180

As the Virgin Mary ruled her husband, woman 'll do the like now.

(741)

¶ Holy writ seith, ' if women souereynte   5181
   Of hir housbondes haue, how þat þei
Vnto housbondes[4] contrarïous be : '
   þe text is such,[5] I woot wel, but what þei ?
     That text I vndir-stonde þus al-wey :   5185
       Whan þat housbondes hem mys-take and erre,
       Ageyn þat vice wyues maken werre.   5187

As to women being contrarious,

[leaf 91 b]

it's only when their husbands go wrong.

(742)

¶ Thogh a woman hir housbonde contrarie   5188
   In his oppynyoun erroneous,
Shul men for þat deme hir his aduersarie ?
   Straw ! be he neuer so harrageous,[6]
     If he & she shul dwellen in on house,   5192
       Goode is he suffre ; therby pees may spring ;
       Housbondes pees is pesible suffryng.   5194

A husband ought to be ruled by his wife.

(743)

¶ By concorde, smale[7] þinges multiplien ;   5195
   And by discorde, hate, ire, and rancour,
Perysshen þinges grete, & wast & dyen.
   Pees hath þe fruyt of eese[8] in his fauour ;
     To gete pees holsome is þe labour,   5199
       And kepe it wel, whan a[9] man hath it cauȝt,
       That ire ne discorde bannysshe it naght.   5201

Concord brings prosperity ; discord ruins it.

---

[1] both H R.   [2] trowe R, trow H.
([3] This is a faint imitation of Chaucer.)   [4] her husbondes R.
[5] is such I wote wele R, I woot wel is schuch H.
[6] outrageous R.   [7] smale R, smal H.   [8] oseese H, ese R.
[9] that a R, a *rubd out of* H.

(744)

Peace is
pleasant to
God.

¶ How plesant to god, is of pees þe myrthe !　　5202
What delyte eeke in pees and vnioun
The prince of pees hath shewëd in his birth,
By angels delitáble song and soun) ;

Also, aftir his resurreccïoun)　　5206

Christ left
Peace on
earth.

He pees bad ; and whan vnto heuen he stigh,
He leftë pees in erthë truëly.[1]　　5208

¶ Et in *terra*
pax homini-
bus.
Pax vobis.
Pacem relin-
quo vobis.

(745)

The peaceful
are Sons of
Christ.

¶ þat ȝift of pees, þat precïouse Iewel,　　5209
If men it kepe, & do it naght away,

[leaf 92 *a*]

Sonës of crist þei may be clept[2] ful wel ;
But strif, which moche is to þe fendës paye,
Among vs feruent is so, welawey !　　5213
We[3] cristen folk, with-inne vs[4] and with-out,
Haue so gret stryfe, þat þer may no pees rout.

¶ Beati paci-
fici &c.

(746)

Internal wars
in England
have slain
thousands.

¶ The ryot þat haþ ben with-in þis lande[5]　　5216
Among our-self, many[6] a wyntrës space,[7]
Hath to þe swerd put many a thousand :
The gredy hert, þat woldë al embrace,
With[8] irous wil, and crabbed palë face,　　5220
And swypir[9] feendly hand with strook vengeáble,
Haþ many a woman maad hem cloþe[10] in sable.

(747)

Ambition and
Greed caused
them.

¶ þis is no doutë, þat ambicïoun　　5223
And couetysë fyre al þis debate ;
Tho two be of wikkéd condicïoun.
No wight halt hym content of his estate ;
Euery man wilneþ to ben éxaltat' ;　　5227
þogh he be gret, ȝit' hirë[11] wolde he goo,
And þeis aren causes of our stryues[12] & woo. 5229

[1] lefte . . . truly R, left . . . truly H.
[2] clept R, clepyd H.　　[3] We R, Whe H.
[4] what within R.　　[5] lande R, londe H.　　[6] full many R.
[7] The rebellions of the Percies against Henry IV.
[8] With R, Wit H.　　[9] swepir R.
[10] made clothed R, maad hem cloþ H.　　[11] hier R.
[12] ben . . . stryfe R.

(748)

¶ Werrë wi*th*in our-Iself is most harmfúl   5230   Internal war is harmful,
And p*er*illous, & most is a-gayn kynde.
þer-wi*th* þis land hath wrastled many a pul ;
þe smert is swich, it may nat out of mynde,
ffor it haþ cast our welthë[1] far be-hynde,   5234   and has wasted our wealth.
And ferther wolë,[2] but thoo werrës stynt ;
No goode may come of werrës wrathful dynt.

(749)

¶ Whilës þat Romaynes were in hert al oo*n*),   5237   While the Romans were united, they ruled the [leaf 92 *b*] World.
And vndeuydid, al[3] hool stode, þei were
Lordës of al þe worlde ; foo was þ*er* non
Out-warde, as who seith, myght hem greue or dere ;
But al sauf welthë[1] may *m*en suffre and bere ;   5241
With[4]-Inne hym-self sprang such deuysïou*n*,   Division ruind em.
þat it hem broughtë[5] to confusiou*n*.   5243

(750)

¶ What causyd hir inwárd werre and rumour[6]   5244   Avarice caused the wars.
But auericë ? she reft hem her wele ;
Whilës þei had in cheerte and fauour
Pro*f*it *com*mun, thei hadden bi þe stele
Prosperite ; but it a-way gan stele   5248
Whan þei him drough to p*ro*fyte singuler,[7]
And of p*ro*fyt *com*mun nat weren cheer.   5250

(751)

¶ *No*/*a* de Auaricia.   ¶ By-hold how[8] auaricë crepith inne,   5251
And kyndlith werre, and quenchiþ vnite !
O fauel ! þou myghtést ben of hir kynne,   Flattery is as bad a Break-peace as Avarice.
ffor swich a breekë[9]-pees as þat is she,
Right swich a-nothir, may I namë þe ;   5255
þou rekkest nat, ne dredest nat, to wende
ffor muk to helle, vnto þe ferthest[10] ende.   5257

---

[1] welthe R, welth H.   [2] wole R, wold H.
[3] all*e* R.   [4] With R, Wit H.
[5] brought H R.   [6] murmur R.
[7] syngulere R, singurer H.   [8] how R, of H.
[9] breke pees R, breek pees H.   [10] into the ferrest R.

(752)

¶ This fauel is of pees a déstourbour; 5258

Twix god and mannës[1] soule he werrë reisith;

This worlde is blent by þis dissymulour;

Vertú he blameþ, ánd vicés he preysith;

Sore in þe bowe of treccherye he teisytñ; 5262

His shot is gay, but it is énvenymed;

His fikil art may nat a-ryght be rymed. 5264

(753)

¶ Vertuouse trouthë,[2] hydë þou þine heede! 5265

þou mayst as wele, thyn art may nat a-vayle;

Out of þis worldës grace art þou as dede:

But fauel, traitour! þi fals gouernaile

Makith ful manny shippës for to saile 5269

In-to þi cofre; warme is þine office;

þat trouthë[3] lesith, wynnë can þi vice. 5271

(754)

¶ Alas! so manny a worthi clerk famóuse, 5272

In Oxinford, and in Cambrigge also,

Stonde[4] vn-avancëd, wher the viciouse

ffauel hath chirches. & preuendres,[5] moo

þan god is plesid with;[6] alasse! of thoo 5276

þat weiuen vertu so to be[7] promoted;

And þei helples, in whom vertu is rooted. 5278

(755)

¶ The knyght or sqwier, on þat othir syde, 5279

Or Ieman, þat haþ in pees or in werris

Dispent with his lorde his blode, but he hyde

þe trouth, and[8] can currey fauel, he nat þe nere is

His lordës grace; and vn-trouth ful fer is 5283

ffrom him, þat worthy corage hath honóured;

Grace of his[9] lorde by fauel is deuóured. 5285

---

[1] mannes R, man H. [2] trouthe R, trouth H.
[3] trouthe R, trouth H. [4] Stonde R, Stode H.
[5] prebendes R. [6] with R, wit H.
[7] wernen . . . so to be R, weiuen (*or* weinen) . . . so be H.
[8] and R, an H. [9] his R, þis H.

(756)

¶ Now vnto my mateere of werre inwarde　　5286 We needn't go back for civil war; it's at our door.
　Resort I ; but to sekë stories olde
Non nede is, syn þis day sharp werre & harde
　Is at þe dore here, as men may be-holde :
　ffrauncë, no wondir þogh þine hertë[1] colde,　5290 France, you're near death!
　　And brenne also :[2] swich is þine agonye,
　　Thi self manaseth þi self for to dye.　　5292

(757)

¶ Thi self destroye, and feble is þi victórye !　5293
　Thow hast in þi self stryven oft[3] or nowe,
And hast appesid al,[4] haue in memórie,　　　[leaf 93 b]
　Thurgh þi prudence ; wost þou nat wel how
Slaghtre is defendid ? and nat rekkest þow　　5297
　To rebelle a-geyn god þat it forbedith ?
　ffor the, myne heuy gost bisily dredith.　　5299 I grieve for you.

(758)

¶ What any part offendid hath to othir,　　　5300 Redress offences fairly.
　Redresse it faire and charytablely ;[5]
By lawe of god, ye ben ech others brothir.　　　You are brethren ;
　O ! now adayës is noon enemye
　Lyke oon þat is to othir of bloodë nye ;　　5304
　　Beth ware ! correct it ! lest men of yow seye,
　　' lo ! whilom this was ffraunce of hye nobley ! '

(759)

¶ I am an Englyssh-man, & am þi foo,　　　　5307 I'm an Englishman, and your foe;
　ffor þou a foo art vnto my lygeánce ;
And yit myn hertë[6] stuffid is with woo　　　　yet I am sorry for your civil war.
　To see þyn vnkyndly disseueraunce :
Accordeth yow ! girdeþ[7] yow with suffraunce ! 5311
　Ye greuë god, and your-self harme & shame,
　And your foos ther-of han disport & game.　5313

---

　　　　　[1] hert H R.　　　[2] also sithen R, also seith H.
[3] ofte R, of H.　　[4] all R.　　[5] charitably R, charytably H.
　　　　　　[6] hert H R.　　[7] gurdeth R.

(760)

¶ Alase ! Also, þe greet dissencïoun,   5314
   The pitous harme, þe hatëful discorde,
Þat hath endurëd twix þis regioun
And othir landës cristen ! he, þat lorde
   Of Remes al is þe auctor of[1] concorde   5318
      And pees, sore is meeuëd þer-*with* ; but we
      Naght dreden for to offend his mageste.   5320

(761)

¶ Off fraunce and englonde, o cristen *princes*,   5321
   Syn þat your style of worthynes is ronge

Thurgh-out þe world, in al þe *pro*uinces,
If þat of yow myghtë[2] be red[3] or songe

That ye were oon in herte, ther nys no[4] tonge   5325
   That myghte expresse, how *pro*fitable and good
      Vnto al peple it were of cristen blood.   5327

(762)

¶ Yeue hem ensamplen ![5] ye ben hir mirrours ;   5328
   They folowen yow : what sorwe lamentable
Is causëd of youre werrës scharpë schoures
   Ther wot no wight, it is irré*pa*rable !

O noble cristen Princes honurable,   5332
   ffor him þat for yow suffred passïo*un*,
      Of cristen blod, haueþ compassïo*un* !   5334

(763)

¶ Allas ! what peple haþ your werrë slayn !   5335
   What cornës wast, and dounë[6] trode & schent !
How many a wif and maide haþ be by layn ![7]
   Castels doun bette, and tymbred houses brent,
      And drawen downe, and al to-tornë[8] and rent ! 5339
         The harm ne may nat rekened be, ne told ;
         This werrë wexiþ al to hoor and old.   5341

---

[1] aH is the actour and R.   [2] myght H R.   [3] radde R.
    [4] is no R, nys H.   [5] ensample R.
[6] wasted and doun*e* R, wast and doun H.   [7] forlayn*e* R.
         [8] aH to-tore R, also torne H.

(764)

¶ To wynnë worldly tresour and richesse,   5342 The winning
  Is of your strif þe[1] longe continuaunce ;   of wealth is the cause of the war.
Wherby it semeth þat ye han scantnesse
  Of good, or ye konne haue no súffisaunce
  Of plente ; and if þér be hábundaunce   5346
    In youre cofres, and in your hertës nede,
    Of lordly[2] cónceit may it not procede.   5348

(765)

¶ Whan Alisaundre deed was, and y-graue,[3]   5349 When Alexander was in his tomb of gold,
  And his toumbe óf gold wroght ful richëly,   [leaf 94 *b*]
As kyngës dignite wole axe and craue,
  Dyuerse philosophres droghen[4] hem nygh
  Therto ; and as oon of hem stood þerby,   5353
    he seidë þus among þe folkës alle :—
    " Seeþ swiche a chaunge is newë now byfalle ![5]

(766)

¶ " This Alisaundre madë yistirday   5356
  Of gold his tresor, but gold makiþ now   gold possest him.
Tresor of him, as ye be-holdë may."
  An[6] othir philosopher seide eek how
  " Al þis world yistirday was nat y-now   5360 Alive, the World couldn't satisfy him:
    To stoppen[7] Alisaundres couetise,
    And now thre elnes of cloþe[8] him suffice."   5362 dead, 3 ells of cloth did.

(767)

¶ O worthi princes two, now takiþ hede !   5363 O Princes, Death can slay you too.
  As hardy, deth is yow for to assaille
As sche[9] dide Alisaundre, whom in drede
  Hadde al þis world ; what myght his force auaille
  A-gayn þe deth ? no thing, sanȝ faille ;   5367
    ffor þogh þat he swerd wer[10] of chiualrie,
    Deth threwe him down to grounde, & lete him lye.

---

[1] your R.   [2] lordes R.   [3] in his graue R.
[4] drowe R, drogh H.   [5] chaunce now newe is falle R.
[6] An R, And H.   [7] stoppen R, stoppe H.
[8] cloth hym do, cloþ him H.   [9] he R.   [10] were R.

REGEMENT.   O

(768)

All life's won
wealth must
be left here:
none goes to
the grave.

¶ With how[1] grete labour, or wiþ how[1] gret peyne,

Men wynnë good, to þe world [þey] leue it schal;

Vnto þe pitte goþ nought but þe careyne:

And þogh gold werë grauen þer-with-al,

Naght myght it helpë: beth nat goldës thral! 5374

Suffiseth to your good,[2] ye prinees boþe;

With pees and restë, armë yow and clothe! 5376

(769)

Peace should
be made at
once.

[leaf 95 a]

¶ Whan ye haue stryue and foughten al your fille,

Pees folwe moot; but good were it, or thanne,

That pees were hadde: what lust han ye to spille

The blood þat crist with his blood boghte, whanne

He on þe croys starf? o lady seint Anne, 5381

Thi doughter preyë to beseche hir sone

To stynte of werrës þe dampnáble wone. 5383

¶ ffinis belli
pax.

(770)

¶ The book of reuelacïouns of Bride 5384

Christ said to
St. Bridget,

Expressith how crist þus seide hir vnto:

" I am pees verray; þere I wole abide,

Where as pees is; non oþer wole I do.

" If France
and England
will peace,
they shall
have it.

Of ffraunce and Engëlond þe kyngës two, 5388

If þei wole haue pees, pees perpetuel

Thei schul han "; thus hir book seiþ, woot I wel;

¶ libro 4° de
reuelacioni-
bus sancte
Brigide, ca-
pitulo cv°
Christus di-
cit, "ego sum
pax," &c.
¶ Si reges
ffrancie &
Anglie volu-
erint habere
pacem, ego
dabo eis per-
petuam pa-
cem: sed pix
vera non po-
test haberi,

(771)

¶ " But verray pees may be had by no way, 5391

But if trouthë and Iustice louëd be;

And for þat á[3] kyng haþ right, forthi may

And they can
have it by
Prince
Henry's
marriage
with French
Katherine."

By matrimoignë pees and vnite

Ben had;[4] cristës plesance is swiche; þus he 5395

That right heir is, may þe remë reioyse,

Cesynge al strif, debate, or werre, or noyse." 5397

nisi veritas
& iusticia
diligantur.
Ideo quia al-
ter Regum
habet iustici-
am, placet
mihi quod
per matrimo-
nium fiat pax,
& sic regnum
ad legitti-
mum here-
dem poterit
peruenire &c.

---

[1] out R.

[2] Chaucer, *Truth* 'Suffiseth to your good, thogh it be smal.'

[3] o R.

[4] Henry V's marriage with Francis's daughter Katherine.

'Cesynge' (l. 5397) turnd out in the end to be 'aggravating.'

(772)

¶ Now syn þe wey is open, as ye see,   5398
  How pees to gete in vertuous manere,
ffor loue of him þat dide vppon þe tree,   For love of
  And of Mary, his blysful modir dere,   Christ, make
    this Mar-
  ffolweþ þat way, and your strif leye on bere; 5402 riage, and
    get Peace!
    Purchaseth pees by wey of marïage,
    And ye þerinne schul fynden auauntage.   5404

(773)

¶ Now, pees! approche, and dryue out werre & strif! Peace, drive
    out strife!
  ffrenchepe! appere, and bannysshë thow hate! Friendship,
    banish Hate.
Tranquillite! reuë þou[1] ire hir lif   [leaf 95 b]
  That feruent is, and leef for to debate!   Tranquility,
    kill Ire!
  Ye thre vertuës, now late see abate   5409
    The malice of þe foulë vices thre,
    þat verray foos ben to al *christ*iante.   5411

(774)

¶ O cristen princes! for þe loue and awe   5412 Christian
    Princes,
  Of him þat is þe king of kingës al,[2]
Nessheth[3] your hertës, and to pees yow drawe!   make peace!
  Considereth what good may þerof fal![2]
  The hony takiþ, and leuyth þe gal![2]   5416
    The sternë iugë in his iugëment
    May doo but right for his punyschëment.   5418

(775)

¶ What desobeïssance and rébellioun,   5419 Rebel not
    against God!
  What wil vnbuxum, what vnkyndënesse,
May he preue in yow, þat destruccïoun
  Don of men, his handwerk, soothly, I gesse.
  It mostë nedës stire his rightwisnesse   5423
    A-geyn yow; stinteþ at his reuerence,
    Sueth his grace and his beneuolence!   5425

---

[1] thou reve R.   [2] all*e*, fall*e*, gall*e* R.   [3] Softeth R.

(776)

Henceforth,
strive only
for Peace!

¶ ffrom hennës-forth lat þere by-twixe yow be   5426
    So vertuous a strif,[1] for cristës sake,
That ye of pees and loue and charite
    May striuë[2]; lat your pite now a-wake,
    That longe haþ slept; and pees bytwixt yow make;

Make war on
Christ's foes,

And on þe foos of crist, your rédemptour,
    Werreth! thére kitheth your vigour!   5432

(777)

the Unbe-
lievers, and
bring them
to Christ's
faith.

¶ Vppon þe mescreantys to makë werre,   5433
    And hem vnto the feith of crist to brynge,
[3]Good were; therynne may ye[4] no thyng erre,
    That were a meritórye werrying;[5]

This is the
way to
Heaven.

That is the wey vn-to the conqueryng   5437
    Of hevenes[6] blyssë, that is endëles,
    To which yow bryngë the[7] auctour of pees. Amen !

Explicit.[3]

[THE ENVOY[8]]

[from MS. Reg. 17 D vi, lf. 101 bk.—The last leaf has been torn
    out of Harl. 4866. Note the change of rymes.]

(778)

O Book, who
gave thee
boldness to
go before the
Prince of
Wales?

Olitell booke, who yafe the hardynesse   5440
    Thy wordës to pronounce in the presence
Of kyngës Impe, and princes worthynesse,
    Syn thou all naked art of eloquence?
    And why approchest thou his excellence   5444
    Vnclothed, saue thy kirtell bare allone?[9]

His patience.

I am right sure his humble paciënce
    The yeueth hardynessë so to done.[10]   5447

---

[1] lyfe R.   [2] be R.
[3—3] In the much later hand than the rest of the poem, the
same as wrote the first leaf.   [4] he R.
    [5] werreying R, werryng H.   [6] heven R.
    [7] the Actour R, thauctour H.
    [8] See Hoccleve's *Minor Poems*, i. 61.   [9] Also Phillipps MS.
    [10] to do so, Phil.

(779)

But o thyng wote I wele : go where thou go,   5448
  I am so priuë [un]to[1] thy sentence,
Thou hast, and art, and wolt ben euermo
  To his hyenesse, of suche beneuolence,   5451
    Though thou not do to hym due reuerence
      In wordes, thy cheerte not is the lesse.
  And yf lust be, to his magnificence,
    Do by thy rede : his welthe it shall witnesse !

Thou art full of good will to him, tho thy words be poor.

(780)

Beseche hym, of his gracious noblesse,   5456
  The holde excused of thyne Innocence
Of endityng ; and with hertes mekenesse,[2]
  If ony thyng the passe of necligence,   5459
    Beseche hym of mercy and indulgence,
      And that, for thy gode hert,[3] he be not fo
  To the þat all seest of loues feruence !
    That knoweth he, that[4] no thyng is hidde fro.

Pray him to excuse thy ignorance,

as it speaks from love, which God knows.

Cest tout.

[1] vn-to, Phillipps MS.   [2] humblesse, Phil.   [3] wil, Phil.
[4] god whom, Phil.

INDEX AND GLOSSARY.

Grisel, 15/401, grizzle
grotte, 153/4249, groat
ground ebb (tide), 25/669
grounded, *p.p.* 60/1662, 74/2041
gru, 70/1939, favour, good word
gruchith, 39/1069, grudges, grumbles
grype, *v. t.* 41/1127, seize, get
guerdoun, 65/1781, reward; 158/4383, 172/4790, pension
guiltless, *n.* 115/3196
gybett, 130/3617, cross
gye, 47/1298, 49/1335, guide
gyed, 14/366, guided; 31/831, treated
Gyle, St., 6/151
Gyles, 75/2052, Egidius de Colonna
gyn, 40/1103, device, tool

hack and hew on a thought, 34/929
half, a goddes, 38/1050, on God's behalf
halve, 45/1246, share
hanaper, 68/1879, a Government office
handwerk, 121/3340
hang in hell, 163/4519
hard as a post, as, 169/4695
hardest, at, 78/2140, at the worst
hardnesse, 35/963, poverty
hardyly, 8/184, boldly
harmful, 125/3471
harrageous, 187/5191, obstreperous
hasp (of a lock), 40/1104
hastid, 159/4417, driven
hastiness, 85/2357
hastyf, 76/2092, hasty
haunted, 113/3126, practist
have: God have his soul, 68/1868
hauynge, 149/4147, property
haw, not worth a, 176/4886
haynous, 107/2961, bitter
he, 72/2002, ? for 'be'
heap of stories, a, 64/1765; of nyce girles, 24/652-3
Heaven's Queen (Mary), 179/4984
heete, 80/2217, promise
held him up, 151/4196
hele, 10/259, conceal
hell: marriage for lust is a, 60/1657
hell to listen to Hoccleve, 38/1034-6
helpless, 10/255
helply, 148/4118, helpful
Hempen lane, 17/453, the gallows
hennes, 46/1274, 47/1276, hence

Henry IV., 30/816
Henry, Prince of Wales, tries to save Badby, p. 12. See 'Prince'
hent, 43/1169, got
herbergage, 46/1264, lodging
herë, *pr.* 9/238, her
here and there, 18/489, all over
herie, 54/1477, bless
Hermenye, 117/3235, Armenia
herne, 171/4765, corner
Herod and Pilate, 183/5074
herte-depe, 5/118
hertyth, 71/1972, cheers
heuye, 391/1064, be heavy, be troubled
hewe, 52/1426, person?
high time, 11/276
hiȝte, 12/302, promist
hilde, 167/4647, pour
hily, 174/4837, highly
his, a man of, 55/1504
Hoccleve wedded, p. 53; names himself, 68/1864; his folly, 157/4360; his annuity in arrear, 158/4383. See 'Annuity.'
hoghte, 52/1441, ought
hog's life, lechery is a, 132/3657
hokirly, 66/1817
holde, 154/4289, house
holde hem, 86/2377, keep, observe, with them
holly, 14/369, wholely
Holofernes, 139/3858
Holy Scripture, 39/1072, 168/4669
homely, *a.* 152/4232; *adv.* 113/3127, familiarly
homicide, 59/1613, 114/3148, 164/4548, man-killer
honde, bore on, 42/1156, accused
honest death, 66/1811
honest poverty, 39/1073
honey & gall, 195/5416
hood, 16/427
hook, with envy as its bait, 79/2183
hool, 3/49, whole, well
hore, 102/2808, continue, go-on long
hore, 5/122, gray-headed
Hospitality, failing, p. 19
hot, 73/2015, fresh, keen
hous, 62/1715, household
housbondly, 36/980, thrifty
housbondrye,36/977,house management, thrift
humble, *n.* 129/3585
Humility, 182/5048

musen, 17/444, muse
My lady changeable, Fortune, 50/1381
mynde, 63/1723, mention
myndes ye, 105/2895, mind's eye
myne, 113/3133, control
mynystre, 133/3692, officer
mys, 48/1303, amiss
mysbare, 128/3559, misconducted
myscherith, 86/2380, discourages
myslokyd on, 26/703
mysrewly, 158/4376, ill-regulated
mysruled, 8/195
mysse-dispendid, 149/4137
mystake him, 112/3089, make a mistake, go wrong
mystook, viii/6, misbehaved
myte, 56/1535, mite; not worth a, 361/977

Nabal, 139/3851
naddest, 62/1718, hadst not
nakid, 119/3290, undrest, made naked
name; nothing like a good one, 147/4085
narwe-clothid, 20/540, with tightish clothes
nay, it is no, 37/1001
nayte (nay R), 122/3374, deny
necessite, 176/4902, need, want
Necessity, make a Virtue of it, 46/1252
need, *n.* 50/1373
Needle and thread, 25/682
neghtburgh, 48/1307, neighbour
Nemo helps Hoccleve's fellows, 54/1487
Nero, 111/3062
nessheth, 195/5412, soften
neuen, *v. t.* 152/4227, name, mention
Nice girls, a heap of, 24/652
nobley, 33/885, nobility
Nobody, 54/1487
nominacioun, 128/3561, mention
noryce, 104/2875, nurse
not, 5/121, know not
nougher, 1/11, nowhere
nouthir, 46/1247, neither
now of dayes, 20/541, nowadays
noyous, 90/2482, hurtful
nuisaunce, 3/58, annoyance
nusance, 30/8101, 125/3462, harm
nycest, 54/1473, most foolish
nycete, 136/3762, folly, lust

nygardie, 48/1306, niggardliness
nyghtertale, 139/3849, night-time
nygon, 74/2033, niggard

o, 52/1416, one
oaths, p. 23-4; nice Girls, 24/652
Oaths tearing God limb from limb, 23/628-630
oblige, *v. t.* 67/1837, bind by bond or deed
obstinacy, 143/3976
obstinat, 8/189
obysaunt, 111/3070, obedient
occident, *n.* 146/4056, west
occupation, lack of, 11/281
of = by, 44/1193, 164/4563, 165/4580; for, 48/1310, 154/4282; from, 90/2485; in, 67/1856; com of, 38/1047, come on!
Ointment of preaching, 52/1429
Olden days, the households of, p. 19
onswre, 2/16, unsure
opinion, 176/4894
opposyd, 15/395, chided
oppression, 92/2541
or, 26/692, 43/1166, ere, before
orient, *n.* 146/4054, east
ornat, *a.* 71/1972
our good old fathers, 14/357
-oure, written and rymed with -ure, 86/2368, 2370-1
out, 10/254, outwardly
oute, 69/1907, put forth
outen, 140/3889, utter
outrage, 151/4201, extravagance
outrance, put to the, 116/3217
over-blind, 32/861
overlook 16/429, look supercili-ously at, or refuse to recognise
ouerschake, 60/1655, satisfied and done with
overterve, 66/1811, roll over or turf over?
ouerthrowe, *v. t.* 55/1526
overthrowyng, *n.* 3/65
Oxford and Cambridge, unbeneficed clerics in, 190/5273

paid, Hoccleve's annuity not, 35/945
pallesie, 135/3735, palsy
pamfilet, 75/2060, Hoccleve's poem
paramours & wives, men have both, 58/1604
parcel (part) play thy, 110/3055

REGEMENT. P

which is which, 17/445
whyl er, 48/1317, some time ago
wind when it blows south and
  north at once, 135/3757-8
wine, effect of, 138/3830-6
winter, 188/5217, year
wisdom, the beginning of, 175/4852
wisseth, 45/1245, teach you
withholde, 46/1250, keep, retain
wityng, 82/2257, knowing, asking
wives, few good now, 135/3756
wold, *p.p.* 39/1075, willd
wolf follows carrion, 111/3064
womb, 137/3802-3, belly
Women, why they're better than
  men, p. 184-7
wone, 113/3130, share, number
work-days, 179/4971
wormes mete, man is, 40/1087
worth, is not, 17/441, is not good
  enough
wos, 18/466, whose
wrake, viii/5, mischief
wrapped, 14/373, involvd; wrapped
  in an heuy drede, 35/959
wrastlen, 20/531, wrestle, struggle
wraþ, 59/1619, make wroth
wreche, 25/671, revenge; 48/1323,
  vengeance
wrestid, 6/130, turnd, twisted
wretched plight, 50/1362
Wretchedness, the worst kind of,
  3/52
Writing: what hard work it is, p.
  36-7; gives you pains all over
  your body, and spoils your eyes,
  p. 38

wyket, 109/3014, gate
wyte, 148/4116, wight
wyte, *n.* 56/1530, blame; 98/2720,
  blamable act

ʒ: myin, 16/407, mine
yᵃ, 38/1045, yes
yafe, 196/5440, gave
yate, 66/1830, a gate
yclomben, 33/904, climbd, risen
ydel, in, 14/367, in vain
ye, 51/1398, eye
ʒee, 108/2979, yea
yeard, old, 67/1858, of many years'
  service
ʒeme, *n.* 133/3684, heed
yemptid, 160/4435, emptied
yerne, 88/2423, eagerly
ʒernest, 51/1407, yearnest
yfraght, 32/858, freighted
yfycched, 32/856, fixt
ʒiftles, 98/2716, giftless
yilde, 57/1580, pay
yment, 72/1978, meant, intended
Ynde, 91/2523, India
ʒok, *n.* 54/1480, yoke, bond
ʒok of mariage, 144/3992
young folk not wise, 6/147
Youth is devoted to the Tavern, p.
  22-3
youth's lusty flowres, 33/906
yoye, 161/4466, joy, heaven
ys, 33/907, ice
Ysaye, 98/2708, Isaiah
yschryue, 65/1802, shriven, shorn
yseid, 72/1991, told

R. CLAY & SONS, LIMITED, LONDON & BUNGAY.